From the Ottoman Empire
to
the Republic of Turkey

Kızıltoprak Stories

by
Nezih H. Neyzi

PEVA PUBLICATIONS
1999

PEVA Publishers wish to express their gratitude to Mr. H. Basri Danışman for the time and valued advice he lavishly bestowed upon them after the sad loss of the author, Nezih H. Neyzi; without his assistance, their task would not have been completed.

Cover: Leyla Hanım at the harmonium and Nezih Neyzi (1935)

PEVA Publications
Peva Building
Imam Adnan Sokak 1
80080 Beyoğlu, Istanbul
Tel.: +90-212-245 66 47
Fax: +90-212-251 84 63

Printed in Turkey by
Onur Grafik Ltd. Şti.
Tel.: +90-212-516 10 72

ISBN: 975-7239-08-9

Nezih Neyzi

Another leaf fell down to earth from the great plane tree that is the **Cumhuriyet**, the Republic.

Nezih Neyzi,

The perfect gentleman of Istanbul, with an enduring smile, the wise man of integrity...

During the hard times of the 1990's, he silently supported the **Cumhuriyet**, and later could witness the achievements of his paper during the last years of his life, living through the days which proved the veracity of the road taken from a broad outlook, and the indispensibility of the Nation's "Enlightenment". He passed away on the threshold of the twentieth century.

He was truly dedicated to Cumhuriyet, the Republic.

* * *

As a child, he lived at Kızıltoprak with his well-to-do family.

How?

Quoting him:

"In our mansion at Kızıltoprak, I talked to the gardener and the cook and listened to the hardships suffered by the common people of Anatolia during the Ottoman period. Famine, disease, and endless battles. Idris the cook had been captivated by the British during the Canal raid. Gardener Süleyman fought at the Dardanelles with his bayonet. Hayrettin Hayreden's eyes were frozen in the cold of Sarıkamış. Kenan the driver was a prisoner in Russia and had escaped from Siberia to Turkey on foot. Brother Ethem, a relative on my father's side, described his escape from Siberia. He also told the story of his voyage to America as the chief engineer of the Gülcemal ship. Years later, my father-in-law General Kemal Doğan related the battle against the British at Mosul and how the Arabs stabbed in the back. My mother-in-law had shown me the coat her husband had worn at the Iraqi front, with a bullet hole in the back. General Kemal Doğan was in Atatürk's team when he landed at Samsun on May 19th. He had fought the French and the Armenians at Çukurova during the War of Independence. He was artillery commander at Sakarya. He enjoyed telling how they had fooled the Greeks by displaying stovepipes in the guise of artillery. He had participated in the Baku invasion. Almost his whole life was spent in the final battles of the Ottomans."

Nezih Neyzi was born into and lived in the atmosphere of a wealthy family with an extensive family tree. He was a privileged person, studied at foreign schools and in foreign countries. But he was a democrat and a populist, also an etatist.

Academician.

Businessman.

Writer.

* * *

Some people enjoy the profoundity of simplicity, disowning ostentation. Nezih Neyzi never lost control when faced with problems, he never abandoned his smile. He had cast the lead in his heart to the deep past of his family. He wrote books to save past events from the depths of oblivion and carried them to the future. As if to prove that affection for the past could not be linked to conservatism, he always looked ahead to the future all his life.

In his book, the **Kızıltoprak Stories**, Nezih Neyzi tells how he had found, among old papers and documents, a book belonging to his mother. On the 13th day of June 1914, she had written the following in her diary:

"The day is ending and I am standing on the balcony of my room at the top floor. The sun is setting gloriously. The sunset is so bright that one can look at it only for a few seconds. The sky is deep blue, there are no clouds and yet no stars have appeared."

When I was a little child, someone had told me that each star in the sky was focused on a human being. Even if not true, the idea had appealed to me.

Last Friday, we saw Nezih Neyzi off on his last journey. It was a still and grey weather. The sky was pressed on us like a heavy lid. Not a single star in the sky. During a cloudy noon, with even the sun in hiding, why on earth should we see stars?

İlhan Selçuk,

Translation by Filiz Ofluoğlu   **Cumhuriyet**, January 31, 1999

Preface

Kızıltoprak means "Reddish Earth". It was the first township on the Berlin-Baghdad railroad. On the Asian shore of Istanbul the railroad began from Haydarpasha terminal and winded through the Anatolian plateau, passed to Aleppo and went back to the Anatolian plateau as far as the present Iraqi border and down to Baghdad. The Germans built this railway and had a concession to exploit all mineral resources 50 kilometers on each side of the railroad. That is why the railroad track winded as much as possible. This, of course, included the oil fields near Mosul at that time still in Ottoman hands.

Kızıltoprak was a dormant little settlement with large gardens and kiosks of the Ottoman administrators and mainly a Muslim section of the city of Istanbul also at that time still called Constantinople by the Christian community. The connection to the city was by railroad from Kızıltoprak station to Haydarpasha terminal and then by boat to the port of Galata. The alternative was to take a horse carriage to Kadıköy ferry station.

I was born in 1923 in Sultanahmet near the Blue Mosque and my parents moved to their maternal household in 1929, so my childhood memories are from Kızıltoprak and its surroundings.

These memoirs are a summary of family tales narrated to me by grandparents and relatives. As a child I would listen to their stories. There was no electricity, no radio and at night the kerosene lamp and candles were the only source of illumination.

My grandmother's mother Leyla Saz Hanım was in her eighties but with a brilliant mind and would tell us stories of her grandfather who was the "tatar" of the sultan. He carried the special messages of the sultan to far flung sections of the empire. My grandmother had travelled with my grandfather Mehmet Ali, who was a governor at Harput in Eastern Anatolia. From here they moved to Yanina (today in northern Greece) and then to Trabzon. All these travels were on carriages and camel caravans. During the occupation of Istanbul after the first world war, my father had to go by boat to Inebolu and then by carriage in two weeks to Ankara. All these stories were complemented from other sources and anecdotes of the cook, the gardener and maids. They represented the soldier fighting in the Dardanelles or a soldier who went to the Suez Canal but was captured by the British. One of the maids had carried ammunition on her back during the liberation war.

There were also other sources of information such as relatives we would visit during the holidays or who would come and stay at Kızıltoprak for a few days. They were people like Hayrettin Bey who was on the Russian front in the first world war and he would tell us the stories of the cold on the Russian frontier where his eyes were almost frozen. Ethem Bey a cousin of my father, who fell prisoner to the Russians, was sent to camps in Siberia, escaped after the revolution and walked to India before coming back to Istanbul. A taxi driver whom my father used quite often was also a prisoner of war in Siberia and somehow managed to walk back to Istanbul. My father-in-law General Kemal Doğan who was an artillery man, had fought on all the fronts starting from Libya against the Italians, then in Iraq against the British, then in the Caucasus up to Baku before returning to Istanbul. He joined the first expedition of Mustafa Kemal Pasha (Atatürk) on May 19, 1919 to Samsun, and he was asked to organise the southern front against the advancing French. After the ceasefire, he joined the war against the invading Greeks on the Aegean front. He would not talk or tell stories but answered my questions in short sentences.

As a child I began to collect old documents, letters, books in old script and family pictures. All these became documents in the preparation of this book. I have tried to narrate the old family tales and thus leave a summary of events to future generations. Otherwise all this unwritten history would be lost with our generation. We had a chance to live and be educated by the last Ottoman generation but we were brought up under a new regime representing the new Turkish state, the Republic of Turkey.

Many reforms started about a hundred years ago under the Ottoman regime but began to take shape under the Republic. All phases of life changed. I have tried to tie Kızıltoprak with the last Ottomans and close the book with the end of this last generation.

I am sure there are omissions or errors in the evaluation of all the changes that took place with the reforms of Atatürk. I have related the life of the last Ottoman administrators as much as possible then took up the reforms of Atatürk and their effect on our daily life at Kızıltoprak. I would like to thank all of my relatives and friends who helped in the preparation of this book.

Nezih H. Neyzi
Levent, Istanbul, 1997

The Turkish Alphabet

Letters	Name	Pronounciation
A a	a	sun, cut, come
B b	be	bed, buy, bill
C c	ce	jar, jelly, jam
Ç ç	çe	church, chapel, child
D d	de	dear, doll, did
E e	e	red, bed, net
F f	fe	fine, fair, foul
G g	ge	gale, good, guy
Ğ ğ	yumuşak ge	(prolongs the preceding vowel) weight, neighbour
H h	he	hard, hill, hell
İ i	i	sit, thin, pin
I ı	ı	Cryil, wanted, syllable
J j	je	pleasure, measure, French: juste, jeune
K k	ke, ka	kite, cold, cat
L l	le	lilac, lull, lily
M m	me	me, mine, mime
N n	ne	nine, no, name
O o	o	poet, author
Ö ö	ö	French: deux, seul, German: Köln, König
P p	pe	pebble, pie, pipe
R r	re	rhyme, red, ready
S s	se	sister, similar, send
Ş ş	şe	shoe, sharp, short
T t	te	tell, truth, time
U u	u	put, foot, bull
Ü ü	ü	French: tu, sur, German: Glück, über
V v	ve	away, vizor, vital
Y y	ye	year, young, youth
Z z	ze	zebra, zero, zeal

Vowel Harmony

The Turkish language is sweet and melodius, mainly due to the laws of vowel harmony, whereby words beginning with front or back vowels preserve the same quality throughout. It is spoken by more than eighty million people from Macedonia to Siberia. Turkish is an easy logical language. There is no gender, no *he*, she or *it*, but one word for all three. The *der, die, das* of German, the nightmare of learner, are not found in Turkish.

There are eight vowels in the Turkish language, which are divided into two groups. The first group is (e, i, ö, ü) forming the front vowels and the second group (a, ı, o, u) forming the back vowels. In Turkish, adjectives are obtained from nouns, and from adjectives and nouns, verbs are created. The language is in conformity with the modern science of phonetic-spelling and pronounciation is regular. It is formed of sounds which are the natural result of the laws of position and inflection of the tongue, and the movements of the lips and jaws, and every word is pronounced as it is written. The only exception is the soft (g), which is written as (ğ) and serves to lengthen the sound of the vowel it follows. The language is based on the principle of vowel harmony. In other words, if the vowel of the first syllable of a word is a front vowel, the vowels of the subsequent syllables have to be front vowels. While, if the vowel of the first syllable of a word is a back vowel, so are the vowels of subsequent syllables. Suffixes have, as a rule, two forms: one with a front vowel and used with front-vowelled words; another with a back vowel, used with back-vowelled words.

Glossary

Ahretlik	: Was a girl who joined a family under the terms of an agreement with her parents. She was brought up and did the work of a maid. When she grew up, her marriage was arranged and she was provided with a dowry.
Avlu	: A small garden enclosed by a wall.
Bacı	: An elderly house maid.
Charshaf	: A loose garment to cover women outdoors.
Courna	: A marble sink used in Turkish baths.
Çeki	.: Two-hundred and fifty kilogram weight unit used in fire wood trade.
Denk	: A bundle consisting of a mattress and some essential articles wrapped in a carpet.
Efe	: A semi-outlaw living in the Aegean area. An efe was a person who would defend the poor and ransom the rich.
Efendi	: Gentleman, Sir.
Evlatlık	: A child adopted as a servant.
Falaka	: A punishment involving beating the feet.
Ferace	: Ladies' outdoor mantle.
Ferman	: Hand written decree of the sultan.
Fodla	: Food given to the poor.
Gecekondu	: A house built overnight.
Göçent	: Migratory tribe.
Hafız	: A person who has memorized the Koran
Halk Evi	: People's Center.
Han	: Caravansaray, khan; inn.
Hodja (Hoca)	: Is a religious instructor, teacher.
İdadi	: A school equivalent to the lycée.
Kabalak	: Head gear of Turkish soldiers in World War I
Kalfa	: Is an experienced servant in charge of housework who supervises the "ahretliks" and other girl servants.
Kalpak	: A head gear made of lamb skin.
Karlık	: Water cooling jar using ice or snow.

Kiosk	: Large house (about 15 to 20 rooms).
Konak	: A small palace (about 40 rooms).
Kurna (Courna)	: A sink made of marble used in Turkish baths.
Lakap	: Surname
Maçuna	: A large wooden barge used to carry goods on the sea.
Maltız	: A brasier made of clay.
Mangal	: A portable charcoal brazier.
Maşa	: Tongs to hold burning wood.
Medrese	: Theological school.
Mektupcu	: Male secretary.
Mesjid	: Small mosque with a symbolic minaret.
Meşlah	: A robe worn by women at ceremonies.
Misakı Milli	: National Union.
Müftü	: Religious affairs director; mufti.
Peçe	: A cover to hide the face of women.
Pilav	: A dish made of rice.
Postnişin	: He who sits on the skin, meaning the leader of a religious order.
Potur and cepken	: A type of national costume, consisting of trousers and vest.
Sahan	: Copper container
Selamlık	: Room reserved exclusively for male guests.
Şalvar	: Baggy pants.
Şehzade	: Son of the sultan; a prince.
Takunya	: Wooden overshoes or sandal.
Taşlık	: A storage room with a stone floor.
Tatar	: A mounted messenger of the sultan.
Tef	: Tambourine.
Tuğra	: Monogram of the sultan.
Türbe	: Name of an area in Istanbul where there is a mausoleum of sultans and high officials of the Ottoman Empire.
Ud	: Musical instrument like a lute.
Yalı	: House on the shores of the Bosphorus.
Yemeni	: Scarf for girls.
Yüklük	: A built-in cupboard to store beddings for guests.

Contents

SECTION I
The Last Ottomans

Chapter 1
First Recollections

I was born at Sultanahmet district of Istanbul in 1341. At that time the Arabic calendar was still in use and my birthday corresponds to December 25, 1923. Istanbul was still the capital of the Ottoman Empire. The last sultan was in Istanbul but the Republic of Turkey was proclaimed in Ankara. It was an interim dark period with many unsettled problems. A few months later Sultan Vahdettin left Istanbul secretly on a British warship. So I began life as the first generation of the Republic of Turkey.

My parents moved from Kızıltoprak to Sultanahmet with my elder brother Ahmet. My father was one of the pioneer Turkish businessmen, a rare occupation among Turkish families. He managed to sell rifle bullets and second hand uniforms to the army of the Republic in Ankara. He found discarded uniforms of the British army in Vienna, and posing as a Jew from Istanbul, selected the uniforms from warehouses. They had to change the buttons of the uniforms which had the insignia of the Anzac, the Australian army who had fought against the Turks in the Dardanelles.

Before going to Vienna, he acquired a western style hat and placed it in a box. After boarding the Orient Express from the European train station at Sirkeci, he took out his fez and put it in the box. His office boy carried the box home. At that time as a Turk he could not wear such a hat in Istanbul but if he wore a fez in Vienna prices would immediately go up. He found the Jewish owners of second hand coats and military uniforms and bargained hard to reduce the prices. The Turkish army needed clothing but there was not enough funds to manufacture or buy new clothing.

So my father brought these bundles of clothes to Istanbul and then by train to Ankara. He also sold five million Mauser rifle bullets. Upon transferring them to Ankara he received a congratulatory note from the general staff for supplying these required items in time and at a very reasonable price.

With the money he earned, he rented the house at Sultanahmet where I was born. We lived in that house for three years but I only remember the incident of the fire. The chimney caught fire and the fire brigade came to save the house. They pumped lots of water to the chimney and the water came down from the stairs like a cascade. To me this was a game and I liked it very much and implored my parents to call the fire brigade again.

I really do not know whether I remember this incident or it was related so many times by my father and mother that I image it vividly. Many years later when I was about 35 years old, I went one day with my mother to Sultanahmet to see the old house. It was being used as an office by the Republican Party. So many people were walking in and out. We entered and went upstairs. No one objected to our presence. When we came to the corner room, my mother said, "This is the room where you were born." The house is still there and now it belongs to the Tourism Administration and they take good care of it. It is one of the few houses that has managed to survive all these years. It is the house just opposite the Marmara University Rectorship building.

My father decided to move to Taksim Square which was being developed at that time. Next to our house there was a cinema which showed silent films accompanied by piano. My father had his office and a telephone on the ground floor. At that time there was a switchboard operator to ask your number. I would ask her, "Girl, is my father there?" I do not remember my father at this house as he was constantly travelling on business. My paternal grandmother had a room of her own in this house. In 1927 my younger brother Ali was born. Then my grandmother Feride Hanım came to stay with us. My grandfather Mehmet Ali would come occasionally but returned to Kızıltoprak. My older brother Ahmet was attending the Galatasaray primary school which taught in French. I remember Ali in my mother's bed. I was living mostly with my nurse

Hediye (a girl that my grandmother had bought in Yanina and given to my mother as a wedding gift). My mother had explained to me that a new brother was coming and I was prepared for this event.

My nurse would take me out for a walk each day. We would try to see the Taksim monument which was under construction. We could look between wooden planks of the fence surrounding the statue. The tramway would go somewhere behind the statue in the direction of Harbiye (Military School). My nurse would lead me to Beyoğlu street which had nice stores and pastry shops. We would buy some cakes and return home.

There was a taxi stand right outside our house. The drivers would frighten my grandmother by blowing their old rubber pouch horns. She would push them away with her umbrella. These are my recollections of the Taksim period of my life.

In 1929, we moved for the last time to Kızıltoprak. There was a big reconstruction going on and the house was being enlarged. This house was bought by my grandparents in 1890 from a man who had two wives. So the house was symetrically built in two sections. The kitchen and wash room were outside the house, so there would be no smell of cooking in the house and the male cook and servants would not go into the house. The back rooms were being enlarged and a third floor was added to house Mehmet Ali Ayni's library and bedroom. My grandmother had her room on the second floor.

When the house was dismantled in 1968, I took away some pieces. From the washroom I took the two marble sinks and brought them to my garden at Levent. I also took the main gate of the house and a "Kafes" lattice that was used in the old houses to prevent strangers from seeing the interior of the house. They are now used as decorations on the walls of our present home in Levent.

Those who remember the house at Kızıltoprak like to see these pieces of the old house and remember the old days.

The old house had fourteen rooms, two bathrooms, several storage rooms and a large cellar to store charcoal and wood for the winter. In the garden beside the kitchen there was a stable for cows and a stable for horses, and there were rooms for the gardener, cook and drivers. A toilet for the servants was also in the garden hidden behind the kitchen. Naturally all these rooms had their furniture. So when we moved from Taksim to Kızıltoprak my mother's furniture went into storage at my fathers' old house also in Kızıltoprak. My grandmother lived there alone and there was plenty of space to store the furniture.

Sometimes we would go with my mother to her mother-in-law's house and look at the furniture and maybe bring back a chair or something to use at the house. To me home was Kızıltoprak. I lived there until I got married in 1950 and moved to Ankara to the office of my father.

My books and belongings remained at Kızıltoprak. I had asked my mother to give me my late uncle's cupboard which had a mirror door and a lock. I stored my hunting apparatus, old school books and toys. It was the only locked place in the house. I had a collection of old lead soldiers and trains and other little things. This cupboard stayed as my "castle" at Kızıltoprak until the house was sold.

When we went to the United States for a year in 1954, we took our furniture to Kızıltoprak for storage. When we came back, we took our furniture from Kızıltoprak to Levent. But it was a small house so I could not bring my old cupboard. There was nothing valuable in it but I left it locked in Kızıltoprak. It contained some old clothing, the swords of Sırrı Pasha (my grandmother's father), old pictures, the eyeglasses of my uncle and grand parents, old hunting gear etc. During the last years of Kızıltoprak thieves entered the house. They broke into my cupboard and stole the ud (lute) of Leyla Hanım. This was a special ud made for my grandmother's mother. It had a flat back so that she could reach the front and play the instrument more easily. They did not take anything else.

By 1968 when it was decided to tear down the house at Kızıltoprak, we had moved to a larger house in Levent so I could bring my cupboard to the new house. Again, it is the only locked place in our home. If a thief comes and breaks it open he will be sorry for his efforts but for me

Kızıltoprak memories stay locked in this old cupboard.

This new house at Levent is full of memories from Kızıltoprak. The largest room is used as a museum containing some furniture that came out of Yıldız Palace, pictures of ancestors and the "fermans" of the sultan given them for decorations or assignments. There is also an order signed by Mustafa Kemal at Uşak in the front lines conveying full colonel's status to my father-in-law Kemal Doğan. We have also many pictures from my wife's side of the family. One of these is an interesting composition because it puts side by side Ottoman administrators like Ismail Pasha, the governor of Crete and Sırrı Pasha, the governor of Baghdad and a general of the liberation army. They are all our dear past relatives. There is a picture of my mother nursing me painted by Belkıs Mustafa one of the first woman painters in Turkey. The picture of Leyla Saz Hanım, my grandmother's mother, shows her with her palace costume and her decorations. It was taken at her son's house, Yusuf Razi Bel. I kept this dress and the small medallion but unfortunately the large medallion was sold many years ago. One picture of her in her youth with her two sons and two daughters is dedicated to her son-in-law Mehmet Ali Ayni. There are the pictures of Ismail Pasha, Leyla Hanım's father in his grand uniform and decorations while serving as the governor of Crete. Then there is the picture of Sırrı Pasha, her husband, again in full uniform as governor of Baghdad. My grandfather Mehmet Ali Ayni is pictured in his governor's uniform with only four medallions as he was still in his early forties.

My library also contains the books of Mehmet Ali Ayni. He was an administrator and a philosopher and published thirty-two books. There are also pictures of my mother in her bridal gown standing alone with a crown on her head. Men were not allowed to come to the wedding until after a special ceremony in which the husband saw his wife for the first time. I have written on the back of these pictures who is who, for when we are gone no one will remember these people in their fezes and old costumes.

All the family stories collected in this book were told in the old

Ottoman style and manner of speech. In school we learned the new modern Turkish which Atatürk had developed with the efforts of the History Foundation and the Turkish Language Foundation. Atatürk's reforms were taking place one after the other. The teaching of Turkish was with the new Latin alphabet that was accepted in 1928. Turkey is one of the few nations that has totally changed its alphabet in a period of two years. While these reforms were going on, we did not hear anything against Atatürk at our house in spite of the fact that my parents had been administrators of the sultans for many generations.

The main reason for this support of the Republic is the big resentment the Istanbul population felt during the occupation of 1919-1923 by British, French and Italian troops after the Allied victory in the first world war. The Ottoman Empire had fought on the side of Germany during this disastrous war. The Sevres Treaty dismantled the empire. Istanbul lived though a difficult period during this war and lost all its territory in Europe and the Middle East. Practically all the nations that were part of the empire joined with the enemy. Even the Muslim Arabs and Albanians did not want the Ottoman administration any more. For centuries we had lived together with these nations. The grim years of occupation was a big humiliation to the Muslim population of Istanbul. On top of this, the Muslims were divided between the supporters of the sultan and the nationalists headed by Mustafa Kemal. All these conflicts and sufferings were narrated to us by the people who lived through these events. Our childhood is full of stories of battles with the Russians, French, British, Italians, Arabs, Greeks and Armenians. Many people went to Yemen and never came back. Others lost their lives in Albania, Greece, Bulgaria or Serbia. Stories of fighting at Musul and Kut described getting wounded and narrowly escaping enemy capture... tales of Arab bands attacking Turkish soldiers... the last train taken by my uncle from Beirut which saved his life - all these were told to us by people who had lived through those difficult days.

These memoirs are put together to relate the difficult period my parents went through during the transition from the Ottoman Empire to the Republic of Turkey. As a member of a family who has lived for many generations in Istanbul, I would like to relate to our children and grand-children the experiences we encountered during this big transformation. I have used the documents, letters, pictures, etc. of my parents and fore-fathers and translated them as carefully as possible in order to relate these first hand experiences accurately.

The documents are in old Ottoman script which remained in use until 1928 when Atatürk introduced the new alphabet.

Atatürk was able to bring new vitality to the Republic by introduc-ing the Latin style alphabet which could be learned more easily by the population. Illiteracy during the Ottoman regime reached 95 percent in certain areas of the empire. Yet the Greeks, Bulgarians, Albanians, Serbs, Armenians and other nationalities in the empire had their private schools and a much higher degree of education.

The new republican generation did not learn the old Ottoman script which was based on the Arabic alphabet. The Ottoman language was a mixture of Turkish, Persian and Arabic. Therefore an educated Ottoman had to learn these three languages and the complicated vocab-ulary and syntax in order to read and write. Hand writing was different from printed text; therefore the chance of learning the Ottoman lan-guage was restricted to the intelligentsia of the country.

Today it is debated whether such a drastic change was necessary to improve the nation. The fact is that now, those who want to learn the old script are free to do so at universities in Istanbul and Ankara. There are also international centers like Kiel in Germany and orientalist depart-ments of many American and British universities teaching the old script. The acid test is that illiteracy in Turkey has dropped to about 20 percent for women and 10 percent for men.

When Atatürk died in 1938, I was a student at the 8th grade of St. Joseph school in Istanbul. I had seen him only in the balcony of his train at Kızıltoprak. The train would go slowly up hill in front of our house where we would wait to wave at him. He would stand in the balcony of the last carriage and wave back at us. Coming down from Ankara the train would pass very quickly but we would understand his coming and going by the sentinels posted on both sides of the railroad.

We took part in his funeral ceremony at the Dolmabahçe Palace. I would listen to anecdotes about him told by my father and my uncle who was Atatürk's doctor. My father had his office in Ankara and my uncle, Dr. Asım Arar, was the undersecretary of the Ministry of Health. My father would see him quite often at Karpiç, a famous restaurant in the thirties run by two White Russians who chose to stay in Turkey. Mustafa Kemal would go to this restaurant and mix with the population of Ankara. My father would listen to his conversation. Once he was invited to his table while he was drawing a sketch of the Italian-Abyssinian war. He gave this sketch to my father who had it framed with a picture of Atatürk. My uncle had closer relations with Mustafa Kemal and was among the doctors who signed his death declaration.

During our youth we experienced the reforms brought by Atatürk and we saw their effects on our daily life. My recollections will be through these years of drastic changes in Turkey.

In 1938 when Atatürk died at the Dolmabahçe Palace, practically all the schools and the population of Istanbul went to parade in front of his catafalc placed in the large reception hall of the palace.

Our entire 8th grade class from St. Joseph went to Dolmabahçe to pay our respects. Our Turkish teacher must have asked us to write an essay after this visit. I am glad I kept this paper all these years because it brings back that day vividly. No one had a camera to take a picture. My paper reads as follows:

MY FEELINGS IN FRONT OF ATATÜRK'S SARCOPHAGUS

"When I learned that we were going to visit Atatürk I was very glad. There was a big preparation at the school. We put on our school uniforms and went to the palace. We entered the main gate and the sea was on our right side. We could see those leaving the palace on our left side. They all looked very sad, some could not hold their tears. Finally we arrived to the entrance of the palace which was guarded by officers in full uniform. When we entered the palace hall the main thing that struck us were the illumination torches. We were advancing at a very slow pace. At that time I felt a pain in my heart. All we could hear was sobbing people and no other voice. Footsteps would not be heard because of very think carpets covering the floor of the palace. High ranking officers were keeping the guard with drawn swords. The sarcophagus was covered with the flag that he had liberated. Our school passed in a solemn parade in front of our esteemed leader and left the palace with great sorrow."

These were my feelings at the age of 15 when we paid our respects to Atatürk for the last time. I am glad our teacher gave us this assignment and my feelings were thus preserved on this faded paper.

Chapter 2
From Ottoman to Republican Rule

In 1923, the Turkish Republic was declared but those that set up this new state were all Ottoman administrators, soldiers, politicians, bureaucrats and some enlightened intelligentsia all brought up during the days of the empire. The common people and peasants were the same as ever.

All decorations, titles, religious sects and organizations were abolished, stopped or closed down. However, the same people were still in existence except for the sultan and his close relatives who had been asked to leave the country. Those involved in religious sects had withdrawn from the public eye or retreated in seclusion. In the eastern part of the country, the landlords and religious leaders did not change their way of life. Even today the big land owners, leaders of various sects and post-nişins* are still in existence and either secretly or openly continue their activities.

Some of the administrators in Istanbul had run away to Ankara during the occupation of the allies and the war of independence (1919-1923). These people had completed their education during the period of the last Ottoman sultans and had the courage and desire to go to Ankara to join Mustafa Kemal. The move of the capital from Istanbul to Ankara symbolizes the passage from Ottoman to Republican rule.

Many years later, in 1952, someone at Doğubayazıt had asked me who the sultan was in Istanbul. He was an illiterate man and lived as a shepherd in the mountains. He did not have much chance to talk with people. He was explaining to me the way of curing sick people by using black sheep skins for some diseases and white sheep skins for other diseases. The sheep would be slaughtered and the skin used as a cover to

---

(*) A post-nişin is the eldest member of a family or sect accepted by his clan as the unofficial leader of his community or congregation.

wrap up the sick person. The sultan had left the country 30 years ago but some people still thought that there would be a sultan somewhere in Istanbul.

During my school days, I was a little puzzled. History lessons attracted my attention. When Ottoman history was taught, during the expansion of the empire the sultans were good and capable people; when the tide turned back and the empire was crumbling the sultans were not good people any more and they were bad managers. In the last years they became traitors. The last sultan was only accepted as the Caliph of Islam and he ran away from Istanbul on a British warship. Thus the Ottoman dynasty came to an end. It was true that the Arabs did not like the sultan, the Iranians had never accepted the caliphate of Istanbul, and other Muslim nations of northern Africa like Algeria and Morocco never accepted the sultan as the religious head of the Muslims. For the Christian subjects of the sultans, the caliphate was irrelevant. As a child, I would think and say that as long as the sultan was strong he was accepted as caliph and as sultan, but after the decline his importance disappeared. During the days of my childhood, I could not figure out these history lessons, was it Ottoman history or was it Turkish history?

I would look at my family. They were all people who had worked under the Ottoman regime. The oldest story that I could gather was the trip of Abdurrahman, the Tartar who carried the sultan's message to the commander of the besieged castle of Morea. He was the grandfather of Leyla Hanım.

After he received the letter, he opened the sole of his boot and placed it between the layers of skin and sowed the boot. He would ride his horse so fast that the belly of the horse would almost touch the ground. He changed his horses at relay stations where a ready saddled horse would be waiting. When he approached Morea and had to change once more his mount, he stopped at the last inn. Many Greeks were gathered there discussing how they would share the spoils of this rider. He knew Greek but pretended not to understand and asked the inn keeper to prepare some food, then pretented to go the toilet. Instead he jumped on the ready saddled horse raced away from the inn. The Greeks started shouting and shooting after him but he was already far away. Finally he came to the castle of Morea which was completely surrounded by Greek rebels. There was no way to enter the castle. He saw a shepherd with his herd of sheep grazing around. He asked the shepherd to slaughter a sheep and sell him the skin. He tied the skin on his back and started crowling among the sheep in the herd. The shepherd was playing his flute and roaming around the castle. The rebels did not care about the shepherd and the herd. They gradually approached the gate of the castle. At the right moment, he jumped up and ran to the gate. When the Turks saw him rushing to the castle they lowered the gate on the moat, opened the gate and he ran inside. The insurgents started shooting after him but it was too late. He delivered the message safely to the commander of the castle.

As a child, I did not understand the use of a letter and asked my grandmother's mother, "What is the use of a letter to the commander of a besieged castle?" "It builds up the morale of the defenders," was the answer.

Leyla Hanım's father was Ismail Pasha, the doctor of the sultans who had circumcised many newborn babies who later became sultans. He was the only man who was accepted to the harem of the palace. He took his daughter Leyla to the Çırağan Palace at the age of four. Münire Sultan, the mother of the sultan, liked this little girl very much and kept her at the palace for many years. She wrote her memoirs (in old script) in a daily paper in Istanbul after the sultans were gone and the harem was closed down. Her son Yusuf Razi Bel translated these memoirs into French and had the book published in Paris in 1928 under the name Le Harem Emperial.

In spite of all this Ottoman influence there was an appreciation of Mustafa Kemal Pasha, referred to as Gazi Pasha at Kızıltoprak. My father was going secretly to Ankara via İnebolu, the only safe port left on the Black Sea. There was no scheduled boat service from Istanbul and sometimes he had to wait for a week until he found a vessel leaving for İnebolu.

13

My uncle, Dr. Asım Arar, had joined the Ankara government and went there with my aunt as an official at the new Ministry of Health. Another uncle, Sırrı Ayni, was educated in Germany during the Ottoman days and worked at the railroad administration with the Germans at Haydarpasha. He later went to Turhal where a new sugar factory was going to be built. The generation before mine did not remain in Istanbul and lead a comfortable life. The only person who could not go to Ankara was my grandfather who was put on retirement by the last Ottoman government. Later he was appointed as chief of the liberaries to classify the old books in the Ottoman script.

As mentioned before, there was a love and respect for Mustafa Kemal at Kızıltoprak. This was mainly due to the bitter memories of the occupation of Istanbul by British, French and Italian troops after world war. My father, mother, grandmother would relate with sorrow those gloomy days. I would hear other tales from the cook, the gardener and helper that came from Anatolia. They had suffered the bitter days of war from 1910 to 1919 during the Ottoman days followed by the liberation war from 1919 to 1923.

Starting from the Italian war in Libya in 1910 and then to Balkan wars of 1912 and the first world war, 1914 to 1919, including the bitter fight in the Arabian peninsula and the Iraq and Russian fronts of the Caucasus, there was continous war for about twenty years, ending only after the defeat of the Greek forces in Anatolia in 1923.

The transformation from the Ottoman Empire to the Turkish Republic is symbolized by reforms that took place after the end of hostilities in 1923. These reforms had an effect on our daily life at Kızıltoprak. There were people who did not approve of these drastic changes. But few dared open heir mouths during the lifetime of Atatürk who died in 1938. Of course, there were some demonstrations against him by some religious people who killed a young officer called Kubilay and his guard during a religions uprising in the Aegean. There were also Kurdish rebellions in the eastern part of the country. The question of the Bosphorus and Dardanelles straits and the Hatay question with Syria

14

were subjects of international political tension. The question of the straits was finally resolved in an agreement signed in Montreux Switzerland in 1936, and the Hatay question was solved with France just after the death of Atatürk. However, it is still a sore point between Turkey and Syria.

After the death of Atatürk, Ismet Pasha (İnönü) was elected president and another difficult period started with the second world war in 1939. İnönü led Turkey through these difficult war years and managed to remain neutral. After the defeat of Germany, Turkey joined with the allies.

In order to understand our present social system, we have to know the historical developments of the last century. The Ottoman Empire started a series of modernization attempts but the reforms were superficial and did not alter the way of life in general. The dismantling of the Empire after the first world war created the following countries: in the Balkans, Albania, Yugoslavia, Romania, Bulgaria and present-day Greece; in the Middle East, Syria, Lebanon, Palestine, Israel (at a later date), Jordan, Saudi Arabia, Iraq, Kuwait, Bahrain, the United Arab Emirates, Yemen; in North Africa, Libya and Egypt. Up to the year 1900 all these countries were controlled from Istanbul. The influence of the sultan changed according to the relations with these countries. There were frequent uprisings and the Anatolian Turks had to go and restore order in these regions. At the end of the first world war, all these territories were separated from the empire and what was left was only a small section of Anatolia. Istanbul was occupied by the allied forces, Western Anatolia was occupied by Greece, the French and Italians took control of southern Turkey, the Russians invaded Eastern Anatolia. Istanbul was occupied from 1919 to 1923. I was born at the end of this unfortunate period and started life as the first generation of the republic with the present borders and the capital city as Ankara.

The alphabet of all these countries that came out of the Ottoman empire stayed as it was; only Turkey changed her alphabet, abandoning the Arab script for the Latin. This was one of many very radical changes.

Most of the Ottoman laws were abolished and new laws based on the Swiss or German codes were accepted and translated to Turkish. The Islamic laws allowing marriage with four wives were also abolished. The calendar changed. The keeping of time changed from the lunar calendar to Greenwich time. All weights and measures shifted to the decimal system. Even the call to prayer from the minaret changed from Arabic to Turkish. There was also a law called the "Hat" law concerning head wear and other customs of dress. The family name was adopted by law. Foreign schools were taken under control of the Ministry of Education and all foreign primary schools were closed.

A law was passed to control navigation on coastal waters. The Ottoman foreign debt administration was closed down. The Turkish Republic paid all the foreign debts in installments that lasted until 1950.

The capital city of the country was changed. This is also a very rare thing to see in the history of nations. Istanbul represented the Ottoman and was occupied by the enemy. During the liberation struggle Atatürk chose Ankara as the capital of the new republic. It was not an easy decision because Ankara was a poor little town in Central Anatolia. There were no adequate buildings to house the government offices. The country was taking a new start and the idea of a new capital was appropriate. People of Istanbul prefer their old town to Ankara. As a coincidence my first daughter was born in Ankara and my second daughter went to Ankara to complete her university education. So now there is a new generation, born and raised in Ankara, who prefer Ankara to Istanbul. For us we still say jokingly, "The best part of going to Ankara is the hope of coming back to Istanbul."

If Atatürk had not changed the Ottoman script, it is most likely that all the reforms would have been wiped out in time. The Ottoman script was only for the intelligentsia and could only be learned with difficulty. The Koran was recited without understanding. For the first time Atatürk asked for a translation of the Koran into Turkish. He did not close down the mosques but the teaching of Arabic was forbidden. He saw that Turkish needed a reform in order to be used by the entire nation. He

16

made primary education free and compulsory. This was essential for the unification of the country. Now, again, there are people that study the Ottoman script and can translate the old documents. The Arabs did not understand or use the Ottoman script. The Turks left in the Balkans and in other parts of the empire also learned the new alphabet and could communicate with their relatives in the homeland.

The last Ottomans are practically all gone. I cannot read the inscriptions on tombstones or on the front of the mosques. I used to go with my mother and she would read with ease these old writings. Sometimes, my grandfather would take me to the cemetery of his parents and would read the inscriptions. I would write them down in my notebook knowing that one day I would need to know who is who. These tombstones, fountains, and other old monuments are becoming archaeological remnants of the past.

In about ten years no one will remain alive from the Ottoman days. All that will stay will be buildings, tombs, museums, some antique furniture, folk dances and music. Anthropologists will find objects during their excavations and will wonder the use of these articles. Therefore I am trying to describe the passage from Ottoman to Republican rule and to explain all the changes that took place with the closing of the Ottoman period.

Chapter 3
Memoirs of Leyla Hanım
(My grandmother's mother)

Since my childhood at the house in Kızıltoprak, I had a liking for souvenirs and old objects. I went to a boarding school at the age of six and maybe this made me attached very much to my mother. My father would be almost always on travels. According to the Ottoman way of life children would not talk much with their father. No questions were asked and you had to obey only. My mother had told me that Sırrı Pasha, the husband of Leyla Hanım, would kiss his children only after they went to sleep so that they would not be spoiled.

My grandfather Mehmet Ali Bey was some one to be avoided and to stay away from. My father was very jovial and friendly but since he also was brought up in the Ottoman style, he would expect us to behave accordingly. When an elderly person entered a room you were supposed to get up and wait until he or she sat down. Every person had a set place in the living room: My grandfather's corner, my grandmother's armchair, Leyla hanım had her own seat. At the table the children were not allowed to talk. They would answer if they were asked a question. The children could not give orders to the maids or servants. You could only ask something from the youngest maid. All these rules were not written but they were known somehow. They were acquired by hearsay or by the advice of our nurse. Whose hand had to be kissed, who should be greeted first and how we should behave was whispered to us by our nurse.

When we were children at Kızıltoprak there was no electricity, city gas or running water. Before the sun set the kerosene lamps would be prepared. Water was pumped from a deep well in the garden. According to the season, charcoal braziers (mangal) were lit or the wood stoves were fired on winter days. There were no radios, iceboxes, televisions and such gadgets in those years. There was more conversation between people. In general people would walk wherever they went, so talking would continue during the walk. There were more visits among relatives and neighbors. As children we had to listen to what was being said. As there were many elderly people in the family, they would tell tales and relate their memories. Whenever we sat with Leyla Hanım, we would ask her to tell a story. Everyone had one or two tales that we knew. We would ask again and again to hear these stories. We would already know where to laugh or where to be sorry. Still we would ask for these tales. After years went by we started giving numbers to these stories. For instance we would say Kızıltoprak No. 27. This was my father's story of the bear at Kastamonu on the road to Ankara from İnebolu. This was a way of joking, as not all stories were numbered, but we would understand from the start which tale was going to be told. It came to a point where we would start laughing before coming to the point. Then at the climax laughing would go into a roar.

My grandmother would tell stories with great excitement and imitations of the characters in the tale. She had travelled a lot during the days of the empire and had met many characters, so she would relate the tale by using local intonations or even swear words! Leyla Hanım would be very upset and would reprimand her daughter saying, "Feride stop now, I will have a stroke!"

One day there was watermelon for dessert. My grandfather objected to the taste of the watermelon and said, "It tastes like the flesh of an old lady." This was very contrary to the Ottoman table manners and Leyla Hanım was very upset and said to her son-in-law "You must have tasted it sir!". In such a situation it would be improper to laugh but it was very, very funny and we almost plunged into our plates in order to keep quiet.

Some tales were about the sons of unknown sultans and their fights with dragons and other creatures. They would also relate funny happenings on their travels. One day my grandmother was going by train from Istanbul to Salonica to visit her brother who was stationed in that city. All train compartments had a door on the side of the car and it was easy to get on and off the train. During the voyage no one could leave the cabin. Uncle Sırrı was only four or five years old and he had to go to the toilet. My grandmother opened up a newspaper and held her child on the paper to relieve him. The paper was then wrapped and thrown out of the cabin window. Suddenly shouts came from the next compartment. The paper had opened up and pasted on their window. Nothing happened to anybody but it was a strange accident and lots of complaints came from the next compartment. This story was told many many times and each time we laughed and laughed. What made it funny was the imitations and expressions of my grandmother.

People at Kızıltoprak had time to read and write. It was natural to see everyone with a book in his hand because all the work was being done by servants, cook and maids. Leyla Hanım would write her poetry on small pieces of paper or on the back of her cigarette box. My grandmother, Feride Hanım, did not write much but she had a notebook where she collected songs, poetry and annecdotes about places where she visited. My mother had always one or two books beside her bed and she had writing paper and envelopes for writing letters to my father. My grandfather had two libraries, one in his guestroom and one next to his bedroom where he did his writing most of the time. He would sit on a large divan cross legged write on his knee in old script. His writing was very quick and articulate. He learned the new alphabet but he was slow with these new characters, so he still used the old script. Unfortunately, Leyla Hanım's music and poetry had all been burned in a fire in her old house at Bostancı. She was trying to recollect and rewrite her songs, music and poetry. My mother and aunt would read in French or English and my uncle would read in German. My grandfather knew French but would ask my mother's help for the translation of some English texts. When the elderly wanted to talk secretly from us they would talk in Greek. Leyla Hanım knew classical Greek but her daughter Feride would speak Istanbul Greek and her mother would correct her. My grandfather knew Arabic and Persian very well and would teach us verses from Persian poets. Every day the Cumhuriyet paper was purchased. The gardener would go and bring a copy from the Kızıltoprak market, as there was still no house to house delivery system of newspapers. My grandfather would bring a copy of Akşam when he returned from work. The newspaper was read first by the elderly. My grandmother would put on her eyeglasses, have a look at the paper and then turn it over to my mother. My mother would read the news loudly and everybody would listen. Then she would shift to the novels that were published in sections each day. After this the crossword puzzle was solved jointly and, perhaps by that time, some of the neighbors would come and try to solve the puzzle together.

Leyla Hanım continued to use the old script while trying to rewrite her poetry and memoirs. I asked my mother and mother- in-law to re-write these in the new alphabet. I kept these notes for years and gradually realized that these manuscripts were not to be found anywhere else. At that time there was no tape or videos to record these old tales and souvenirs. There were also no home film cameras. All that remained was old and new script documents, letters and black and white snapshots or photographs taken at studios in town. Later my mother and uncle had cameras and liked to take pictures.

They made several family albums and when Kızıltoprak was being closed down I took and safeguarded all these albums. No one else was interested in these old papers and pictures. There was also a question of storage space. Luckily I could send a lot of furniture and trunks to my brother-in-law's cold storage depot at Yalova. That place had a large attic were I could store whatever was left from Kızıltoprak. Whenever I found time, using the documents that my mother and my mother-in- law had written in the new script, I tried to learn the old script. I learned to decipher some, but it requires much more practice to read and understand the old Turkish. The year I went to school the old script was stopped so what I could learn was at home with a special teacher. I have tried to select examples from Ottoman life from these documents.

I will start with Leyla Hanım's memoirs which had been translated to the new script by my mother. This document reflects the experiences of Ismail Pasha a governor sent to the island of Crete by the sultan, her father, Ismail Pasha the chief physician of the sultan and was later a governor of several provinces. Now I will leave you to read the memoirs of Leyla Hanım as they were written down by her. Excerpts from Leyla Saz Hanım's diary:

"I think I was born some time between sixty and sixty-five (1860-1865). According to the customs of the period, I was brought up by nurses, wet-nurses, and servants. My father (Ismail Pasha) was the chief physician of the sultan, and Münire Sultan (the sultan's mother) took me to the palace when I was four years old. This gave me the chance to observe the way of life in the palace and I will write about it in later years. I cannot remember when I started to read and write, but at the time of the latest revolt in Bosnia- Herzegovina, Ömer Efendi and Sabit Efendi who were my father's assistants, used to give me private lessons.

"When my father was appointed the governor of Izmir, he took me along. According to the fashion in those days, I was dressed like a boy. I shared my father's room and a male nurse took care of me. Later, my mother and my brothers joined us and we lived in Izmir for some time.

"We returned to Istanbul at the time of the conquest of Sebastopol. When I was introduced to Sultan Mecid I was dressed as a "zeybek" in the traditional costume of the Aegean region. He made me recite some classical poetry.

"In those years I had already started composing some music and had learned to play the piano. I also began taking painting lessons from Dellasuda Faik Pasha, a very famous artist. He must have been bored with me and, after a while, started sending one of his assistants, a doctor called Yanko, to continue with the lessons; but my grandmother, my aunt and my father soon forbade me to go further in painting. I continued to take piano lessons from Therese Roma who lived in the Kadıköy section of Istanbul. My sister and I used to play "in four hands". As there were no players of European music among Muslim families during the reign of Sultan Mecid, the princes Aziz and Murat and İlhami Pasha were very fond of listening to our music.

"I would spend approximately nine months of the year in the

22

palace; I gave piano lessons to the sultans Refia, Münire, and Behice and helped them with their dictation. I spent most of my time with Murat Efendi (the sultan's son) and his wives. They would ask me to play the piano or make some paintings. During those days I was unaware of the goings on around me and enjoyed life very much. But one night I felt very humiliated. Someone had dropped a love letter into the room of Murat Efendi and made him believe that it was from me. That evening we played the piano; he asked his brother Kemalettin Efendi to dance with me and we had a very good time. After everyone retired to his quarters, a girl brought me a thank you note written in a very kind manner. I had seen such notes before but had never received one and I asked the girl what it was all about. I never had such desires and hopes. When I enquired further, the girl giggled and said she could not reveal any names but it was the answer to my note. I could not explain to the carrier of the message and I had no chance of clarifying the situation so I had to bear this audacity. The next evening I could not join the group because I did not know what was written in the love letter; I was very ashamed. Anyway, I was invited and had to go. His attitude was not changed and everything went on as usual but whenever he looked at me, I felt like disappearing somewhere. The earlier years of my life were spent among the children of the sultan; our relations were on a brotherly basis. A lady of Hamid Efendi was invited to our house. She was the type who would make friends easily and tease anyone she met. This was a kind of game among ladies of the palace. One day I saw her talking to two young men and I found one of them rather attractive. Later on, I had a chance to talk to them and liked their conversation. I had never considered myself as a grown up nor thought of falling in love or being loved but, somehow, I began to think of this person quite often. I learned from my sister that my uncle also knew him; he was Sadullah Bey, the son of Esat Pasha. My uncle thought positively about our marriage. I must admit that I was very pleased. But Sadullah Bey knew nothing about these developments.

"In the meantime, my father was appointed the Governor of the

Island of Crete. Again I was going along with my father. I went to Münire Sultan to pay her a farewell visit - at that time she was the wife of İbrahim Pasha. Sultan Mecid died that night. I experienced the calamity in the palace. I took leave next morning and a few weeks later we sailed for Crete on the imperial frigate Keyvan.

"On the boat my father introduced to me a Christian lady whose name was Elizabeth Verf. She did not know Turkish and I did not know any of the languages she spoke. She was a well educated person and I was impressed with her immediately. She wrote down the Greek and French alphabets and demonstrated the sounds they represented. During the few days we were on the boat, I had learned the syllables in those languages.

"When we reached Crete she became my governess. She had a writing cabinet placed in a small room where I studied with her every morning. I was spending the rest of the day sewing and attending feasts.

"Elizabeth Verf, the Christian ladies of Crete and I would go to the sea-baths which were a little outside the town. After we had a swim, we would find a rock on the shore to sit on and she read me Robinson Crusoe. I could not understand all of it. The whole summer went on like this. Then, in the winter, my grandmother forbade me the lessons. When the old lady returned to Istanbul, we continued our lessons. The concubines in the house would often come and knock on the door wishing to relieve me - they thought I had enough and was getting bored! We did not mind them and continued with our lessons. I pleaded for a calligraphy teacher and my father invited Esad Efendi of Candia (he is now the Chief Accountant of Jerusalem) from the secondary school in Crete.

"After reading some literary books, I started scribbling some verses myself but I never dared show them to anybody. One day my father noticed my writings and asked me to recite. He liked them and I was very happy. He showed them to Sadık Efendi who was the son of Kutbi Efendi, the famous poet in Crete. Gradually I began to learn to write poetry and songs. Within one year, I had learned to speak Greek and begun to understand French. The ladies of Crete would come to me to have their dresses cut to measure.

"Soon after our arrival in Crete, I heard that Sadullah Bey had been married. I was very sad but tried not to think much about it. I was asked to marry Hilmi Bey, the son of Mustafa Pasha, but my father would not consent. In the year eighty (1880), we went to Istanbul on leave for two months and returned. While we were making preparations to entertain Sultan Abdülaziz on his return journey from Egypt, his daughter Mürşide Sultan came to stay with us in Crete for a convalescence. In eighty-three (1883), upon the encouragement of my father, I wrote a poem for Sultan Aziz and sent it to the Mother Sultan. Sultan Aziz liked it very much and sent me a gift of a coffeecup holder engraved with diamonds. I also sent two songs to Fatma Sultan and heard that she was very pleased. As a souvenir she sent me a medallion which I still keep. During the local revolt in Crete, I was the translator and secret secretary to my father.

"At any rate, my life in Crete was not in vain. Foreign ladies resident in Crete and travelling ones passing through used to visit and stay with us. I had met the Countess Tene who was later condemned to death in Tripoli. Madame la Countess de Schatz who resided in Crete liked me very much. One day she saw my headgear and asked me what it was called and I replied, "Garibaldi". She happened to be a close friend of Garibaldi and they were corresponding with each other. Soon after, she conveyed me his greetings."

The notes of Leyla throw light on the life of the young Leyla and reflect her close relations with the royal family at the Çırağan Palace.

I compared her notes with "Voyage du Sultan Abd-ul-Aziz de Stamboul au Caire", the diary of the French professor L. Gardey who kept and published a diary of the trip of Sultan Abdülaziz from İstanbul to Egypt and back. It is the diary kept by this French teacher during the trip from Istanbul to Cairo and back. He had presented a copy to the Governor of Crete with his handwritten dedication, "A son Excellence Ismail Pasha, gouverneur de l'ile de Crete - homage de mes sentiment les plus distingues". The book was published in Paris in 1865. Professor

Gardey describes the trip in detail and states that at the last minute the steamer which carried Sultan Aziz diverted her route to İzmir and did not stop at Candia, Crete. There were a lot of preparations to greet the sultan in their home. They bought new tableware and so on to receive the sultan and his entourage. However, after I read this diary, I understood why the sultan did not step on Cretan soil. It is clear that the European powers did not want the sultan to set foot on the island because they wanted to annex this island to Greece at that time. Ismail Pasha, who was originally from the island of Samos and of Greek descent, was sent to calm down a rebellion but the rebellion started after he had returned to Istanbul. The Turkish armada was followed by one British and one French destroyer. Information contained in the notes of Leyla Saz and the book by Professor Gardey, who was teaching at the Imperial School of Engineering of Istanbul at the time, coincide on a detail of history. They supplement each other and give us a true picture of the events, reflecting a certain period of the Ottoman Empire.

I was very fortunate to have had the privilege of knowing and talking to my great grandmother Leyla Saz in her later years and listening to her music which she composed and played on the old harmonium which her father had given to her in 1867 when she was still a young girl. She would tell me and my brothers fairy tales as well as accounts of her ancestors. I would plead with her to play "the march" which was the "March of Crete" that she had composed. She never refused; she would take her cane and walk with difficulty to her small organ and play it with the enthusiasm of a young girl. She died in 1936 at Kızıltoprak, Istanbul, in my grandparents' house, where four generations of our family were living together under one roof.

An example of her letter writing is given in the following pages. These are three letters she wrote to her daughter Feride who was in Trabzon. These letters were written during the Balkan War. The date on the envelope stamp shows 25.11.12 (1912), issued in old Turkish and French by the postal administration. The cost of the stamp was 20 para (one kurush consisted of 40 para and one hundred kurush was one lira).

The stationery used is an old letterhead printed in Yanina. This paper and envelope must have come back from Yanina to Kızıltoprak when my grandfather was appointed as governor to Trabzon. She simply deleted the word Yanina.

The letter starts with a "B" which is an abbreviation for "Bismillahirahmanirahim", meaning, "in the name of God the Provider and Protector".

"My dear daughter Feride,

"You must have worried after you left since I was left alone in the house. I started immediately to tidy the place. In the first hours I felt very lonely and I almost got lost in the empty house. I tried to do things and thus kept busy. Until the night I found something to do but many times I had tears in my eyes. At last the first night passed and the next day Emine Hanım came. Our old maid Şerif came. On Friday night the children came.

"One gets used to every situation. We are all in good health. Now the children are getting ready to go to school. I am invited to Nasib Hanımefendi and I will not be able to visit your brother. There are exams at the school and Nezihe prefers to study here in solitude. This week we plan to go to Nişantaşı but you send your letters here. İlyas the cook prepares our food. He also helps with heavy work in the house. For the time being that is the situation.

"Yesterday Hasan Bey came, they are all fine. I am sending to you the card that came from Selahattin. I believe Mehmet Ali bey found him a good job. Today Nasib Hanımefendi came over. Ilhami Bey got wounded on the Çatalca front from his leg, Şerif Pasha informed by telegraph. He still could not return to Istanbul. Your cable informing your arrival to Trabzon has just arrived. You should see our joy and happiness. I kiss the eyes of Mehmet Ali Bey. The girls both are kissing your hands and Sırrı kissing your eyes. The day that you left I could not comprehend the notes of Sırrı that came from Galatasaray. After you left I collected the papers that were here and there and the report was the first one that came to my attention. I had ordered İlyas to say that I am not at home to whoever comes. Everything is upside down and I am completely alone. How did you like Trabzon? Who have you seen? Hasan çavuş (a helper) took the filberts you sent to Sırrı. İlyas is alright. Mustafa will go to Kartal on the 29th of the month. I think I will stop this letter here. Şerif, Sıdıka and Emine are kissing the hem of your skirt and they send "selam" to Elif.

"Leyla"

It is understood from the letter that Leyla Hanım stayed with the children at Kızıltoprak when her daughter and son-in-law went to Trabzon. M.A. Ayni was transferred from Yanina to Trabzon. My mother, aunt and uncle stayed in Istanbul to continue their schooling. Leyla Hanım left her house at Bostancı and moved to Kızıltoprak to take care of the children. The Balkan war was at its worst stage. The Bulgarian army advanced as far as Çatalca which is very near Istanbul. Istanbul feels the atmosphere of the war but life continues. At home the cook, maids and servants do the work. My mother brought me to the world ten years after these events. She would always relate those days. Her grandmother took very good care of them and they were under her influence because her parents were somewhere else in the empire. While my grandfather and grandmother went from assignment to assignment, their maternal grandmother took care of them and they liked her very much. That is how they completed their education at the British High School for Girls in Istanbul. Leyla Hanım describes these difficult days in a letter dated 10.2.1913 to Trabzon. The enemy was approaching the gates of Istanbul the capital, and the empire was in great danger. It was not yet finished but the end was visible and, worst of all, the future unknown. She was in Istanbul but her daughter and son-in-law were in Trabzon. That was the last duty of my grandfather. He was put to retirement after this position. There is another letter from Leyla Hanım to her daughter:

"My dear Feride,

"B (Bismillahirrahmanirrahim)

"Your letter of 19th October has arrived. I was very glad about your good news. We are also in good health. I am sure you are informed about the war news. It seems there are 100.000 soldiers between Istanbul and Izmit. They are transporting as much as needed to the European side by boat. They are advancing from several points towards the enemy. They have also organized some groups and they are going to demolish the railroad which is under Bulgarian control. Thus they will stop the advance of enemy troops. At night they are being transported from Anatolia to Istanbul. I believe they are also bringing cannons. There is no torch illimunation as it was done previously. They are coming quietly after midnight. The chief of staff Enver has selected 40,000 soldiers, keeping them as reserves under his command. There are many people from high and middle income families who register as volunteers. The son of doctor Hilmi Pasha left Kızıltoprak the other day against the will of his family. He even tried to commit suicide but was not successful. This time he ran away without the consent of his family. There was a neighbor at Harput whose name now escapes me, but their son Firuz also went as a volunteer. There are many who want to go to the front as volunteers. I hope they will be successful. Yesterday your brother Yusuf came for a visit. He says that news can only come after a period of three or four days. This time we hope to succeed. They are all men of war and active. The first news of success will encourage the soldiers. Everything will change for the better. When I asked him if there is a hope on the side of the government, he was very much offended and said that people of Kızıltoprak are always on the negative side. Of course I am very much concerned. Should anything happen I will do all I can to save the children. For the time being the danger is not very imminent, otherwise I would take the children and go further to a safe place. You also are uneasy, I know, but I will take control of things if necessary. It is not necessary that you should return now and at any rate do not leave your work at the Red Crescent. Of course, I know you miss your children but please be patient. It is easy to come from Trabzon. You can jump on a foreign boat and come over to Istanbul quickly. Do not worry, if necessary I will take the children and come over to you. For the time being we should be patient. Yesterday the three of them with Mustafa on their control came to me with joy and happiness. They were very glad to see the letters. They had lots of lessons to prepare and to memorize, so they could not write a note. Yusuf measured Refika; she is one meter and 59 centimeters tall and reached the height of her elder sister. Sırrı was only one meter and 39 centimeters. They are all very healthy. They have rosy cheeks but Sırrı has a problem. He has difficulty to understand French and grammar is too complicated. He is very much afraid that he will be detained. They have placed two sons of the sultans on both of his sides, one the son of Sultan Hamid and the other the son of Süleyman Efendi, brother of Sultan Mecid. They were very well dressed and when we said that the trousers should be mended Sırrı was very upset. He was looking to me and then to his uncle. On Sunday the shops are closed, so I said to him to wear his old trousers and I would buy new ones and send him on Wednesday. He was very happy but he was eyeing his uncle. When he also confirmed, then he relaxed. We had a good laugh. Yusuf was going to take them to the cinema but they did not want to return late to school. So he promised to take them another day. He got used to me but he still misses you very much. He is very close to his sisters. He tells what he needs, so please do not worry about him. My husband sent 15 liras to cover our expenses. Mustafa went to get it. I had paid the increased taxes on our konak so I was a little tight. I am now allright and I paid the salary of Mustafa. It seems he also wants two salaries from you. I gave him his October and November salaries of two liras each.

"I would like you to order two silver teacup holders like the ones you sent to the children. You might send them with someone who is coming back. I had them weighed and each one costs four mecidiye (20 kuruş). This makes eight mecidiye and I will send it by post. I will send it to the name of Hasan. The same greetings like before, Mustafa and Dilber kiss your skirt's hem. We are suffering a shortage of house help but the name Peymane is not appealing to me. I am afraid she will resemble the old Peymane.* Our Dilber is running all the time. She is very good at heavy

---

(*) They must be looking for a maid to be brought from Trabzon.

30

house work. I try to overlook her errors. 28 November, 328. Leyla".

In old letters there was no address or name of street. The postal service was also very expensive. The stamp of 20 para compares to 56,000 TL. with today's rate (One gold is 11,250,000 lira in 1997). The address on the envelope is as follows:

"To the wife of his Excellency the Governor of Trabzon, Mr. Mehmet Ali Ayni".

This letter reached Trabzon and my grandmother kept it for many years. She brought it back to Kızıltoprak. My mother kept her mother's old papers and letters. Luckily Kızıltoprak did not burn down and these letters stayed in a bag in my granmother's wardrobe. I had taken this furniture to Yalova and then twenty years later brought them to Levent. Gradually, as much as I would have time, I went though these letters and read them with my mother-in-law. Now I am relating to you this letter written to her daughter on 28.2.1913. The first world war is still not declared but the Balkan war is at its peak and Istanbul is under danger of occupation by the Bulgarian army. The postal administration is still a capitulation administration under French control and they collect their interest with the revenue obtained from postal services.

As with all the correspondence, the letter "B" stands on the top. (There is no punctuation in the hand writing of the Ottoman script. In the old script they leave a little distance and that is how you understand the end of a sentence).

"My dear Feride,

"I am glad to receive your letter and we also are in good health. This weekend I was alone with Sırrı. The girls will visit their uncle this weekend. I did not see anybody these last days. So there is no gossip. The newspapers are all empty and they make me very nervous. It gives me great pain. But still I send a man to the gate when I hear the voice of the newspaper man. At night I go to bed with several newspapers. Life goes on with grief and sorrow. There are people who are still running after their own benefit and do not care. They are after fame or gains. I cannot describe how sad this makes me. I feel guilty that I came to this world as a human being. Again I complained too much. I am very glad to hear about your Red Crescent activities. I am sure you will be successful. Please control the accounts very strictly. You should write to Princess Nimet Hanım who is the president of the association. Your husband can tell you more about this. The other day a bullet was shot from a Russian warship to the minaret of Valide Sultan mosque. Also there was an attack by a Russian soldier to a lady in charshaf. There were a lot of complaints but the newspapers do not write anything. This shows that these Russians are helping the Bulgarians. It is not a good sign but we cannot do anything to stop them. We are keeping our nerves under control. If fate will show us utter defeat it will be a shame to have lost so many lives and end up in disaster. They say that there will be no unrest within Istanbul city. I am not worried about it but I feel very sorry for those on the fighting front. I am sure that all the places that we have lost will never come back. At least I pray that these lives will not go to waste. I am completely in distress. I want to say much more but it affects my heart. My pen is running on the paper, I cannot stop it. Leyla, year 328 month 9".

I will end the memories of Leyla Hanım with this letter. News of her death in Cumhuriyet newspaper in December 1936 was published on page 2 with a picture of the funeral services. My grandfather and the hodja of the mosque are at the head of a group of men taking part in the funeral. At that time women did not participate in funeral ceremonies. Since children also were not brought to the funerals, I had to stay at home.

The news is as follows: YESTERDAY THE FUNERAL OF LEYLA SAZ TOOK PLACE

"We inform with regret that our poet Leyla hanım's funeral took place yesterday. With the participation of her relatives and friends she was taken from the house of her son-in-law Mehmet Ali Ayni to Kadıköy where she was transferred to a boat and taken to Sirkeci. From there the funeral prayers took place at the Nuruosmaniye mosque. After the prayers, she was taken to her eternal resting place. We are very sorry to have lost Leyla Hanım at the age of eighty-four. She was very well known in the society and had helped many people during her lifetime. She was liked by all relatives and friends and her death is a big loss. We give our condolecences to her family."*

This is how the life of Leyla Saz ended. Her nickname was Mimi at home and it was a show of affection to her by her grandchildren.

Her son Yusuf Razi had translated her memoirs into French and published them in Paris under the title Le Harem Emperial. A French writer Albert Cahuet wrote an article about her in La Petite Illustration in the September 12, 1925, issue. This book was later translated into Turkish and published in Istanbul under the title of "Inside the Harem". This article on Leyla Hanım in French is reproduced in the appendix of this book. It was later translated from French into English by a New York banker, Landon Thomas and published in 1990 as The Imperial Harem of the Sultans: Daily Life at the Çırağan Palace during the 19th Century by PEVA Publications in Istanbul.

_____

(*) Her grave is at the Edirnekapı cemetery and is surrounded by the graves of her daughter Feride Mehmet Ali, her son Yusuf Razi Bel and her granddaughter Leyla Hayreden. [The author of this book, Nezih Neyzi, who passed away on January 28, 1999 now rests in the same plot.]

Chapter 4
Memoirs of Ismail Pasha the Doctor
(Father of Leyla Hanım)

What we knew about the life of Ismail Pasha at Kızıltoprak was the version told by Yusuf Razi Bel his grandson, presented here in a later chapter (page 89). I learned more details about him twenty years after the dismantling of the house at Kızıltoprak.

Uncle Yusuf had prepared a "Livre de Famille," that is a diary of the family in French. The section that I found was titled, "My maternal grandfather, The Doctor Ismail Pasha." He also wrote a section on his father Sırrı Pasha. These are typewritten notes and I believe they were never printed.

Apart from this French version there are other notes titled "To be sent to Mr. Midhat Cemal." Most probably this was meant to be published in a magazine.

In the French version Yusuf Razi relates that he saw his grandfather and that he remembers him. He saw his grandfather the last time at the age of eight. He remembers his face and his voice and adds, "In those days children could rarely see their father."

Ismail Pasha had a stroke at his office at the Sublime Port (the prime ministry) in February, 1874. He was laid down for a few days at his office then they brought him to his konak (big house) at Beşiktaş. My grandfather took me to his grave on a bayram day (holiday) many years ago. It is at an enclosed cemetery called a "Türbe" in old Istanbul.

Ismail Pasha was born on the island of Khios in 1807. An Izmir surgeon who was visiting the island regularly adopted him and brought him to Izmir. He was trained at the medical school at Topkapı Palace and became a surgeon. He conducted the circumcision of the sons of the sultan and thus became the sultan's doctor. He was sent to Paris for further training and then he went to Pisa Medical School in Italy and obtained a certificate on gynecology.

Leyla Hanım told her son Yusuf Razi that her father had taken care of the mother of the sultan. He took her to Yalova thermal baths which he had reconstructed with a decree of the sultan. The bath at Yalova is still called the "Mother's Bath" because of this event. He stayed forty days with the mother sultan and brought her back after she was completely cured. The sultan, very satisfied with this cure, bought Ismail Pasha a konak at Beşiktaş and awarded him a medal.

The positions occupied by Ismail Pasha were:

1848 Minister of Education and Minister of Public Works
1849 Minister of Trade
1851 Member of the High Commission of "Scientists"
1852 Minister of the School of Medicine
1853 Governor of Izmir
1857 Minister of Trade
1860 Member of Ministers of the Court
1861 Governor of Crete for six years before the revolution
1867 Minister of Interior
1868 Governor of Izmir

During this appointment Sırrı Bey had been transfered from Yanina to Izmir to work as secretary to Ismail Pasha. He decided to marry Sırrı Bey to his daughter Leyla and thus make him his son-in-law.

1871 Governor of Salonica (He resigned after 5 months)
1872 Minister of Interior
1873 Head of the Istanbul Municipality
1879 Died of a stroke at the Sublime Port

Ismail Pasha had been to France, Italy and England. He had visited factories in these countries and became well informed about the industries of Europe. He was very witty and was accepted in international circles both at home and abroad. At that time he was referred to as His Exellency. He was very influential during the reign of Sultan Mecid. After the throning of Sultan Aziz he was appointed Governor of Crete in order to get him away from Istanbul. But he was very much liked by the mother sultan and the sultan so after some years he was recalled to

Istanbul again and given very high positions.

Ismail Pasha had many friends like the great Reşit Pasha and Fuat Pasha who were influential people of the time. But he had also opponents who were jealous of him because of his closeness to the sultan's family and the palace. When he was appointed Governor of Izmir he was successful in arresting famous bandits who were hiding in the mountains. He would take care of the sick while he was serving in Izmir, not charging any fees to the poor and providing their medicines.

One day his son-in-law Sırrı Pasha saw a hodja massaging his forehead and reciting some prayers. After the man left, he asked his father-in-law, "Sir, you are a doctor, how do you accept the treatment of an illiterate man?" He replied, "My son, this man has acquired a way of making a good massage with his hands and he is very experienced. I do not mind his reciting prayers, his massage is excellent. I had a headache and he made me relax, let him say some prayers, I do not mind".

Sultan Mecid was very much afraid of owls and their cry. One day an owl began singing in the garden of the palace while Ismail Pasha was present. The sultan got very upset because this meant a bad omen. Ismail Pasha immediately looked out of the window and said "His excellency this was not an owl it was a "Kerkenez" bird, the owl's voice is different." The sultan calmed down.

Ismail Pasha had related to his family strange situations that would happen at the harem. The ladies at the harem were rather uneducated and not accustomed to talking with men. So when they were sick and had to be examined they would not reply to the questions of the doctor. Questions on eating habits were answered very generally and they would protest to the questioning of the doctor.

The problem of bowel removal and the answers given were quite unrelated. For instance when the doctor asked if she "went out" regularly or not this was mixed up with going out of the harem and they would say "whenever there is a religious holiday, or whenever the sultan would allow." Finally the doctor would have to ask more directly in order to get an answer on the state of the bowel movements.

Ismail Pasha was a connoisseur of good food. He always found well trained cooks and he would give them advice on cooking. Some of these master cooks were turned over to the palace kitchen. Those who had eaten at his house would describe the special meal that was prepared.

Ismail Pasha was also a close friend of Namık Kemal who was a famous poet and writer of his day. When he was the minister of interior he was not very strict to the "Young Turks". This was one of the reasons why he was taken away from this position.

Ismail Pasha had made the circumcisions of Sultan Mecid and Sultan Reşat when they were little boys. He had met Sultan Abdülhamid but had not made his circumcision.

All these anacdotes reveal how close Ismail Pasha was to the royal family. I had heard these anecdotes from Uncle Yusuf Razi himself. After her house at Bostancı burned down, Leyla Hanım did not build a new house but rather would stay in winter with her son Yusuf Razi in Nuruosmaniye and in summer with her daughter at Kızıltoprak. She did not carry any furniture because she had her piano at Kızıltoprak and her portable harmonium in her large bedroom at Nuruosmaniye. During the winter of 1936 while my father and mother went to London on a business trip, I used to visit Leyla Hanım each weekend. On Saturday afternoon I would go straight to Uncle Yusuf's house. She would play her "Crete" march on the harmonium. She would relate tales of her grandfather Tatar Abdurrahman or tell other tales. On these occasions, I could see and get to know Uncle Yusuf and his family better. During the summer Uncle Yusuf would come often to Kızıltoprak to see his mother and sister Feride, my grandmother. Uncle Yusuf Razi was married in France during his education at the Ecoles des Pont et Chausse in Paris. His wife's name was Marie Bel but her Turkish name was İsmet Hanım. The house of Yusuf Razi was full of furniture and the walls of the living room were covered with big pictures of Sırrı Pasha, his father, and Ismail Pasha, his grandfather. The house was full of family pictures, stamp collections, tiles, clocks and many other old objects.

Leyla Hanım had her room on the same floor where the dining

room and the guest rooms were. She would take her cane and walk to the dining room from her bedroom. After dinner she would go to the living room or return to her room. I had a feeling that there was a distance between her and the French daughter-in-law but nothing was said in this respect. There was a big white ceramic wood stove in the middle hall which heated the whole floor. There was a partition at the staircase leading to the third floor where Yusuf Razi had his bedroom, working studio and a guest room. Sometimes his daughter, also named Leyla, or his son Ismail would come and stay in this room. The daughter Leyla married with Hayrettin Hayreden and we saw each other quite often. They used to visit my parents at Kızıltoprak. After the death of Hayrettin Bey, I kept in touch with the younger Leyla and saw her up to her last days. She would come to visit us and tell old tales to my children. She gave me some of the old papers of her father Yusuf Razi. If she had not given these documents it would be impossible for me to give an exact account of the family ancestors. Tales were told at Kızıltoprak but the exact dates and places of travel, their positions, etc. were not clear to me. All came from these documents supplied by her. It is much safer to relate from old written documents than to rely on tales and hearsay.

The wife of Ismail Pasha was Nefise Hanım, the daughter of Tatar Abdurrahman Ağa. My mother's first name was Nefise derived from the mother of Leyla Saz Hanım.

Among these papers I found a letter dated May 15, 1854, written in French by the English Consul General to the Governor of Izmir, Ismail Pasha. The letter is on the subject of hay to be purchased from the Aegean area and loaded on a boat at the Dardanelles. The consul asks Ismail Pasha not to charge the usual tax of the port because this shipment of hay is for the British cavalry horses at Sıvastapol. They are going to fight the Russians together with the French and Ottoman armies.

These are the famous horses of the light brigade that had a disastrous fate at this war at Sıvastapol. They were all killed because of a faulty maneuver. I found a book by Cecil Woodham named The Reason Why in which he describes this war and the fate of these horses.

If Leyla Hanım had not kept these papers, I would never have seen this letter in French written by the British Consul General at the Dardanelles in 1854. At that time the borders of Izmir district extended up to the Dardanelles.

Chapter 5
Sırrı Pasha (The husband of Leyla Saz)
(My great-grandfather)

I owe these memoirs to Uncle Yusuf Razi and to his daughter Leyla
Hayreden who would give me now and again old manuscripts and pictures. In general I would not even have time to read these but would
store them somewhere. In her last years I was very busy as the general
manager of the Maritime Bank. Funny enough, I did not at that time
know that the Yalova thermal baths were built by Ismail Pasha. These
baths were run by the bank and as my duty I would take care of them
and do the necessary repairs.

Uncle Yusuf had prepared a "LIVRE DE FAMILLE," or Family
Notebook in French, a section of which is devoted to his father Sırrı
Pasha and starts as "MON PERE SIRRI PASHA." Most probably he pre-
pared it for a French magazine.

He was born to a Turkish family in the year 1843 or 1844 in the
town of Hegire, Crete. Yusuf Razi had a chance to talk with his father's
brother, Nuri Pasha who also confirmed that the family was brought
over from Konya after the conquest of Crete. They were among the first
Turkish settlers coming from Central Anatolia. Sırrı Pasha's father died
when he was 12 years old and the children were brought up by their
eldest sister. One of the brothers had a little business in Candia. One of
the older brothers became a governor at Bilecik and Kütahya. His name
was Fuat Pasha and he was the one who built the tile covered government office building at Kütahya. Years later, to commemorate his name
a statue was erected at Kütahya. We were invited for this ceremony but
as I was very busy at the School of Business Administration I could not
participate. I went sometime ago and took a picture of the statue with
my daughters Furuğ and Füsun.

Fuat Pasha never got married. Nuri Pasha married the daughter of
Abidin Pasha from Preveze (now in Greece). Abidin Pasha, became the

Minister of Foreign Affairs and governor of the Aegean islands. Later he became governor of Ankara and Adana. Fuat Pasha and Nuri Pasha are buried at the Rumelihisar cemetery and I went and found the tombstones a few years ago among all the family graves. Sırrı Pasha is with his second wife and Kamuran Bey, his son from his second wife, are side by side. Bülent Kandiyeli the son of the second wife had told me about the place of these graves. I had known Kamuran Bey in Kızıltoprak as he would came and visit his step sister Feride, my grandmother. Many years later I met with Bülent Kandiyeli accidentally in Ankara. We were both working at the Ministry of Transportation.

Sırrı Efendi took his education at Candia, and learned Arabic and Persian and wore a turban. All his life he wrote literary and religious books. He also pointed to the fact that Turkish should be simplified and relieved from the Arabic influence. He tried to simplify the flowery Ottoman language with its never-ending sentences. Yusuf Razi refers to his father's efforts to simplify the Turkish language as an indication that he can be looked upon as a leader of this simplification movement.

Sırrı Pasha published his correspondence with the Russian general Stolyfrine in his book in 1894. He was at that time governor of Diyarbakır and the book was published by the official government printing house.

He made the agreement with the Russian general for the delivery of Varna and Çumla after the Russian war. This was a lengthy agreement because the cities were going to be delivered in peace. This gave the right to the Turkish army to take back all its soldiers and ammunition. There was no other transportation than horse carriages belonging to the farmers. The harvest season was on, so they had to wait until the end of the harvest to rent the carriages. The Russians were getting impatiant for the Turks to evacuate the cities, but Sırrı Pasha handled the situation gracefully and the Russian Czar sent him a medal for his efforts.

In 1876 he was appointed as governor of Karesi (Balıkesir) and the following year was transferred to Trabzon. At that time Trabzon was a very difficult place to manage because the Russians were invading

Georgia and all the Muslim population was pushed out to Turkey. At the same time they were instigating the Christian population in and around Trabzon to migrate to Georgia. There was also internal fighting among Georgian regional landlords which made the situation worse. Sırrı Pasha's correspondence with the Sublime Port is also very interesting. There was a rival person in Trabzon called Çürüksulu Ali Pasha who was complaining to the Sublime Port and wanted Sırı Pasha to be called back. Finally Sırrı Pasha was called back to Istanbul. Yusuf Razi describes these days of intrigue. There was a big party at the house of Çürüksulu in Trabzon and at night they threw illuminating shots. They aimed these shots to the house of Sırrı Pasha.

Sırrı Pasha explains these intrigues and the reaction of the local population. He came back to the "Konak" at Beşiktaş and after three months he got appointed as governor to Kastamonu. As it was winter, he left his family in Istanbul and went alone to Kastamonu. The roads at that time in Anatolia were very primitive and that is why they waited until summer to move the family. The houses at Kastamonu were very difficult to heat in the winter. Leyla hanım took her son Yusuf Razi from the Galatasaray school on the way to Kastamonu. Yusuf Razi enjoyed this trip very much. He was a boarding student at Galatasaray so this trip was a good outing for him. Specially the pine forests between Ankara and Kastamonu were very impressive. They encountered heavy rain on the way to Kastamonu and water got into all the trunks. The trunks were placed on wagons pulled by buffalos and the rivers flooded. The wagons got stuck in the mud. So they could arrive two days after they reached Kastamonu with horse carriages. All of Leyla Hanım's dresses were ruined when the water caused the colors to run.

They were very happy at Kastamonu. The population was all Turkish and therefore there were no foreign consulates. Consulates would always cause some problem or another.

The climate also was very nice and the air very clean. Life was also very inexpensive because of the abundance of fruits and vegetables. There was only one important problem and that was the population had contacted syphillis. This disease is called "Frengi" which means "from the French." It seems it was brought by the crusaders when they were going to Jerusalem. Soldiers that came back from the military also spread the disease. It took at least half a century to eradicate this disease. At that time there were no medicines to prevent spread of the disease among the population. They even had two sets of glasses and coffee cups. The glasses and cups of guests to the home were kept separate and washed separately.

Sırrı Pasha was also happy with his post at Kastamonu, but this stay did not last very long before he was transferred to Trabzon in 1883, for a second time. From Trabzon he was sent to Ankara as a governor. While his father was in Trabzon, Yusuf Razi again stayed at Galatasaray in Istanbul as a boarder. In summer the two brothers Yusuf Razi and Vedat took a French boat (Messagerie Maritime) to Trabzon. Once when Leyla hanım was going to Trabzon accompanied by her nurse and the nurse's husband, a practical surgeon named İbrahim Efendi, they encountered Sırrı Pasha on the way at Samsun and he was in pain. At that time the district of Trabzon extended as far as Samsun. İbrahim Efendi examined Sırrı Pasha and found a boil on his midriff. He immediately opened up the boil and cleaned the wound. Yusuf Razi relates that by chance his father's life was saved, as the boil would have poisoned his blood.

During his second appointment at Trabzon the situation was calmer. The refugees that came during his first appointment had settled down. So he found time for public works and started building a road to connect the port of Trabzon to the interior city of Erzurum. Even at that time the transit road from Trabzon to Iran had become important. This road would be impassable during winter months and would close down. There was also no road to Sivas. He started the road to Sivas from both ends, with the cooperation of the Sivas governor Halil Pasha. The roads to Ordu and to Giresun were also completed. Previously the only transportation was by sea between these towns. He also connected Ordu to the towns in the interior of the country.

Yusuf Razi writes: "I remember vividly the day my father Sırrı Pasha and Halil Pasha met at Giresun." I would never have thought that I would write these memoirs based on the writings of Uncle Yusuf. We met one day at the funeral of a relative at the Beyazıt mosque and he told me, "My dear Nezih, you will not understand now, but we started coming to these funeral ceremonies too often; you are still too young to understand this situation." God bless his soul, he is buried at the cemetery next to the grave of his beloved mother. Many years later his daughter Leyla was also placed in his grave. During religious holidays I go to visit this cemetery at Edirnekapı. My grandmother also is near by in the same lot.

I had also listened to some anecdotes on the private life of Sırrı Pasha from my mother. Sırrı Pasha was very fond of good eating. He would ask the maids to peel the grapes one by one and take out their seeds. Then these cleaned grapes would be placed in a bowl. The pasha would eat the grapes with a spoon. During cold winter nights when he went to bed he had one concubine lying on one side and another concubine on the other side. I must have looked at my mother with my tongue in cheek so she had to give an explanation and said, "in order not to catch cold."

While writing about Sırrı Pasha, I must also mention his brother Ahmet Fuat Pasha who also held important positions during the Ottoman regime. One day my cousin Rasih İleri informed that he was going to Kütahya to take part in the ceremony unveiling the statue of Ahmet Fuat Pasha. The governor of Kütahya had placed an announcement in the papers on January 4, 1961, inviting all relatives of Ahmet Fuat Pasha to take part in this ceremony. I was very busy at the School of Business Administration of Istanbul University. I was the assistant director in charge of the newly starting management courses. So I could not go to Kütahya at that time.

The ad said that during the years 1892-1908, the governor of Kütahya was Ahmet Fuat Pasha from Crete. He had the city hall built and covered it with tiles which made Kütahya famous. He also made the green mosque, a school building, built the river banks in the city, made

a new park and many other social buildings. In appreciation of his services the city had his statue erected and wanted to inaugurate it in the
presence of his descendants. He had also another brother, Nuri Bey, who
was a member of the national senate. Nuri Bey had three children, Celal
Nuri, Sedat Nuri and Suphi Nuri.

Chapter 6
Memoirs of Feride Mehmet Ali Ayni
(My grandmother)

I remember her always active and doing something. She never used the word impossible and always found a solution to the problems of life. Although she was the daughter of a pasha, she never stayed behind and went together with my grandfather to all his assignments in far flung sections of the empire. She always collected local songs and customs of the places that she went and wrote them down in her notebook. My mother safeguarded this notebook and I have translated it to new Turkish for future generations.

When my grandfather was appointed to Harput one could only go there on horseback. If you were to go by carriage, one of the wheels would extend beyond the precipice when turning around the mountain. I have managed to keep two leather trunks that were mounted on mule back to travel in these areas. Detailed descriptions of these trunks and other things are included in the section on objects found at Kızıltoprak.

While in Harput she was collecting local songs, one of which is against the fez, the head wear worn by Ottoman men. I have tried to translate this song into English:

Harput March 26, 326 (1898)
I mounted a swing in the garden
I put on my head a nice "Kalpak" (1)
The hair on the Kalpak is very bright
The lining is of silk
The fezes will be left soon
The Austrian trader will be broke (2)

---

(1) A hat of lamb skin
(2) The fez was imported from Austria

Don't worry, don't worry, don't worry
It is no use to wear the fez
The fez is no longer fashionable
The artificial dye is running (3)
It is now very visible
No use, no use, no use!
No use to wear this fez anymore.

There are several play songs collected at Harput. These were short dancing songs used on the stage and sung by dancers with musical accompaniment. There are "gazels" which are sung without accompaniment. There is also a song "Çiftetelli" which is a type of belly dance. There are many Harput songs which deal with relations with Armenians as it was a mixed city of Armenians and Turks.

My grandmother had her calling card printed and of course there is no address or phone number. Her name and Kızıltoprak was sufficient for the card at that time.

There is also her handwritten letter to her father in Baghdad. She is thanking her father for the nice earrings that he sent her for the Ramazan holiday. She also says that she fasted during the whole month of the Ramazan. She says that her sister is taking medicines and therefore cannot fast. She says that her sister is at the "konak" at Beşiktaş and that she is staying with her mother at the yalı (a house on the shore of the Bosphorus). It is the house of her aunt at Kanlıca. She says that her mother is looking for a house with a garden. The letter is dated 1902.

At that time the empire extended from the Adriatic Sea to the Persian Gulf. The Balkan War had not yet started. The governor of Baghdad controlled what is now Iraq and other lands on the Persian Gulf. She had two sons and two daughters and chose to stay at the konak at Beşiktaş (Istanbul.) This home was next to the mosque at Beşiktaş where the Migros supermarket is now. In that area the Beşiktaş

---

(3) The red color of the fez would run at the first rain

47

municipality named one street after Leyla Hanım.

My grandmother rented a floor of the yalı from her cousin. In the years 1936 to 1942 she used to go there in the summers. We also would go and stay with her. She had a row boat and a boat man. The Bosphorus was full of fish and lobster. We would swim and catch fish and lobsters practically the whole summer.

In those days, there was no out board engine. We had to row the boat to reach nearby markets or to get fresh water from a spring.

In 1987 a Russian ship crashed into this yalı. Luckily the owners were sleeping in the back rooms. The Russians paid an indemnity so it was well restored and still stands today. It belongs to the children of my grandmother's cousin.

My grandmother writes to her father about finding a house with a garden. At that time a garden was considered as 5 to 6 acres. Finally Leyla Hanım bought the property at Bostancı and had a house built by her son Vedat Tek who was the chief architect of the sultan.

I remember this place. My mother took me there one spring day, probably about 1940. It took about a quarter of an hour's walk from the Bostancı train station. It was on a hill overlooking the Marmara Sea and the Princes' islands. The garden was surrounded by stone walls. In those days, Bostancı was full of vegetable gardens and empty fields. Once when Leyla Hanım was away some thieves broke into the house, stole the furniture and then set the house on fire. All that was left were the stone walls, some walnut and almond tress in the garden, and the marble stairs of the entrance gate. Wild grass had grown all over the garden. In the grass white daisies had bloomed cheerfully. We collected some of the wild flowers and returned home. I felt that my mother was very sad but did not say anything, not to make me sad. During the first world war, my grandmother sold her golden bracelets and bought sixteen cows. She had a stable made in the garden of the house at Kızıltoprak. There was a shortage of food and prices went very high. So she had gardeners and helpers and began to sell milk to the market. She would also make butter and yogurt from the milk. This way the family did not suffer from hunger during those difficult years. I do not remember the cows but I remember the stable very well. We used to store our bicycles and other garden things for many years in that stable. She died in 1942 when we were at school at Robert College. The dean called me from the study hall in the morning and asked me to go home. My mother had telephoned to the school. So I went home and took part at the funeral of my grandmother. My grandfather was still alive and I had grown up enough to take part in a funeral. She was brought to a grave next to her mother at the Edirnekapı cemetery. [Nezih H. Neyzi now rests in this grave with his grandmother]

Chapter 7
Memoirs of Prof. Mehmet Ali Ayni
(My grandfather)

I never forgot a tale that my mother told me many times. When they went to Yanina they took a Greek ship from Istanbul. At that time there were no Turkish passenger boats operating to the Adriatic Sea and therefore they were obliged to take this boat. The trip took a few days. During the journey a Greek speaker got up in the dining room and lectured against the Turks.

At that time the Balkan War had not yet started. There was no Albania. Albania was governed from Yanina. My grandfather was transfered from the town of Bitlis in Eastern Anatolia to the town of Yanina. The trip from Bitlis to Aleppo had to be made with horse carriages and camels. Then they could take the train from Aleppo to Istanbul. After they reached the port of Preveze on the Adriatic they took a "lando" carriage drawn by two horses to Yanina. This was a relatively more comfortable carriage with glass windows and a door so that passengers would be safe from rain or wind but the driver was still out in the open. They only took my mother to Yanina and her sister and brother stayed with Leyla Hanım in Istanbul. My mother would relate the trip with anxiety because they would see the glitter of the rifles of the bandits in the mountain tops. There were soldiers in front and at the back of the "lando" carriage to protect the governor. The Greek bandits did not dare attack such a large contingent of soldiers. On the road they stayed overnight at Laros then the next day they arrived safely to Yanina.

My grandfather is not the last Ottoman governor to Yanina. The one after him was arrested by the Greek rebels during the Balkan War and he was hanged. My grandfather was transferred just before the Balkan War and was lucky to save his life. Trabzon also was a problem area. The boundaries were from Samsun in the west to Batum. It was the last administrative post at the Russian frontier. Both Greek and

Armenian rebel groups were fighting against the Ottomans in this area.

The duty of the governor of Trabzon was to support the fighting army in the Balkans. They were trying to supply medical help through the Red Crescent. My grandmother was also working in that organization as seen from the letter of Leyla Hanım to her daughter.

My grandfather was an enlightened administrator in the last period of the empire. He worked through the ranks in various sections of the empire and advanced gradually. Of course, his father-in-law Sırrı Pasha must have been instrumental in his advancement. He was an ardent reader of philosophy and had a large library mainly of French books part of which I was able to keep. I can see from notes on the margins of the books that he had read them thoroughly. After he was put to early retirement he was appointed as professor to Istanbul university which was the only university in the empire. His last position was the head of the classification commission which made an inventory of the old books collected during the years at the main library in Istanbul.

Since we lived together at his house, I had the chance to see and talk with him as much as possible. He would ask me to take his manuscripts to the printer which was on the European side of Istanbul, and bring back the proofs from the printer. It was difficult for him to take the train from Kızıltoprak, then the boat and then walk to the printer. Sitting on his arm chair cross legged, he would say to me, "Kukush take these papers to the printer and bring back the proofs." "Kukush" was my nickname at home. He was writing Milliyetçilik (Nationalism) at that time. This was his last book.

The last time I saw him was on the subway in Beyoğlu. He stopped and we had a little chat. I was going home and it must have been a weekend. He was going to the hospital for a treatment. He looked sick and tired, and he had his cane in his hand and a hand bag. I was very young and eager to go home to see my mother. It did not occur to me to offer him a hand and go to the hospital together. He could not return home from the hospital. He was buried at the Zincirlikuyu cemetery which is very near where we live at Levent. In 1943 this cemetery was newly opened up and considered very well organized but it was too far away from Kızıltoprak.

We would have conversations with my grandfather. I would ask him, "What would you do when you were appointed to an unknown place?" He would think for a while and not answer immediately. He would slap his hand to his knee and say, "Construction." In later years when I studied his documents and the faded old pictures that he took during his assigments, I would see him in front of many construction sites. This was either a ground breaking or an opening ceremony of an official building or bridge. Wherever he went he built a school or a mosque, government building, prison, fountain or library and thus created jobs at his place of work.

He also found time to read and write. He published thirty-one books during his lifetime. Besides these he has written many articles in magazines and newspapers. Those published after 1928 are in new script and two are in French, published in Paris.

He was born in Serfice in southern Macedonia, which is now in Greece. His family migrated from Konya and settled at Serfice many years ago. In 1960 I was invited to a congress in Athens and we decided to drive from Istanbul to Athens. On the road we stopped at coffee houses and talked with the Turks that remained in Greece after the first world war. They were under constant supervision of Greek priests and we could not talk at ease. We went up to Kozani and then took the south road towards Athens. The town of Serfice is off the main road. So we took a side road and arrived at Servia which is the present name of the town. We sat at a coffee house outside the town and talked with the owner. We were a little afraid to drive into the town because of the Cyprus problems which were just starting. The word Istanbul was written on our plates. I know a little Greek, so could converse with the coffee house owner. He said not to worry and to go into the village. He said there are not too many people left in the town. When I inquired about the reason, he said that the Greeks left after the Turks left the place. I inquired again and he said that there was not anybody left to sell something. We went into the town which had only one main street. There were very few old people seated in front of half closed shops and they were playing "tavla" the back gammon game. I inquired about the Turkish section which was at the left of this street. There was one fountain left from the old days. All the Turkish houses were burnt and the garden walls were falling down. There was a mosque on the next hill and a tree had grown on its dome. It was quite a bizzare and lonely place. Years later, I read a book by an Armenian writer Aram Andonyan on the history of the Balkan War.

Another Armenian called Zaven Biberyan had translated it to Turkish. It has a section on Servia and describes the awful events that took place in Servia during that war. The Greeks that entered the town started killing all the Muslim population. All the Muslim houses were pillaged and burnt down. These were the victory celebrations of the Greeks and lasted the whole night. At the time of the visit, I did not know about the atrocities but what I saw made me feel very bad. The state of the Turkish section of the town was evidence of some awful events. Bad things were not told to us when we were young. I took the picture of the fountain to show to my great uncle Hasan Tahsin Ayni who was still alive. He looked at it and said, "I was very young when we left Serfice so I cannot remember."

Another place where I "met" my grandfather was at Bitlis. This is a town near Lake Van where I was in charge of building a shipyard to construct ferry boats to carry the train from one side of the lake to the other. The railroad leading to Iran comes to Tatvan, a town under the administration of Bitlis that is on the shore of the lake. The train is put on the boat and crosses to Van where the railroad starts again towards Teheran.

We had completed a boat and went to the lake to celebrate the inaguration of the boat. Then we went to Bitlis with Minister of Transportation Ferda Güley. We entered the room of the governor and I was taken by suprise. The picture of my grandfather was hanging on the wall. He had died many years earlier but his picture was still on the wall.

All the other governors had a standard photograph except my grandfather. They had found a picture of him in the garden of his house at Kızıltoprak. This was quite a surprise for me. Later on, in 1984 when I went again to Bitlis to conduct a study, I visited the governor. While he was talking on the phone, I looked at the pictures on the wall. My grandfather was there but they had found a more formal picture of him. He had served in that area at Harput and Mamuretül Aziz which is now called Elazığ. I had obtained a lot of information about these regions from my grandmother and grandfather. Later on when I was working as a government official in these areas this knowledge was very useful.

In 1869, my grandfather and his mother Refika Hanım went with his father to Yemen where he had a business. My grandfather learned French at Yemen from a Bulgarian doctor. After staying a few years they returned to Serfice. Ever since the establishment of the Greek Kingdom in 1821 there had been no peace in southern Macedonia.

In 1874 my grandfather's family decided to move to Salonica which was a safer place. Thus they avoided the atrocities of the massacre of Serfice. My grandfather's father had a wholesale business and therefore travelled a lot in the empire. Mehmet Ali was sent to the İmperial School of Government in Istanbul and graduated in 1881. He was appointed to a position in Edirne and started teaching history. He then was transferred to Dedeağaç (now Alexandropolis in Greece). From there he was appointed to a school in Aleppo. After a year he got appointed to Diyarbakır and it took him six days on horseback to reach Sırrı Pasha the governor of the area. Mehmet Ali did not know that this man was going to be his father-in-law. There they became very friendly with the poet Süleyman Nazif. They had a life long friendship and corresponded even when they were away from each other. Mehmet Ali shifted from teaching to administration by becoming the secretary of Sırrı Pasha.

In 1952 I went to Diyarbakır for a survey and visited the library and the museum of Ziya Gökalp, a famous local writer and poet. When I asked the librarian for the book of Sırrı Pasha he was a little astonished and said, "These days no one has asked for this book (Letters of Sırrı

Pasha)." It is of course in old script. I copied the title page of the book and showed it to my mother. She confirmed that this was the book of her grandfather and gave me a copy of the book which I still keep in my library.

My grandfather had some advice to his grandsons: "Write a book," he would say. When I was young I did not appreciate what he was saying: "You will die and disappear, but your work will remain." We never thought of dying at the age of 15 or 20. He was encouraging us and he had my younger brother Ali's story printed on paper that had been left over from one of his books. This was a small child's story called On the Plains of Siberia. It was inspired most probably from the stories of our relatives and acquaintances who had fallen prisoners of war to the Russians and managed to escape and come back. Sırrı Pasha, the governor of Diyarbakır, decided to marry his younger daughter Feride to his secretary, Mehmet Ali Ayni. That is how he became the son-in-law of Leyla Hanım. After marriage he was transferred to Istanbul, then to Kosovo in 1896, later to Üsküp (Skopje) and to Pizren. From there he was transferred to the Ministry Education in Istanbul. The minister had declared at a meeting in the palace that there were 35,000 schools in the empire. When the minister asked Mehmet Ali Ayni to confirm this statement, he was working in the statistics section of the ministry. He had produced statistics on schools and the figure was much below what the minister had stated. When he was asked to change the figures he stated that he would not change a word. On this incident he was transfered to Taif in 1903. He took an Austrian boat which was very comfortable for that time because the Austrian Empire had ports on the Adriatic and had made a fleet of luxury passenger boats. They crossed the Suez Canal and reached Aden. From there he had to transfer to a dilapidated local boat to go to Hodeida. From there it took him five days' travel on mule back, crossing the desert of Yemen with great difficulty. He had an escort of a few gendarmes and he took two masseurs. Because he was not accustomed to such long journeys on mule back, they would apply a massage at the inn where they stayed at night so that he could continue the trip the next day. My grandfather would relate strange stories of this desert town. In order to work he would sit on a big earthenware jar full of water which was placed on the floor of the room. There was a large wicker hung on the ceiling which could be pulled by a rope to give some breeze. At intervals they would throw a pail of water on the wicker. This would cool the room a little bit. After a while he got appointed to Kut-al Amara which is now in Iraq north of Baghdad on the Tigris River.

There were two Arab clans living in that area: the El-bu Muhammed and the Benilam. He tried hard to calm down the disputes between these clans. He later described to us the poverty of the people living there. He would see the poor management the Ottoman Empire had and he would feel very sorry. Although this town was tied to Baghdad, in reality there were two ruling clans. Our army was not in real control of the area. He was the governor but all that he could do was to repair the government building. His knowledge of Arabic and Persian helped him a lot in these assignments. He could not do much with his force of ten soldiers and an old cannon. When the two clans started fighting each other, he could not intervene. He would wait until they got to bitter fighting, then fire the cannon which made a big noise. The horses of the Arabs would get frightened and start running right and left. The cannon would turn upside down so it would take a long time to load again. The Arabs would not dare attack him because of this terrible noise.

After a year he returned to Istanbul and got appointed to Carassi which is now called Balıkesir in the Aegean region. He took his wife and daughter, my mother, to this assignment. My mother would relate their going to Susurluk and other nice picnic areas in the vicinity. They grew very nice melons in the area. They would send melons to the sultan at Yıldız Palace in Istanbul. My grandfather had large albums made to show his activities. Sultan Abdülhamid collected picture albums from governors to see what was being done.

Many years later, Yıldız Palace became a museum and the director asked me if I had any of my grandfather's albums. The albums at Yıldız had been taken to the Topkapı Museum when the sultans went away. I found an album in the trunks of my grandmother and donated it to the Yıldız museum. That copy had remained at our house in Kızıltoprak.

When Mehmet Ali Ayni came to Balıkesir he experienced the worst of the rebellions which was conducted by Çakırcalı Efe. This bandit would stop voyagers or organize attacks on farms. The officer in charge of arresting this bandit also revolted and took to the mountains. Sultan Abdülhamid issued a pardon to Çakırcalı Efe. At the declaration of the "Constitution" all bandits were pardoned and they came down from the mountains. As an administrator of the last Ottoman era my granfather experienced all the difficulties running a country with a defunct organization. These bandits in the European part of the empire gathered at Salonica. One of them was Yorgi Atinelli, a Greek from Ayvalık. The İttihat and Terakki Party* was hoping that upon receiving pardons these bandits would go back to a normal life. Just at the time when Mehmet Ali Ayni was transferred to Lazikiye (Latakia, now in Syria), this Yorgi Atinelli started taking ransoms from rich Greek people and from the church in Balıkesir. My grandfather took his family to Istanbul and went to Ayvalık to take control of the situation. A·tobacco trader was helping my grandfather. At that time tobacco traders were smuggling tobacco from the French monopoly. This was another anomaly of the Ottoman administration. The capitulation administration had obtained the right to control the transportation of tobacco and thus collect taxes. They had their own police force to control this trade. This trader had been saved from prison by Cemal Bey in Balıkesir who was the assistant of my grandfather. This trader convinced Atinelli to stop his illegal activities. The Greek mayor of Ayvalık was surprised to see this bandit finally under control. Cemal Bey had sent a cable to Atinelli and asked him to keep quiet while the governor was in town. Of course, such personal interventions did not solve the root of the social disorder and the bandit resumed his operations as soon as my grandfather left Ayvalık.

(*) Union and Progress Party.

57

During his appointment at Latakia my grandfather was faced with the Armenian problem. To explain this complicated issue, I will leave you to the text of my grandfather himself which was published in his memoirs:

"THE EFFECTS OF RELIGIOUS DISORDERS ON LATAKIA"

Religious disorders create great animosities. History can give many examples. There was a disagreement between the Nusayri believers and the Şafii believers among the Arabs living around Latakia. During the reign of Abdülhamid they were teaching the Şafii beliefs in the schools of Nusayri villages.Nusayri beliefs were not recognized. In official correspondence they were referred to as "Hüdayi" (men of God). This aggravated the animosity between these two groups.

Within a few days of his arrival to Latakia, representatives of the Nusayri came to visit the governor and asked him to erase the Hüdayi inscription from their official registry. They were also not satisfied with the election of their representative to the National Assembly, Druze leader Emin Mehmed Arslan, and said he could not represent the Nusayri.

The uprising of the fundamentalist Muslims in Istanbul on March 31 had its effects on Latakia. The rebellious mulla* had killed Arslan Bey the deputy from Latakia. They mistook him for Hüseyin Cahit who was a famous newspaper reporter in these days. There were also rumors that the Nusayri people would attack the town at any moment. The governor was very upset and tried to control the situation. He was suspecting that the French consul general was instigating these disturbances.

On one Friday a message came from the French consul asking permission to visit a certain village and requesting gendarmes be assigned to guard him. The governor was going to ask the head of the gendarmes for help but he had suspicions. Why should this consul general want to go by boat to a distant village four to five hours away under this hot

---

(*) Religious scholars or disciples.

sun? This cannot be just a pleasure trip, so what was the reason? He could not solve the question and decided to take a stroll with his carriage around the city and invited the müftü* of Latakia to join him in this outing. When the müftü arrived they took the carriage together outside the city.

The prairies around the city were very pleasant. After driving for about half an hour they saw a group of people approaching in the distance; there were forty to fifty people. He stopped the carriage and waited until they came closer. He saw that they were mostly women and children with only a few men. He asked who they were. Where they were coming from? Where were they going? He understood that they were Armenians from Keseb village near Aleppo. They had been attacked by Arabs from the Şeyh village on April 10, 1325, Friday. A few thousand Armenians had run away from this area to save their lives. They reached the seashore near Antakya and then started walking to Latakia.

He could not continue his outing any more. To take care of this group of people, he left the gendarmes and police who were accompanying him and returned to Latakia. "I instructed them not to move until I came back. I did not enter the city, instead went and visited the old army barracks built by Mehmet Ali Pasha, the governor of Egypt when he conquered Syria. This was an old dilapidated building but could house a few thousand people. After inspecting this building, I went to the city mayor and instructed him to collect all the bread possible from the bakeries and bring as much as possible water to the old barracks. Then I returned to the place where I left the Armenians. By that time more women and children had joined this group and they were maybe three to four hundered people". He instructed them to follow him and took them to the barracks. "I noticed that Arab women were cursing and gesticulating to me from the top of their houses but did not reply or do anything. When I reached the barracks, the bread and water were already there. Without further consideration, I took off my jacket and

---

(*) Religious affairs director.

59

started distributing the bread and water to these poor hungry people. The mayor and some of his assistants were helping. I settled the Armenians to the halls of the old barrack and firmly instructed the gendarmes not to let anyone in or out of the building... I returned home very tired..."

In his memoirs my grandfather tells how he sent these Armenians on a French battleship to Marseille. He had big problems taking care of them. At last, after communicating with the administration of Aleppo and making the necessary preparations at Keseb, he was able to send some of the Armenians back home. While the Armenians were in Latakia, a great amount of relief help had been sent from America such as flour, biscuits and other foods, tools and equipment.

My grandfather's first post as governor was Mamûratül-Aziz (Elazığ).

While they were travelling to Malatya to reach Elazığ they had to stay at Hısnımansur. They were hosted at the konak of Hacı Bekir Ağa who was the head-man of the town and chief of the whole area. He was opposing the settlement of a group of people who had migrated from Montenegro in the Balkans. His first job as a governor was to form two villages, one under the name of Kirkori and the other as Mülk and settle these refugees. After a period of ten years he heard that this man Hacı Bekir had annihilated the village of Mülk. Many years later this same Hacı Bekir had joined the Şeyh Sait British instigated uprisings and was arrested and hanged.

He was faced with the Armenian problem on another occasion. This time he was trying to build a road to Aleppo which was the main trading center. Minister of Transportation Halacıyan, who was an Armenian, stopped the construction activities. It seems the ministry had an agreement with the French tobacco monopoly for construction of three thousand kilometers of roads and my grandfather's road was not within this plan. The excuse was that there was no budgeted money for this road.

There were plans to improve Dersim (present-day Tunceli), an area that has a concentration of Kurdish tribes. They were planning a road construction between Elazığ and Erzincan, starting from both ends, but the same minister stopped the activities. These examples show how the Ottoman administration had deteriorated. Maybe when looked at as separate items they are not very important, but when the question is studied with a broad outlook, one can see how it was planned to cripple the empire.

On September 23, 1327 (1909), grandfather was transferred to Bitlis as governor general. He stayed a short time at Bitlis before being appointed as governor general to Yanina which was at that time a very critical post. Both Italy and Greece wanted to get hold of Yanina. There was no Albania yet established as a separate country. The whole Eastern Balkan area was governed from Yanina which had a mixed population of Albanians, Greeks, Turks and Serbs. These people had lived together for several centuries in and around Janina. I could count about twenty minarets of mosques in an old picture postcard of Yanina which shows that there was quite a concentration of Muslims in that city.

When Mehmet Ali Ayni arrived in Yanina he found the situation deplorable. The Greek population was almost in revolt with the influence of the Etniki Eterya Association. They were constantly attacking and killing the Muslim population. In schools the children were instigated against the Turks. They were encouraged to form bandit groups and cause assassinations. Those same tactics were applied in the years 1950-1960 by the Greeks in Cyprus.

M.A. Ayni was trying to do the following: 1. Inspect the Greek schools 2. Close the Greek consulates of Ergeri, Berat and Avlonya. 3. Settle down the Montenegrans. The Greeks were opposing the settlement of this population. 4. Make an agreement with the Greek government to return criminals for trial. 5. Take the law suits of the Ottoman Greeks to the official Ottoman court house.

After arriving at Yanina, he sent the following cable to the Ministry of the Interior in Istanbul: "There is no uprising at Yanya, Preveze and Reşadiye districts. In Ergani and Berat some Albanians are trying to

61

instigate the people to ask for concessions and autonomy. For this reason we have to collect forces in these areas."

My grandfather studied the local situation and sent a detailed report to the Sublime Port. He said that the Albanians wanted a separation from the Ottoman Empire. They were afraid that the Turks would be pushed to Asia and they wanted to stay in their place. The request of independence of the Albanians was supported by the European powers who were also encouraging the other nationalities in the Balkans to separate from the Ottoman Empire. Austria and Italy were pushing Albanians to request their independence. In America they had formed associations which worked for the cause of the Albanians. There is an interesting section of this report.

My grandfather reports that the Albanians were claiming to have come from an ancient group of European people and they were not related to the Turks. They believed that in the event the Turks were pushed back to Asia, they would be able to remain in their lands. Albanians wanted an autonomous situation, they requested independent schooling and large representation at the Ottoman Grand National Assembly. These requests were aimed at obtaining complete autonomy which was also encouraged by the foreign powers. They were objecting to the elections but the real aim was independence.

He had advised the Sublime Port not to refuse the Albanian requests and to try to set up an autonomous area under the leadership of the sultan. The Albanians had requested a prince for their country.

My grandfather had foreseen that the Balkan area would be lost in the long run. But his duty as the governor general of Yanina was to stop the uprisings that were taking place in the region. The reason for the eventual loss of Albania and the Balkans is the wrong administration of Sultan Abdülhamid who ruled the empire for thirty-five years but did not care for the education and other requirements of the country. He led a period of complete suppression to all his subjects which resulted in unrest all over the empire.

Recently we saw the dismembering of Yugoslavia and the unrest of the Albanians still continues. The reason is that after the Balkan War there was an unrealistic distribution of the Ottoman lands. Albanians are now scattered in Macedonia and Greece. Ethnic wars and unrest still continue in the Balkans.

Publications of Prof. Mehmet Ali Ayni

In 1942 Istanbul University made a jubilee for his 75th birthday. It was made at the Eminönü Halk Evi (People Center) which was a meeting place of the Halk Party but used for all sorts of social events. Many of his friends gave talks which I did not understand very well and I was a little bored at this official birthday party.

On that occasion, a magazine called İş, Felsefe, Ahlak ve İçtimaiyat. (Business, Philosophy, Ethics and Social Affairs) published by Halil Ayhan contained all the works of my grandfather. At that time, he had many students and assistants at Istanbul University where he was teaching theology. They all knew the old script, so it was not too difficult to prepare a list of his publications. I had been able to collect almost all his books and recently, upon hearing that one of his books was on sale at an auction, I immediately purchased it to complete my set.

The list is quite impressive:

1- Theoretical and Practical Statistics, translated from Maurice Block, Printed in Istanbul by Karabet Printing Shop, 1886.

2- Information on Public Works, a text book printed at the Aleppo Government Printing House, 1890.

3- Small General History, a translation of the book by E.Lavisse, printed at the Kastamonu Government Printing House, 1897.

4- The Poor, a translation of the book by the famous Loliee, printed at the Kastamonu Government Printing House, 1897.

5- History of Literature, a translation of the book by Loliee, Kastamonu Government Printing House, 1897.

6- Lessons in Agriculture, co-authored with Captain Mehmet Kemalettin, Kastamonu Government Printing House, 1903.

7- İmam Gazali, Istanbul, State Printing House, 1908.

8- Rules of Republic, Istanbul Kader Printing House, 1910.

9- Principles of Politics and Ethics, a translation of the book by Maurice Block, 1910.

10-Science and Philosophy, a translation of the book by Ch. Bardell, Istanbul 1913. With introductions of Harputi Abdullatif Ef., Head of the Religions Dept., Istanbul University and Veled Çelebi Head of the Konya Whirling Dervishes. This is the first book on positivism in Turkey.

11-Farabi, Istanbul, 1914.

12-Critique and Opinions, Istanbul, 1915.

13-Lessons of Psychology, a translation, State Printing House, 1916.

14-Why I Love Şeyhül Ekber (A. Reşit also translated this book into French), Istanbul, 1923. This book was reprinted in Istanbul in 1995.

15-Hacı Bayram Veli, Istanbul, 1924

16-What is Scepticism, Pessimism and Laicism, Istanbul, 1924.

17-History of Philosophy, Istanbul, 1925

18-History of Religions, Istanbul, 1926.

19-History of Istanbul University, Istanbul, 1926.

20-Turkish Logic Scientists, Istanbul, 1928.

21-Lessons of Ethics, Istanbul, 1930.

22-Celaleddin Devrani, Belgium, Louvain, 1930.

23-The Philosophy of Muhiddini Arabi (in French), Paris, 1935

24-Ismail Hakkı, Paris (in French), 1935

25-What is Democracy?, Istanbul, 1938

26-Everyday Reading, Istanbul, 1938.

27-Abdül Kadir Geylani, A great Saint of Islam, co-authored with Simone Münir, Paris, 1939.

28- Turkish Ethics Teachers, Istanbul, 1939.

29-"Lessons of Political History," Istanbul, 1939. Teaching notes at the Academy of War. (Not published)

30-Nationalism, Istanbul, 1943. (Reprinted in simplified version in 1997).

31-Turkish Saints, Ismail Hakkı, Istanbul 1944.

Besides the above works, he wrote many articles in the publications of the Faculty of Liberal Arts and Theology of Istanbul University on topics of philosophy and ethics. He also published many articles in newspapers. Many of his books have been reprinted in simplified Turkish of today.

Ali Kemali Aksüt wrote a book titled Prof. M.A. Ayni, His Life and Works, which was published in 1944. My grandfather provided many documents to be placed in this publication. I benefited a great deal from this book in the preparation of his memoirs.

Chapter 8
Memoirs of Yusuf Razi Bel
(My great uncle, the son of Leylâ Hanım)

Yusuf Razi Bel was a short little person. Most probably he resembled his mother who was not a tall lady. He would always be well trimmed and very meticulous. At Kızıltoprak, we would go to the train station to meet him. He would be accompanied sometimes by his daughter Leyla or granddaughter Siret.

We would always take the short cut from the station, that is, a walk over the rails, to reach our front gate in the shortest possible distance. Uncle Yusuf Razi would always take the road at the back of the station, walk under the railroad bridge, climb the little hill and reach the front gate with a long deviation. He would also advise us to use this road which of course was safer but longer. I do not remember ever taking this long way. Anyway nobody other than Yusuf Razi would ever choose the long road.

Yusuf Razi was sent to Paris by his father Sırrı Pasha to study engineering. His male nurse who had accompanied him would carry his ablution pitcher and wooden shoes to wash for the prayers. All this did not fit life in Paris so he sent his male nurse back to Istanbul and finally married a French girl. I knew this French lady who was much taller than Uncle Yusuf Razi. When he brought her back to Istanbul and they came to the konak in Beşiktaş his father Sırrı Pasha got very angry and said, "Is this what you found in Paris?" The father insisted that she should be taken immediately to the chief of Islam and converted to Mohammedanism. Actually this was a simple procedure and all she had to do was to repeat "Lailahi illallah, Muhamedûn Resül Allah" that is "There is only one God and Muhammed is his prophet". She repeated these words with a French accent and the formality was over. But she never left her cross which was always on her bed top on the wall and she was taken to the French Catholic cemetery when she died.

God bless these beloved people. My grandfather liked to tease her very much. Her Muslim name became İsmet, her actual name was Marie Bel. Yusuf Razi chose the word Bel as their family name in 1936 when all Turkish families had to improvise a family name. My grandfather would say for instance toward the end of lunch, "The rudder of Normandie (the famous French transatlantic boat) is not functioning properly and is not working anymore." This, of course, was just a joke but she would take it seriously and protest half in French and half in Turkish.

Although Yusuf Razi was our great uncle we would call him Uncle Yusuf because we felt very close. In winter Leyla Hanım would move to his house where she had a permanent room. She had most of her belongings there including the small foot pedalled harmonium. One day we visited her with Uncle Sırrı (my mother's younger brother) and he took a picture of me with her while she was playing the harmonium. Uncle Yusuf was also a renowned photographer. He was for a while the correspondent of the French magazine l'Illustration. It would take ages for him to take a photograph. He was very meticulous and would never snap the picture until all the light and pose was perfect. Leyla, the daughter of Yusuf Razi, kept her father's papers as much as she could and before her death gave me some of these documents. That is how I have been able to obtain the information about Sırrı Pasha, her grandfather.

Yusuf Razi was the appointed mayor of Istanbul from 1919 to 1922. The area where he lived was the French zone and, as his wife was French, he had good relations with the French. He was also close to the palace because of his mother and grandfather.

As I mentioned before he was a very meticulous man and investigated every problem of life. When he was appointed mayor he invited my father with great haste and asked him how much he should give as a tip to the drivers and other attendants at the municipality. The French army was planning to occupy the municipal building as their headquarters. He wrote a letter of protest to the commander of the French army and explained the difficulties that this action would create. The original letter in French appears in the appendix.

The British commander wanted to occupy the house of his brother Vedat and settle his officers. Yusuf Razi immediately informed his brother, and in one night Vedat, who was an architect, brought his men and diminished the space of the house by constructing interior walls. The British officers had been visiting various houses with an Armenian translator in order to report to their superiors which buildings to occupy. By the time they came to Vedat Bey's house, he had managed to put up these walls and partitions, thus reducing the capacity of the house.

In order to hide the freshly constructed walls, he put carpets on the walls and over the doorways that had been closed off. The officers found the space too small and left. This house is still standing. Vedat Bey's daughter Selime opened a restaurant on the ground floor called Yekta, and the floors above have been turned into offices.

Yusuf Razi was one of the founders of the Turkish Automobile and Touring Club. He was also writing articles for the publicatons of this association. His daughter Leyla had kept a personal record register of the Ottoman period on Yusuf Razi and gave them to me before her death.

During the Ottoman period, the Diyarbakır and Baghdad administrations covered what is now Iraq and Mardin, Bitlis, Tunceli, Siirt, Elazığ and Malatya in Turkey. Now this area is further divided to Batman and Şırnak. Sırrı Pasha had served in both those vilayets (districts) of Diyarbakır and Bağdad. His son had kept a copy of a report he wrote to the Sublime Port after he retuned to Istanbul.

The following are the official record of Yusuf Razi and the report of Sırrı Pasha.

Official Record of Yusuf Razi

Registry No.75

Page 253

Yusuf Razi is the son of Sırrı Pasha the governor of Diyarbakır. He was born in one thousand two hundred eighty seven which corresponds to 1870. His birth certificate proves that he was born in the city of Felicity (Istanbul).

He began his education at Rusçuk primary school, then transferred to the Imperial College (Galatasaray). After obtaining his diploma from this school in the sections of science, he went to the government administration school. Then he went to Paris for two years at a school of engineering and obtained his diploma from this institution. He can read and write in Turkish and in French.

Yusuf Razi was appointed in the year 1320 (1903) in August by imperial decree numbered 1318 to Kosovo, Manastır and Salonica as inspector of public works.

He also gave lessons at the imperial school of engineering with a salary of four hundred kuruş, then in 1336 he became the mayor of Istanbul by an imperial decree and his salary was one thousand five hundred kuruş (in 1919).

Ministry of Interior 14 October 338 (1921), Section of Employment and Personal Records (Signature).

Here is the report of Sırrı Pasha to the Sadrazam (Prime Minister) at the Sublime Port after his return from Diyarbakır:

As it is known, the Ottoman Kurdistan is divided into two sections. One part consists of Diyarbakır, Bitlis, Van, Erzurum and the other part, of Mosul and Baghdad administrative areas. The Armenians are settled mostly in the first section of this area. In the other section there are Geldani, Assyrian people who are a non-Muslim population of the empire. There are also a minority of these people in the first section. Although the districts of Mamuretül-Aziz (Elazığ), Sivas, Ankara, and Konya are not tied to Kurdistan, for instance, the mountain of Dersim attached to Mamuretül-Aziz is settled by Kurdish people and in other districts in the area there are roaming Kurdish tribes.

The Kurdish tribes may be dispersed in various areas but they are attached to one clan and although they are far away from each other they always keep in touch and help each other in times of distress.

These Kurdish tribes are under two or three groups and those that are settled in villages are engaged in agriculture and handicraft. They are under the rule of one reknowned chief but they are also attached to the government. There are very few who are disobedient.

There is another group of Kurds who live in tents and migrate with their animals according to the seasons of the year. They roam around with their herds and are called "göçent" (migrant) by the local people. They all belong to tribes whose chiefs have absolute authority and collect a tax from the members. These tribal chiefs are very powerful and rich. For instance, if the government were to offer them a salary of seven or eight thousand kuruş on the condition of settling down in an area, they would not accept this offer. They always prefer to be the free chiefs of their tribes.

There is a third section who are neither settled in villages nor roaming with the herds. They are just unsettled people, going from place to place.

The vagabond tribes are mostly in the Baghdad area. In some cases these Kurdish tribes are at war with each other due to an old dispute about land holdings or grazing area.

These Kurdish tribes are very ancient and if there is a disagreement on one subject they will start a bitter fight. This might cause a lot of damage to each other and their surrounding area. They lose a great number of their people and cause great destruction to the houses and fields. This situation results in unrest and restrains the development of the area.

The tribes that are settled down and engaged in agriculture and handicraft do not engage in such fighting and resemble other parts of Anatolia.

As to the vagabond Kurds they resemble more the Gazze and Shemir Arabs. While they are moving around they might cause harm to the settled areas and there can be some fighting between them and settled people. In some villages where the population is not Muslim they prefer to sell their land to a chief of the area in order to obtain his protection but as you know the government does not approve of such transactions.

When we compare the nations that are settled in this area, for instance in Mamuretül-Aziz, the ratio of the Christians such as Armenians and others, is about 5 percent of the total population. For instance in the Diyarbakır area the population is about 403,800 people and out of these the Armenian population comes up to 44,858 people, including men and women. If it were possible to register the migrating population this ratio would come to about one to ten.

The Armenians who are settled in towns are mostly engaged in handicrafts and some of them have accumulated a lot of wealth but the peasants are very poor. The Muslim population is not engaged in handicrafts but mostly in agriculture and owns most of the land.

Unfortunately, because of poverty, the land is gradually being bought by the Christian population.

As to fierceness and fighting capacity no one can surpass the Muslim population. It is evident that among the Christian population no one will gather ten people and cause trouble. On the other hand, there are Kurdish tribal leaders who can get together 10,000 people and be at the disposal of the government.

Therefore, in an area where the Christians outnumber the Muslim population (God Forbid), if they were to annihilate the Muslim population, this news would spread to other areas and most likely the Muslims would unite and in a few days put the Christians to the sword. There is no probability of such an event either now or in the future. The Kurdish people are very fierce and proud and even do not call the Christians as Christians but call them reaya (people of the soil).

The Kurdish people would not accept the dominance of any other people and look down on the Armenians. It is also evident that the people of this area accept the clothing and customs of the majority. For instance, in the city of Diyarbakır most of the people speak either Kurdish or Arabic and even the Armenians and other nationalities accept and use these languages and customs. Even if they know Turkish they shift to Arabic language. The teaching at the schools is also completely in Arabic. The various minorities teach their language in their schools and their priests also use their own language. The local population do use their Armenian or Assyrian languanges, preferring to shift to Arabic.

This is due to the long-term influence of Arabs since the invasion of this area by the Abbasids.

Also the leaders of the population deal mostly with the Arab world and thus fall under their influence. Mardin, for instance, is at the edge of the desert of Syria and the Şemri tribe roam in this area and visit Mosul and Dirya. Due to this mixing of the population for centuries even the local Kurds have accepted the Arab language and customs. For the same reasons the Christian population have also accepted the Arabic language and way of life. It is also interesting that the Şemri tribe have gained influence in this area by migrating once in winter and once in summer. In some of their visits they approach the villages, sell their products and purchase their requirements and then retreat to the desert. They also destroy the area where they travel and can cause damage to the crops and to the villages they visit. This constant destruction lead to the impoverishment of the area which was very prosperous in previous years. The migrating populations make no contribution to the country yet, on the contrary, cause a lot of damage. The reason why this Şemri tribe is increasing is that due to the damage caused to the area, the population gradually sell their land and join this tribe. These Şemri people are such a nuisance that it is impossible for these poor people to come back and settle on their lands.

This report to the prime minister of the Ottoman administration shows the pitiful situation of the country in those days. Because this tribe could not be controlled they drew on the population of the settled villages and the government could not protect them. Finally these people had to join this unproductive tribe. This led to anarchy in the area. The attitude of the governor is also interesting. He looks at the population of the area as Muslim and Christian. He appeared anxious that clashes might arise between these two groups. He did not think of starting Turkish education in the schools and accepted the fact that this area was under Arab influence. Yet this governor, Sırrı Pasha, was interested in literature and produced publications in simplified Turkish. Letters of Sırrı Pasha was an important document of his day. He wrote many pamphlets of explanations of the Koran. He was also engaged in public works. He constructed a dam in Baghdad that is still used. The place is still called "Sırriye" after his name. He also left behind other buildings and constructions in this area. His son Yusuf Razi kept a copy of the above report written to the Sublime Port. His daughter Leyla was a close cousin of my mother, so we were in touch until they passed away. I listened to the stories on Baghdad and Diyarbakır, first from Uncle Yusuf Razi, then from his daughter Leyla.

The wife of Sırrı Pasha, Leyla Saz, did not go to Diyarbakır and Baghdad with her husband. Instead she took permission from the sultan and retired into seclusion at the house she had built in Bostancı. She understood that her husband had a second wife and that is why she did not go to these assignments. Many years ago at Kızıltoprak, I met Kamuran Bey, the son of Sırrı Pasha from this second wife. As the step brother of my grandmother, he would come and visit her sometimes. When there was a television program on Leyla Saz, my cousin Ismail Arar and I were interviewed together. The children of Kamuran Bey saw this program and came and found us. It seems we were working at the same ministry in Ankara. We were taking part in the same meetings without knowing each other. Mr. Bülent Kandiyeli, the son of Kamuran Bey, was the chief of the legal department of the Ministry of Transportation.

I will close the section on Sırrı Pasha with some examples of his writings and some anecdotes about him that I learned in areas where he had been an administrator.

On October 29, 1975, Tillo Kaptan (captain), the head of the Göliş (Lake Workers) Labor Union, related many stories to me. He had been a captain for many years on the ships that plied between Tatvan and Van. He became the leader of the labor union working on these lake boats. I had been removed from my position as general manager of the Maritime Bank and transferred to the Ministry of Transportation in Ankara as an

73

advisor to the Minister. Because of this I had decided to open a law suit against the Minister of Transportation and Prime Minister M. Süleyman Demirel (now the president of the Turkish Republic). In short, I was persona nongrata at the Ministry which put me in a difficult situation and I had to be very careful in my relations. We decided to go to Lake Van during the Republic Day vacation along with my doctor friend Sami Uçar. In spite of the fact that I had been removed from active duty, Captain Tillo and his friends came to the airport to meet us and kept us company during our stay in the Lake Van area. They took us to Ahdamar, the only island on this lake. Armenian King Haygak had a church built on this island. It is a unique church with outside murals depicting stories from the Bible. This king must have had megalomania because he put his picture above the statue of Christ. We made a tour of the island and the church which is still preserved and made a contest with pistol shots.

On that day in 1975 at Ahdamar Island, Tillo related stories that he had heard from his father. I noted these stories after returning to the hotel at Tatvan. They reveal another aspect of the accounts that Sırrı Pasha had left us. It shows how the Armenians sided with the Russians and took part in atrocities against the people they lived together with for generations. Sırrı Pasha never thought of such a possibility during his administration. What is propagated as the Armenian massacre to the whole world is actually a question of a life and death struggle during the Russian invasion.

The stories related by Tillo are unheard of tales, events that took place very far away from Istanbul.

THE DEFENSE OF MUTKİ*

These are the words of Mr. Tillo, the head of the Labor Union in Lake Van: "My grandfather told me. I was 14 years old and I remember

---

(*) Mutki was the poorest village in the Tatvan district of Bitlis.

74

very well. The Russians and the Armenians had approached the village. We started to evacuate the sheep towards Siirt. My grandfather wanted to have a shot at the enemy and then retreat towards Siirt but on the way he was caught between two fires. He hid behind a stone and could not move any more. Bullets were pouring like rain from all sides. He was thinking what to do behind the stone. As a last resort he took out the ramrod of his gun. He placed his fez on top of the ramrod and gradually elevated the fez above the stone.

A bullet pierced the fez immediately. He dropped the fez to the side of the stone towards the back. The Armenian who was shooting began to come out of his hiding place. He shot him immediately with his rifle. With one bullet he had finished the man. He started shooting as much as he could. The Russian group and the other Armenians decided to withdraw. The fez is still at our home with a hole in it. Thus the village was saved from being completely burned down.

THE FATE OF İBO

İbo had a good Armenian neighbor in the village where he lived. During the war they heard that the Russian army was coming near their village. The Armenian friend told him not to worry and that they would protect them. Thus İbo was relieved and did not worry any more. When the Russian soldiers approached the village, the Armenian went to greet the invaders. They started coming towards İbo's house together with two Russian officers. İbo immediately asked his daughter to prepare milk and coffee in order to offer to their guests. He thought this would be a proper way to meet the invaders. When the Armenian came to the door, his daughter was ready with the milk and coffee. The Armenian hit the girl with a kick and threw her to the floor. İbo was shocked.

İbo had two wives and a daughter. The Armenian said to İbo, "you prepare your daughter to give to me and your wives to these Russian officers." İbo did not know what to say while his daughter was running away. She asked her father to give the pistols to her. The daughter and the wives killed the Armenian and the Russian officers. By that time the house was surrounded so they could not get out.

Ibo started shooting up to the last bullet. When he realized that be could not hold out any more he shot his daughter and his wives and then committed suicide.

THE QUESTION OF RELIGION

There was a flat and hollow ground on top of a mountain, similar to the Nemrut mountain top (it must be a crater). After the Russians left, they collected Armenians and brought them to this place. My grandfather was also there and he saw an Armenian young man, a very nice looking boy. He knew that they would all be put to death. He could not accept to end the life of this young man. He approached him and said to his ear in a low voice. "They are going to kill all of you, if you accept to become a Muslim, I can save you." The boy said no. He repeated his offer three times and he refused each time. At the end he said, "The sin is not mine anymore." The youth closed his face with his hands and my grandfather shot him to death. He related this sad story himself to Tillo. All of them were shot on this hilltop. You can still see their bones at this location.

Some Armenians managed to stay at Mutki in spite of all difficulties. They left only in 1956. The chief of the town made them an offer, saying, "We lived so many years together. Become Muslims and stay here." They refused. Then they were asked to leave. They moved to Istanbul. But in another village a few Armenian families decided to stay and converted. Their grandchildren have now become the "mufti" of the village. Their names became Ahmet, Mehmet or Hüseyin. They mixed completely with the local population. The families knew their ancestors but there was no problem any more.

They became very good Muslims. The grandfather wished that this could have been done many years before and thought how nice it would have been.

76

ARMENIAN HARD WORK AND PERSEVERANCE

There was a long trench to be dug from one hilltop to the other. An Armenian youth dug this entire trench without stopping a moment. No one could endure such an arduous task. He continued digging until he was bent down. He finished the work and got up. At this moment he broke his back, fell down and died.

An ağa (chief) asked an Armenian to build a mill. The grinding stone started to turn. It was a very heavy piece of stone. Everyone wondered how this heavy stone had been lifted and placed here. The Armenian was very strong. The ağa did not want to pay the money and he declared his intention openly. The Armenian said "Give." The ağa did not seem to hear. One day the ağa went to the mill and to his astonishment he could not find the stone. The Armenian showed him the stone. He had thrown the stone at such a place down the river that no one could remove it from that spot. No one was strong enough to bring back the stone. The ağa said that he would pay the money. They agreed on the amount to be paid. The strong Armenian went and managed to get the stone back to its place and the mill started working again. The ağa paid him his debt.

PERSISTANCE

The Russians and Armenians surrounded the village. A Turkish man got three guns and enough ammunition and got up on a hilltop. He started firing from that spot.

One of the guns went very hot and could not fire anymore. He took the second gun and continued firing. The second gun also got hot. He took up his third gun and resumed the fire. Pretty soon the ammunition was exhausted. They could not get the man down from this hilltop. When he had no bullets left they came on him at the hilltop but he had a sword. He drew his sword and killed many on the spot but at the end he was killed and became a martyr. Another source on this subject is

Prof. Caleb Frank Gates, director of Robert College for many years, who wrote a book titled Not to Me Only. He relates how they had come to Harput to join the American missionary school there and conducted missionary activities in the Eastern Anatolia area.* He also tells about Cyrus Hamlin, founder of Robert College, his activities during the Crimean war and how they set up Robert College in Istanbul and Armenia College in Harput. In Anatolia, Syria and Iraq they set up 24 Protestant churches, 32 chapels and 5 centers. This activity stretched as far as Mosul where the Anglican Church was established. They could not go further south because the British missionaries were active in Mosul and Baghdad.

In these religious centers only Armenians were educated and given assistance. They were thus getting further apart from the local people with whom they had coexisted for generations. When you read between the lines of this book, you seem to see the same type of operation as today's Peace Corps. However, after they spread into Anatolia, the differences arising between religious groups became more apparent and unrest spread in Anatolia.

Dr. Gates also writes in his book (p.242) that Kurdish people did not have a written language and alphabet. In order to write Kurdish they sometimes used Armenian, sometimes English. In another place (page 134), he relates the activities of Armenians who came over from Iran and killed the Kurdish population in the villages, including women and children. The Turkish military had to surround these bandits and exterminate them. Mr. C.F. Gates was the manager of the college in Harput from 1894 to 1902. They had changed the name from Armenia College to Tigris College.

When his appointment came to an end at Harput he became the director of Robert College. At this school his job was to educate Bulgarian and Greek children to be sent to their respective newly inde-

---

(*) Caleb Frank Gates, Not To Me Only, Princeton University Press, Princeton, 1940, pages 42, 60, 134, 139.

pendent countries. He explains this activity with great enthusiasm in his memoirs.

The bureaucrats of the first Kingdom of Bulgaria were all men educated at Robert College. Gates' book shows the important effect of the Christian churches that had come for the preservation of their respective religious faiths but in actual practice they had a great influence in the dismemberment of the Ottoman Empire.

An Armenian anarchist confirms what a Bulgarian anarchist says and states that this is the truth: "An action that creates horror is better than horror without success." The book explains how the church helped the Bulgarian and Armenian terrorists.

The sad part is that Gates presented himself as a friend of the Turks. During the occupation of Istanbul by the Allies, he worked for the American mandate proposal. As the book was printed in 1940 he also confirms that he was mistaken during the early years of his life and admits that he could not foresee that Atatürk and İnönü would be able to create a new Turkey. In 1913, the Ottoman Empire had not yet entered the first world war but had lost great amounts of land in the Balkans. The great powers of these days, England, France and Italy, were making preparations to carve up the remaining Ottoman lands. In case the Ottoman Empire would be divided up, the Black Sea area was to be given to Russia. Germany and Russia were in competition and both sides tried to attract the Armenians to their side. The Aegean area was settled already by a Greek population. In the Taurus area there were Armenians and Kurdish people. Both the Germans and the Russians were interested in the areas where Armenians and Kurds were concentrated. The German government appointed a diplomat called Dr. Lepsics who was very much interested in the Armenian cause. In order not to alienate the Ottoman government, this diplomat was instructed to work under cover. At that time the Armenian chief priest complained to the Sublime Port about the Balkan refugees being settled in the future Armenian areas and the arms being obtained by the local Turkish population. He asked for bandits in the Bitlis, Erzurum, Van and Adana areas to be brought under control.

Russian Ambassador Sazanof also complained to the Sublime Port and informed Berlin about his complaints. France and England then joined the Russians in these complaints. The German government in Berlin questioned the Russian ambassador Serbief about the preservation of the Ottoman borders and safe-guarding the rights of the sultan. The Germans' ultimate aim was to get Turkey in the First World War on their side.

Six powers organized a meeting in Istanbul and the Russian delegate gave a proposal to the Turkish government for reforms to be applied to the Armenian population. The proposal was to separate six counties of the empire near the Russian frontier and set up a new state whose head would be a Christian subject of the Ottoman Empire. It said it would be even better to appoint a European to this position. This administrator would set up an army composed of Armenians only and appoint judges to the courts. There would be a national assembly composed of local Christian and Muslim citizens. Each nationality would have their own schools giving education in Turkish, Armenian and Kurdish. The people would be treated with equality in the courts. Another commission would be set up to deal with the problems of land distribution.*

The Germans were opposed to this proposal because this would be the beginning of the dismemberment of the Ottoman Empire. They sent a memorandum of disagreement to Russia. This commission which was assembled at Yeniköy in Istanbul was already a source of disagreement. On July 3, Austria, Germany and Turkey declared that they would not accept the conditions of this commission. Dr. Lepsics, the German delegate, proposed to the Russian delegation to withdraw their proposal but gave a stern note to the Sublime Port to stop the settlement of refugees in the Armenian area.

Finally the German delegation proposed to have inspectors in two eastern districts and to exercise equal rights to the two parties. Those discussions took five months and resulted in an agreement signed on

(*) M. Henri Hauser, Histoire Diplomatique de L' Europe (1871-1914), Les Presses Universitaires de France, Paris, 1924, pp.326-327.

February 8, 1914, between Russia and Turkey. Upon this agreement an understanding was reached on two inspectors who would investigate in the two eastern districts and would have their staff regulate the local military affairs and also disperse the Kurdish bands (outside of the military maneuvers). They would also work on the improvement of the local languages. New schools would be financed from the income of local taxes, and there would be equal participation in the local assembly among Christians and Muslims.

This agreement was never put into effect because of the declaration of the first world war, but it is an interesting document for learning how the foreign powers were imposing their plans on the Ottoman Empire.

DEATH OF YUSUF RAZİ BEY

Previously, the Muslim population did not give death announcements to the newspapers. Death was a family affair and people would inform their relatives about the day, place and time of prayers. If the deceased was an important person, the papers would write it as a news item or there would be writers who would later write about the person. There was no custom then of companies placing large death announcements in the newspapers. When Uncle Yusuf Razi died, an article written by Ercüment Ekrem Talu appeared in the magazine of the Touring Club.

YUSUF RAZİ BEY

"Yesterday, the deceased Yusuf Razi Bey closed his books at the age of over eighty and reached eternity. He belonged to a family who was famous in the fields of literature, architecture and science. His father, who was a man of the administration, also wrote books on religion and on management. His books are Sırrı Furkan and Sırrı Kur'an and Mektubat (Letters). His uncle was a vizier and pasha, his brother the architect Vedat; his cousins, Celal Nuri, Suphi Nuri and the painter

81

Sedat Nuri. Besides these, Yusuf Razi's mother was a reknowned poetess and composer, Leyla Saz.

"Who would not envy such a man who was brought up in this environment and added his capacities? The late Yusuf Razi would feel this envy and would like to hide it in his modesty. He was one of the oldest graduates of the Galatasaray school, the imperial lycee. He would attend always the alumni days and the "pilav" ceremonies. In later years he would be very visible with his white hair, moustache and beard with a smiling face. His memory was very clear and would tell us anecdotes about the school in the old days. We all wanted to join the table where he would sit in order to listen to his tales.

"He knew French as his mother tongue and he had graduated from a French university in the field of engineering. We have heard of his skill in his profession from various reliable sources. His students at the engineering school would also confirm that he was a good teacher. He was also versed in fine arts and appreciated music. He was a "connoisseur" in the fine arts. With his capacities he was also liked by the foreign community. He would correspond with the highest authorities in science and fine arts with his friends in the West. Before the war, he was the correspondent of Illustration for many years. With his articles and photographs he was a perfect public relations man for Turkey.

"When my friend the French writer Mr. Claude Farrère came to Istanbul he visited Yusuf Razi Bey and said, 'This little man is a complete world.' He was amazed with his culture and personality. He would take part in all discussions and always come up with bright ideas.

"During the dark days of the occupation of Istanbul he acted as mayor of the city. He was not successful in this position because he was not an administrator. He did not accept any other administrative position after this experience.

"In recent years one could see the load of the events on his shoulders. The loss of his brother Vedat and of his cousin was too much for him and he did not appear in public lately.

"Finally we heard on Monday evening that he had passed away.

82

With the death of Yusuf Razi we lost one of the last "efendi" persons in our society.

"We will feel this more and more because it is not possible to replace such persons. God bless his soul."

The author of the article, Mr. Talu, also included a picture of Yusuf Razi and wrote under it: "The Late Yusuf Razi, a founding member of our Association T.T.O.K."

In 1921, during the dark days of the occupation of Istanbul, when Yusuf Razi Bey was appointed mayor of Istanbul, British, French and Italian forces were present in the city. There was also one American battleship. Istanbul was divided into three occupation zones: The French took under control the Eminönü side, the British took the Beyoğlu side and the Italians, the Kadıköy side. As the French embassy was on the Beyoğlu side, the French needed to also have an administration building in Eminönü. They decided to occupy the municipal building and informed Yusuf Razi to vacate the premises in January 1921. The fact that his wife was French made it easier for him to communicate with the French occupation army. Maybe that is why he was assigned to this post. Uncle Yusuf Razi wrote a very eloquent letter to the head of the occupation forces. He explained the mistake of depriving the municipality of its location and said this would disrupt all municipal services. Yusuf Razi did not remain long in this position. The original letters in French is in the appendix.

Among the papers given to me by his daughter Leyla, there was a letter of invitation by the sultan's son to a dinner at the Dolmabahçe Palace. The country was going to pieces but life at the imperial palace went on as usual.

The envelope is written in French and designates the Dolmabahçe Palace as the residence of "His Excellency the Caliph".

The invitation is written to Yusuf Razi Beyefendi personally and it is for a lunch to be served at the Bağlarbaşı residence of the "Şehzade" (the son of the sultan) in honor of Abdülhak Hamid the poet and to commemorate his new book titled Finten.

On the menu attached to the invitation, there is a crown and it says it is for the "morning meal" on the 28th of September 1332 (1915). The menu is as follows:

Bean soup with cream

Pasha börek with cheese

Sea bass with mayonnaise

Asparagus

Fresh beans

German dessert with chestnut

Pilaf with pistachios and nuts

Ice cream

Fruits

The Istanbul municipality published a book on all appointed mayors of Istanbul during the Ottoman Empire. Yusuf Razi is also recorded in this book with all the details that took place during his administration.

Yusuf Razi had to move the municipal administration to another building and leave his place to the French occupying forces. The French also requested that he leave the furniture on the premises. The first building that he found could not house all the municipal departments so he moved some departments to the municipality of Beyoğlu district.

The reason the French were able to occupy the municipality was that they had asked the government for a list of possible buildings to use as their headquarters, and the municipal offices of Yusuf Razi were put on the list. Yusuf Razi was very much offended. In general, he was fed up with the bureaucracy. One day someone came to his room while he was busy with his papers. He did not even see the man. After a while he noticed the visitor. He asked him what he wanted. The man handed him a decree that showed his appointment as mayor of Istanbul. After reading the document, Yusuf Razi got up and said "Oh? is that so!", and he left the building immediately.

Chapter 9
The memoirs of Nihat Vedat Tek
(The grandson of Leyla Saz and son of Vedat Tek, the chief architect of the Sultan)

Nihat Bey is the son of my grandmother's brother Vedat Tek. In our youth we were taken each bayram (religious holiday) to the house of Vedat Tek. We did not have at that time the habit of taking trips outside Istanbul for vacations. We would go to the bayram prayers at the Kızıltoprak mosque and then kiss the hands of the elders in the house.

Bayram was a time for greetings in each other's homes. In general the visits started with my father's mother, Saime Hanım, who also lived nearby at Kızıltoprak. Then we would go and visit the relatives on the other side of the Bosphorus with my mother or grandmother. I would see Nihat Bey at his father's house at Nişantaşı or in the summer at Büyük Ada (one of the Princes' Islands). The bayrams rotate during the year according to the Arabic calendar. We did not see Nihat Tek for many years because he worked outside Istanbul. In his last years he was retired and would come to visit my mother, his cousin. Apart from these visits we would not see each other so often.

His father had constructed the ferryboat stations at Moda and Haydarpasha. He helped me on the restoration of these landing stations when I was in charge of the Maritime Bank.

Besides, he took care of his grandmother repairing the grave of Leyla Hanım which had been made by his father, the chief architect, many years before. A tree had grown on the grave and distorted the stones. So, we began to see each other more on the occasion of the repair of the grave and restoration of the ferryboat stations. He was a little younger than my mother and told me many family stories that I was not aware of. Some aspects of the family were not told to us at Kızıltoprak. The family tree was not discussed or was even kept away from the children. We could not ask our parents about every detail. Some facts were told to me by my mother after I grew up, but not the full details. One also tends to forget many of the stories after years go by. It was good to recapitulate with Nihat Tek and we were corresponding with him as well which even made it better. He would write in his own style of language, which had changed over the years.

The letters of Nihat Vedat Tek were very long, usually several pages single spaced type written. He would forget and write the same story again and again. These were his last years and he was hospitalized after these letters reached me. He passed away at the Haydarpasha hospital. Here are some passages from his letters:

Diploma Engineer A. Nihat Vedat Tek

Istanbul

March 2, 1978

Dear cousin Nezih, In our time, that is while your dear mother, father, grandmother, grandfather and Mimi (Leyla Saz) were alive, we would never address our elders as "thou" we would say always "you". Naturally they would address us as "thou". When our elders entered the room, we the youngsters would get up immediately.

I cannot compare myself with them, never, but will relate to you what I have seen and heard. For this reason, dear Nezih, if I address to you as "thou" please do not be offended.*

Your grandmother would come to our house and would stay a few nights. She would take us to the theater at Şehzadebaşı in a two-horse coach. Your grandmother's eyes were green, mine are also green and so was Vedat my father's. It seems Sırrı Pasha also had green eyes.

I do not know if I wrote to you earlier but your mother had told me this story herself. After the marriage of my father, the mother of the sultan asked for Leyla Hanım and said that the Sultan heard that his chief architect got married but did not yet bring his wife to pay her respects. You would not know these formalities but in the palace the custom was to present his wife to the mother sultan, who replaced the queen in the

---

(*) In informal relations one uses the word "Sen" as thou; in formal speech "Sen" becomes "Siz" as "you".

Ottoman court. Leyla Hanım asked her son to take his wife to the palace and perform the ceremony of kissing the skirt of the sultan. When my father asked mother to accompany him to the palace for this ceremony, my mother was very timid and did not want to go. So Mimi took your mother Nezihe and her sister Refika, dressed them both according to the palace fashion that is in ferace* and meşlah** and went to the mother sultan at Dolmabahçe. Later they were accepted by Sultan Mehmed Reşat. Mimi presented her granddaughter Nezihe as my mother and only Refika as her granddaughter. Thus your mother was presented to the sultan as the wife of Vedat my father.

At that time, your mother and her sister were grown up and well cultured, nice girls. They were attending the English High School. My great Uncle Mehmet Ali was very upset when he heard that his daughters wore hats and went out to picnics.

Mimi showed them how to act in the court. When they were accepted into the presence of the sultan, Mimi started to bend down to kiss the hem of his redengot but the sultan got up and held Leyla Hanım by the arm and kissed her hand saying, "One cannot allow Leyla Hanım to kiss the hem, but her hand should be kissed."

The eunuch standing behind Leyla Hanım made a sign which mant that the "audience" was over. Mimi and her granddaughters walked backwards without turning their backs to the sultan and left the room. Oh! I forgot, the sultan accepted your mother as my mother, complemented her and asked about who the other nice girl was. Leyla Hanım said "She is my granddaughter and your humble servant."

The chief of the treasury was waiting outside in the corridor with a golden tray on which there were red silk purses to be given as gifts to the visitors. The chief of treasury gave each one a purse and she and Mimi kissed each other. The treasurer was at the top of the protocol list , in the palace. While they were walking along the long corridor of the

---

(*)   Ferace: ladies' outdoor mantle.
(**)   Meşlah: a gown worn at official visits.

palace Mimi said to her granddaughters that these purses would be much heavier during the reign of Sultan Mecid and Abdülhamid. These red purses each contained 50 gold pieces of one quarter denomination.

Sırrı Pasha went to Baghdad after he served in Adana. His brother Nuri Pasha had three sons and one of them, Sedat Nuri İleri, was an agricultural engineer put in charge of the palace farms. He was also a painter and cartoonist. His son Refik İleri died (in Brindisi) when he was returning by car from Düsseldorf, Germany to Ankara. One of his daughters is now working at the Hilton as a guide. His son went to the USA and never returned. While Refik İleri was a consul general in Baghdad, he met some people who claimed to be the sons of Sırrı Pasha. These two men who spoke very good Turkish mentioned that their father Sırrı Pasha had constructed a dam and they were very proud of him. The name of this dam was "Sırriye". I will write about this to the son of Kamuran Bey, Bülent Bey, in Ankara.

Dear Nezih, please excuse me, I have to type this letter so that you can read easily.

While closing my letter, I would like to point out the following: (The letter is single spaced and five pages long. He gives details on repairs of the ferryboat stations of Moda and Haydarpasha).

Another letter of Nihat Vedat Tek is very revealing about some facts that I did not know about our family until I was over fifty years old.

My dear cousin Nezih, I would like to thank you for your kind reception when I visited you at the Maritime Bank. We the old people appreciate greatly such events. I had heard about your mother's illness when I was working in Adana. I wrote to her and she had told me that she appreciated this letter very much. I used to visit her quite often while she stayed at the Emlak apartment in Nişantaşı. We would always relate past events to each other. I can never forget your father Muzaffer Bey who was such a fine gentleman. In his old age he would come and visit me and we would go out together. He would always talk about you with satisfaction. You all are like your parents, I would like to congratulate you.

Dear Nezih, at my last visit, I had given you some facts on the mother of Ismail Pasha and I had left you her photograph. You were very busy and that is why I did not want to take too much of your time. There were also other people in your room so I preferred not to talk.

Now, I would like to give you some more information about our family. What I am going to tell you was told to me both by Mimi and by Afife Hanım, the daughter of Sadrazam Kadri Cenani Pasha. They had heard this story from their mother.

Ismail Pasha is from the island of Khios (Sakız Island). He belongs to a well known family of the island (Rodokanaki). His mother is also from the same island from the Metaxas family. The picture I gave you belongs to the grandmother of Mimi, her name was Kiveli.

At that time a doctor from Izmir would visit the island each month and take care of the sick people. The church bells of the island would be used to announce the arrival of the doctor. The doctor from Izmir would go by carriage to Çeşme and from there would visit the houses on the island. It is written in history books that the local population revolted against the Ottoman administration. A fleet was sent to the island to control this revolt. During this period of unrest the family asked the doctor to take their son (Sotiri) with him to Izmir. The doctor was a kind person and very rich. They implored the doctor to take this child with him and save his life. The name of the boy was changed to Ismail and he went to Izmir with the doctor. The doctor had property and lands in Aydın and in Egypt. He had no children, so he adopted Ismail and sent him to school. He finished the Rüştiye (equivalent to lycee) in Izmir but during this time both the doctor and his wife passed away. Ismail inherited all the wealth of the doctor. He decided to go to Istanbul for further education and enrolled in the imperial school of medicine. Then he went to further his education at Pisa in Italy and later went to Paris to become a gynecologist. The ambassador to Paris Münir Pasha met this young man who was very intelligent and friendly. He recommended this young doctor to the palace. The sultan accepted him and appointed him as the chief of medicine of the palace.

He was later appointed to Crete and to Izmir as governor. He took Mimi with him during these trips. Mimi relates in her memoirs their trip to the island of Crete. He then became the mayor of Istanbul and was minister of the interior for some time. He was also minister of trade and public works. For a short while he acted as Sadrazam (Chief of Ministers).

My Uncle Yusuf Razi was also mayor of Istanbul for some years. Adviye Hanım, daughter of Ismail Pasha and elder sister of Mimi, married Kadri Cenani from Antep who later became the Sadrazam. He also acted as the mayor of Istanbul. So you can find their pictures at the museum of the municipality at Saraçhane, Fatih.

If you have time, you can find him in the great Larousse encylopedia, in French, a section of two pages under the title Ottoman scientist and writers. He is also mentioned in the German Das Grosse Brockhaus encyclopedia.

Ismail Pasha has published five or six books. I am sure your cousin Ismail has a copy of these books. My sister Saadet has also a copy of these books. I gave to my daughter Nermin the book on medicine by Ismail Pasha.

Mimi would tell us that Ismail Pasha's relatives came to visit him in Izmir and in Istanbul. He gave them gifts and sent them back to the island. Ismail Pasha knew Greek very well, but during his term of office at the island of Crete he did not use his Greek and used interpreters. Mimi also knew very good Greek and could read and write in Greek. In the Ottoman register, Ismail Pasha is referred to as a convert servant of the palace. Uncle Yusuf Razi has this record.

Dear Nezih, I understood that you are interested in the history of our family, so I am taking so much of your time. The first daughter of Ismail Pasha, Adviye Hanım married İsmail Cenani who was the chief of protocol of Sultan Reşad. His son Kadri Cenani is still alive. He lives at Kanlıca on the Bosphorus in his father's "yalı". He is retired from the Shell Company and is a very cultured person. Ismail Pasha had also a son Fuat Bey, a colonel in the navy. From his first wife he had a son called Hayrettin who married our cousin Nazime and died a few years ago. From his second wife he had a daughter and a son. The daughter resembles very much your grandmother Feride. I did not meet the son. They live at Dudullu near Çamlıca. "

I had listened many times to my mother telling about their visit to the palace. With small differences these tales are similar. We had heard that Ismail Pasha was a convert but the details were never told us. I also owe thanks to Nihat Tek for the picture of the mother of Ismail Pasha which I had never seen before.

There is another letter from Nihat Vedat Tek dated January 31, 1978 from Maçka in Istanbul.

"The other day, I noticed in the papers that the great man of state Mr. Bülent Ecevit made a correction of the last administration. I hope you will reach higher positions in the future.

Dear Nezih, do not be alarmed at the (injustice) made to you. Both your uncles Vedat and Yusuf Razi have been subjected to worse conditions. These dear people passed early because of these illtreatments. Only great Atatürk invited my father Vedat and won his heart."

Nihat Vedat Tek had related to me how he went to Dolmabahçe Palace with his father Vedat. He stayed in the garden and waited for his father. Vedat Bey went inside and was escorted to the death room of Mustafa Kemal Atatürk. They were not on speaking terms as he had left the construction of Ankara Palace half finished and returned to Istanbul. The Ministry of Defence was paying for the expenses of the construction of the hotel, but he had spent all his personal money and had not been reimbursed by the ministry. Finally he left Ankara and returned to Istanbul with the plans of the construction. The ministry had to find another architect to continue the work.

Atatürk wanted to part with Vedat Bey in good terms. He said to him from his death bed that he knew the difficulties that he had faced and understood why he left Ankara. So they exchanged a few words of kindness and Vedat Tek asked for leave. Although Vedat Tek had been the chief architect of the Ottoman Sultan, he went for the construction of the new hotel in Ankara. The building is still standing near Ulus square in front of the first Grand National Assembly. It is now used as a government guest house and for official functions of the government.

Nihat Bey was one of the last representative of stereotypical Ottomans. He liked to tell stories of his memories about life at the palace and had great admiration for the old days. Of course, he could not forget the good old times and the splendor that came with the Ottoman dynasty. Their youth was spent in the last part of the Ottoman days when Istanbul was still the capital of an empire. The generation before us was born and raised with the Ottoman family traditions and they had closed their eyes during the early Republic days. They were in a way squeezed between two different periods. Our generation, which was the first generation of the Republic, was brought up by the last Ottomans and inevitably was influenced by them. What we named "old Turkish" was their natural writing. What we called "new Turkish" was the use of Latin letters to write Turkish. The old generation continued to use the Arabic letters until they died away. Once you became accustomed to it, old Turkish was like stenography and you could write very quickly. Writing with Latin letters was a very slow process for them. Gradually the language also changed and many Arabic root words were replaced by their Turkish counterparts. To understand the Ottoman language, we have to learn the old alphabet and increase our vocabulary of words in Arabic and Persian. The writing was different for printing and hand writing. This made it complicated and required a long period of learning. This language and writing gradually disappeared like the Ottoman Empire.

In 1983, my daughter Furuğ went to the island of Khios (Sakız Island) the birth place of Ismail Pasha. She inquired and found that Metaxas is a very familiar name. The name Rodokanaki was a native name of the island. They said that "They were a poor fisherman family and migrated to London". Some years ago, I looked at the London telephone directory and found several Rodokanaki registered numbers. I could not call any of them because I did not know where to start but I knew that the information gathered by my daughter was correct.

People that she met at the island were very friendly. They did not even want to believe that she was a tourist. She looked so much like the local people. Furuğ also felt very much at home.

Chapter 10
Memoirs of Nezihe Neyzi
(My mother)

Among my mother's old papers, I found one of her notebooks. The notebook must have been given to her by her brother Sırrı Ayni because there is an inscription on the first page saying "Lycee Imperial Ottoman. Classe de 2me Pre. Ire Don No. 356 appartenant a Sirry". Underneath it is written "Given to Nazy". In this way, I found the French writing of our family name long before the promulgation of the family name law. Of course at that time no one was thinking that the nickname given to my mother would be our family name in years to come.

On the back cover of the notebook there is an old Turkish inscription saying "Mektebi Sultani" which is the old name of the Galatasary school of today. The handwriting continues: "Second preparatory class, owner's name: Necip Sırrı".

Somehow this notebook has survived over the years and without being lost or burned in a fire which was very common in Istanbul, without being thrown away among old papers. My mother kept her diary in English. So I use her writing which does not need any translation. The diary is dated June 13, 1914 and is titled "Recollections of Certain Days".

June 13th, 1914

It is evening. I am standing on the doorstep of the front balcony in my room at the top of the house in Kızıltoprak.

The sunset is glorious. First there is a line of red, fire- like, on the horizon, which mixes, higher up, with yellowish pink light having so much brightness about it that one can hardly look at it for a few seconds. The sky is deep blue everywhere, not a speck of cloud nor a star is to be seen. On the right hand side stands the Moda point and bay leading into the Yogourtjı river. On the left Feneraki stretches out into the deep blue sea. The lantern in the lighthouse is lit. It is shining like an early star quite lonely in the skies. Three maounas with full open sails are gliding along the sea behind each other. The first is tied on to a steamer and the next two to one another, but as the steamer is very small it is hardly visible and the maounas seem to speed along by themselves. They are sharply outlined against the blue hazed with pink horizon. They look like happy children, light of heart, running along in a beautiful garden, their bright colored dresses flying behind them. The children, of course, would be more picturesque, the resemblance between the two is the light and swift motion of both. It has become rather dark now. I can see no more to write so I shall go downstairs.

* * *

Prinkipo,* June

In the morning I got up at five. The weather was fine, the sun had risen but was not hot yet. There was a gentle breeze, very refreshing. At six I made my appearance in the general sitting room in my dressing-grown (do not think it very shocking). The old gentleman and the lady were there, one on each sofa by the windows facing the sea. I sat still for some time and then took up my sewing. It was a blouse to be finished. I finished it and then wore it.

At noon the weather got very hot. Refika, Meliha and I went into our bedroom (we had one room for us) and did a few gymnastic exercises. Then, we heard a great deal of bustle. We all jumped up and asked what it was all about.

The matter was that four ladies and a child, whom they know very little, had come. These people were relations of M.'s supposed future fiance. They were asked to stay for lunch. We had a pleasant time with them. After they went away we lied down but chatted the whole time. I saw a big insect on M.'s collar and jumped up to catch it, she also jumped up. We lied down again and chatted on. R. and N. went to see Azime but M. and I pleaded a head-ache.

(*) The Greek name for Büyükada, the Big Island.

We sat with her on the terrace facing the sea, Halki and the coast of Asia. It is a splendid view and I am longing to write poetries about it.

A pretty little sailing boat
Sliding on the sea by the coast
Looks like a graceful white bird,
Light and easy in its motion,
And ready to fly off when it likes.
There are no other boats to be seen.
Our little pretty sailing-boat
Is lonely on the sea.

I wrote this little poetry but it is not a good one, then M. wanted me to write one for her so I wrote this:

To Meliha
On a chair a sweet young girl reclines
But to talk, a lot she declines,
She is thinking of her future
And is all in a rapture.

The pretty girl is good and kind,
I cannot any words find
To describe her sincerity
And also generosity.

The next day after the day of which is written above we went for a walk in the morning to Dill.* The road was very lonely after we had left the houses behind us so we played running until we got tired. Then M. and I stood side by side and had our photos taken by R. We walked on until we reached the sea and again climbed on the top of the rocks

(*) Dill is the name of a semi-island extension on the South Side of Büyükada (Prinkipo)

stretching into the sea and again had our photos taken in different positions. After that we had a swing each in our turn. It was so lovely to swing high up in the air with that lovely view in front seen from among the sweet smelling pine trees. Prinkipo really is a romantic place and encourages one to dream and imagine lovely and poetic things. Then we went by the laterna* and asked the man if he would play us the One-Step. He did and I had such a strong desire to dance that I began fidgeting my feet and at last got up and pretended to walk, but it was with the time of the One-Step that I was walking. Then M. insisted that I should dance as there was nobody about except a few Greek women and an old man sitting with his back to us. One of the Greek women there wanted to dance with me but she only knew Polka. So we danced that for a little while. When she got tired she thanked me and went away. Then R. and I danced the One-Step. The other Greek women who were with the old man came up to us and paid us a lot of compliments for dancing so well. None of them know how to dance and only one had once been to a ball. They were young women, very pleasant and good-looking, especially the one who was the other two sisters' cousin. She was very shy and blushed up to her ears every time she spoke. After some time they departed with the old gentleman who was their father.

We had a very pleasant morning that day and returned home quite very gay and happy.

* * *

August

Grannie, Mother and Broe went to Prinkipo to Uncle Vedad's. Aunt Fatma who was there the night before also went away. Father, R. and I were left at home. F. also went away after lunch to the mosque. R. and I were sitting in our room when the door opened and we saw Sherif and a girl come in. I took them to the sitting room as our room was rather untidy. In the course of our talk Sherif mentioned that she had bought a

_____

(*) Laterna is an old mechanical music box.

very pretty stuff for Sıdıka, her daughter, to make a blouse. We asked her to describe it. She did accordingly. We thought it to be very lovely and wanted to make a dress of it for ourselves. She said she would go and get some for us if we really wanted. We gave her some money and she went. After she was gone I played piano and the girl whom Sherif had brought with her sang. Then I played violin. She taught me a new song which I liked very much and learnt it immediately. Sherif came back soon and brought the stuff we wanted. R. wanted hers to be cut out instantly so that she may sew and wear it as soon as possible.

After the visitors went away, I went to see Mebroure. I took her photo. Then we went with her to Fatma's. There also I took the photo of Sabire hanım, a friend of Fatma's. After we stayed there a little, I returned home.

At night after dinner I cut out my dress and sewed it in three hours. The next day R. also finished hers. The trains were used to bring in soldiers so we had to go with the boat from Calamish.*

* * *

August 31st.

A few days ago R. and I were at Mme Burhaneddin's. When we were taking leave to return home I asked her and Mme Daniche to come to us to tea on Monday. On Sunday a thought came into my mind that I should invite some more people and have a little party. So I went to Fatma's. She accepted my invitation. Just as we were going with her to Sadık beys to ask Iffet Hanım and Mme Nejmeddin, we saw the same persons downstairs, came to see Fatma. We stayed there of course, and I told them of my intention. They said they would come, with pleasure.

This morning I wanted to get some biscuits and sandwiches for tea. I took Father's permission to go to Kadi-keuy with R. We walked as far as the Yogourtji bridge then instead of going to Kadikeuy we took the

---

(*) During the first world war, railroads were used for military transport. So the transportation to the center of town was by sea. Calamish was the nearest boat landing.

road to Moda, knowing that we could find what we wanted there more easily than in Kadikeuy.

At the end of the meadow near the river there is Belkis and Saadet's grandmother's house. They sometimes come and stay with her for some time. Thinking they might be there I went in to call them also, but did not find them.

We walked on to Moda and got sweets, chocolate and biscuits. On our way home we called Pakize Hanım and made her an invitation for the next day. She declined as she was waiting for visitors.

On Monday afternoon Mebroure was the first to come. She had a lovely red dress on which suited her perfectly. Then followed Mmes Daniche and B., then Iffet Hanım and Mme Nejmeddin. The latter seeing the open music on the piano wanted us to play. R. played a few songs with Mebroure accompanying with violin and I sang. They liked it very much and praised us all. After that Grannie came and we chattered on till tea-time.

After tea I took my visitors up to my sitting-room. There they saw my little collection of books, about a hundred and fifty or so in all. They were very glad to find among them interesting books and which they would like to read. I lent a book to each of them, but none of them know English unfortunately, they only took Turkish and French books. The excitement over the books over, I showed them my albums, of snapshots of countries, old costumes, etc. My visitors were both enchanted and surprised to see that I possessed so many. The fact is, they were brought to me by Grannie after her journey in Egypt and Austria, and by father after his journey in Egypt to different parts of the world, which are frequent. Then talked along and laughed without any one of us thinking about the time when one noticed that the sun was nearly setting and that it was quite time that they should be back at home. We all got up and went downstairs. I accompanied them to the garden gate and from there they all departed their own way thanking me for my kind reception.

* * *

January 6th, 1915

Yesterday afternoon there was a very big meeting in the lecture-room in the University held by Bessim Omar Pasha. Belkis and I after having a little lunch in the hall of our Studio (I have been following the drawing courses in the University for a month) went to the conference hall. It was half past twelve and there were so many people. We found a place and sat down. The lecture began at two. After an hour's lecture, they showed us by projection different scenes where the Red Crescent had helped wounded soldiers and refugees, and also the persons who first thought of making a club to help people in distress. As the pictures were shown Dr. Bessim Pasha was explaining to us what they were and who they were. There was so much talking that we could hardly hear him speak, then at last he got angry and said that he would not say any more because they did not listen. I and Belkis were very ashamed of this but others did not seem to mind it and they still went on talking.

After it was all over we returned home to my uncle's. At dinner Uncle said that he had seen Bessim Pasha and he was very cross with the ladies and was saying that trying to improve the ladies on their opinions or help to the distressed, it is like trying to tow a boat in a current.

Anyhow I hope he will change his mind and try it again.

* * *

Dec. 10th 1915

Since eleven months I have not written in this book. What a long time! There seems to be no interesting things to write about. I have left the drawing school and I changed the school where I was teaching. Now I go to the Bezmi Alem twice a week, on Mondays and Tuesday. Altogether it is eight hours a week. At first I did not want to go, I made a lot of fuss; cried and did not go for two days but afterwards I continued. Now I am used to the school, I like my pupils and they seem to like me too. Especially the ones in the last class are very nice girls and they

100

work hard. Between the lessons there is an interval of ten minutes, at those times I either go to the teachers' sitting-room or else to the Art School's rooms where Belkis and Refika are, I chat with them there until the bell rings for the next lesson. The other days I often go to the cinema and when I am at home I go to see Mebroure.

* * *

Dec. 18th 1916

Yesterday we came back from Grannie. The other day we had gone to her and also to Ness and her mother. Today I went to the cinema with our neighbour Huesnie Hanım. There were two nice dramas. Tomorrow Mother, Refika and I will go to a concert in Tepe-Bachi. Some of our aunts also will go. We are hoping to have a nice time. I shall write down all that we shall see there.

* * *

Jan. 6th 1916

We went that day to Tepe-Bachi, but I forgot to write about it immediately after. There was Turkish music first, then a gentleman recited a very funny story called "Travelling without knowing where". Afterwards Professor Hegue played piano, then Mr. Laghos played violin. Some time after the "Tableaus Vivants" began. The first one was representing an old Turkish Sultana in an oval frame, then a girl sitting down, lastly there were groups of four or five girls with the Sultana reclining on a sofa and her attendants playing music and dancing. They were all very pretty. First they were holding white lights, then pink, blue and all sorts of colours. The audience applauded very loudly and screamed out bis* so we saw nearly every one of them twice. One of the young girls in them was reported to be the most beautiful woman of Pera but we did not find her so pretty.

Uncle had promised us to send his motor-car to fetch us. When we

_____

(*) Bis is a request to repeat a performance.

came out of the theatre the motor was not there, so we waited, ten minutes, half an hour then one hour passed and still it did not come. At last we decided to go in a tram. We reached home very late, it was dark and lights were lit everywhere.

* * *

Jan. 6th 1916

To-day we went to the Cimena in Kush-dili with Mother, aunt (hala) Refika, Njdette and I. There was a drama of Henry Porten the German actress, and three comical things.

* * *

Jan. 29th 1916

About a month ago I went out with mother to visit the neighbours, but we had a hope that visitors would come to see us, so we stayed at home if they called to come and see us. We were just ringing the bell of a neighbour's door when I saw the gardener coming towards us. I asked him who had come and he said Fatma Hanım and Mebroure Hanım had come to see me. So I went home. Just when we had begun talking and playing piano and singing Hedie ran into the room saying that visitors were coming. I rushed out of the room, when I got to the top of the stairs I saw them coming up. Well I had to say them good-afternoon and make them walk into the sitting room. We sent the gardener in haste to go and call mother. The room was very untidy. All the notes were lying pell-mell on the sofa, wood was lying about near the stove. I begged their pardon for all these and said as it was the heated room I took them in there. They were three ladies, one of them a young girl and the other two married young ladies. They had come from Eren-keuy to see me. At last mother came, we talked with them and they stayed about half an hour more and then went away. After they were gone mother said to me that some one else also had asked for me in marriage that day. These days so many people have come out altogether that we don't know what to do.

* * *

102

Feb. 9th

Last week on Thursday Nessibe Hanım got married. Uncle asked one of his friends to lend him a steamer for that day as we were going to take her to Beycos. All of us, aunts, cousins except Bickie, because she had to stay at home and look after Assim who was ill, went to Sirkedji and got into the steamer. The weather was very fine so we could stay on deck. We went along the Roumeli shore and then crossed over to Beycos. When we landed we saw the people waiting for us with carriages. We drove to the house, which was on a hill. It had a nice view. We took out our charshaf, and after sitting for some time we dressed Nesibe Hanım in her bridal dress. There were relations of the bridegroom's, Albanian, one of them was his aunt, there were his daughters and some other people. Then seyirdjies* (the lookers as they call them) began coming. Such funny dressed people, I thought I was in a province somewhere. The bridegroom at last came and they made coltuk (the bride and bridegroom going arm in arm in their room and after two or three minutes the bridegroom goes away, throwing money over his head). It was half past three at that time, we got ready to go, took leave and went back again with the little steamer.

These days there seem to be many weddings. Yesterday also we have been to a wedding in Bostandji. It was Sabiha's, Nessime's cousin. She got married with a naval officer. Her white dress had suited her very nicely and she was very pretty. We could stay there a very little time, as we had to catch the train for the return.

* * *

March 11th 1916

This date is the date of my bethrothal day. It was on a Friday, the weather was very fine, the sun was shining the whole day. I was hoping my life to be also always sunshiny and bright. How excited I was..

* * *

(*) People who are not invited to a wedding but come from the vicinity just to look on.

March 11th 1917

Now it is just one year and two days since I am bethrothed. Unfortunately, last year when I had begun writing all what I felt and thought that day, visitors had come, so I had to leave off. I dont't know why, but afterwards I could write no more.

I will write now of this year. Oh! how happy I am. I love my Mazy so much and he loves me too. We are so contented of our life, and hope always to be so. In two and a half months it will be one year since we are married. We are so pleased. As days and months pass we know each other better, and our love for each other grows warmer and deeper.

On Sunday which was our bethrothal day Mazy stayed at home, pretending he had a head-ache. We had invited for the evening R. and I. so that we might play piano and violin and have a nice time. I wore that evening my white bride-dress and Mazy wore his smoking. Our visitors came. We talked for about half an hour of the war, of everything being expensive, and of this and the other. Then Mazy began saying "begin, the musicians!" joking. At first I played violin alone, and afterwards we played with the piano together. Mazy and I tried to dance a little but as he does not know it yet, it was just fun. We enjoyed ourselves quietly that night. It was an intimate evening. Our concert went untill ten o'clock. Then we had our dinner and went to bed at half past eleven. All of us were pleased of our evening. We hope to have an intimate gathering every year the eleventh of March and play music and sing and have a jolly time all together"

* * *

My mother wrote her memoirs in English because she was a graduate of the English High School for Girls of Constantinople. In fact she was the first Turkish girl to graduate from that school in 1912. At that time Muslim families did not send their children to missionary schools of the American, French, Italian, Austrian and German. These schools catered more to the Christian communities of Istanbul.

Chapter 11
Memoirs of Muzaffer Halim Neyzi
(My father)

My father was a typical Ottoman gentleman. His father Halim Bey and his mother Saime Hanım were both from Kızıltoprak and the family lived in Istanbul for at least three or four generations. Boys born in Istanbul ("The City of Felicity") were exempt from military service. It was not free to come and settle in Istanbul. People from other parts of the country could not just move to Istanbul. So my father was not drafted to the army but during the war in the Dardanelles where 280,000 men died, the Istanbul men of eighteen and over were drafted. He was in uniform but by the time they were going to be sent to the front the war at the Dardanelles ended. So he was never sent to the front.

He was brought up in Kızıltoprak which was a part of the city where middle and high income families lived in villas with gardens. The population was not dense and the means of public transportation was limited to the train and ferryboats. There were many vineyards and vegetable gardens and open space where wheat and other cereals were cultivated. Practically every house had a vegetable garden. When we took walks around Kızıltoprak with our parents my father would tell us the names of the owners of all the houses.

As years went by and new houses began to be built, he felt very sad because he could not recognize the owners of the new buildings. As a young man, my father wanted to learn languages and registered secretly at the German school. After a few weeks his parents realized what had happened and they immediately took him out of the school. They could not understand why he should learn a foreign language. "Is he going to be a waiter?" they asked each other. At that time Turkish families did not send their children to foreign schools. So he had to go to the Vefa (İdadi) school which is equivalent to a present lycee. That is why he was very eager for us to learn languages and registered me and my brothers at St.

105

Joseph and then to Robert College.

With a friend of his he opened a shop in Kadıköy to sell tailor's accessories and cloth. He wanted to be a businessman but when he wanted to marry my mother, the family of my mother objected to this retail shop and said that he should take a decent job and then they would consent to the marriage. So my father left the partnership and became an accountant at the Ministry of Post and Telegraph. Then there was consent for the marriage.

Before the occupation of Istanbul in 1919 my father had joined the İttihad ve Terakki Party.* He and his friends set up a branch of the party at Kızıltoprak.

During the occupation of Istanbul he started going to Ankara by boat from Istanbul via İnebolu. This was the safest way to go to Ankara because of the Greek invasion in the Aegean area. Plus there were many outlaws and bandits blocking the way road of travellers. These were difficult times for the Ottoman Empire. My father's mission was to support the republican army in Ankara by supplying military uniforms, water jugs, tents and ammunition. The cost of all this equipment was more than two million liras. He would pose as an Armenian businessman in order to board a boat going to İnebolu. Travellers were controlled by British officers with their Armenian translator. My father claimed to be from the central Anatolian town of Karaman where Greeks and Armenians were talking Turkish only. These trips were very difficult because the small boats leaving for to İnebolu had no schedule. They would start when there were enough passengers on board. So sometimes he had to wait for a few days on board before the journey started. There was no port at İnebolu. The boats would stop on the sea and wait for row boats to come and take the passengers and cargo. In rough weather, the waves would lift the boat and the small row boats and passengers were literally thrown into the row boat and caught by the sailors to prevent their falling into the water. Then at İnebolu they had to wait again

---

(*) Union and Progress Party

to form a group of at least fifteen people to start the journey to Ankara. The only transportation available were horse drawn carriages. Each traveller rented a carriage and placed his belongings in the wagon; only after a caravan was formed would they start the journey. There were many bandits and outlaws roaming around the country, but they would not dare attack a large group.

The road was a muddy path through mountains covered with pine trees. There were no bridges over the rivers and creeks, so they had to cross the water at safe places. At night they had to stay at inns where they could find fodder for the horses. Usually they would carry their own food as there were no restaurants of any sort.

The forests were full of bears and wolves. At Kastamonu a peasant explained to my father about what to do against a bear attack. He was explaining as if it were a very simple operation. He said you have to wait until the bear comes near you, gets up on its hind legs and opens its mouth. Then you have to stick your right fist down its throat and with your left hand just open up its stomach with your knife. Then, he said, the bear cannot breathe and falls down. My father would tell this story at every occasion and act like the peasant whom he met on the mountain road to Ankara.

He also went to Ankara though the ports of Antalya and Trabzon to deliver the military supplies so much needed by the army of the newly developing Republic of Turkey under the leadership of Atatürk. To obtain these uniforms he had to go to London, Paris and Vienna. He had a story about the Vienna trip. He had what he called a "European hat". Before taking the Orient Express at Sirkeci, Istanbul, the last stop on the European railroad, he would come with his fez. He could not go out of the house without a fez as it would look very awkward in Istanbul. His office boy would carry the hat in a box to the train. He would take the box from the window, place the fez in it and take the hat to his compartment. When he came back, the operation was reverse. He returned the hat to the box and came out of the train wearing his red fez.

At Vienna he would pose as a poor Jew from Istanbul. If the

Austrians had seen him with a fez, the price of the second hand uniforms would have gone up. He had to work in warehouses to select the bundles of discarded uniforms of the Anzac from the Dardanelles battle front. He had brought home one of the large overcoats which my mother had dyed black and removed the military buttons of the Anzac. This coat was hanging in the corridor and anyone going out shortly to the garden at Kızıltoprak could use it. Many years later when we moved the old trunks from Kızıltoprak to Levent, I found a box containing the buttons that my mother had saved from this Anzac overcoat. Each button has a map of Australia on it and a crown on top with the writing, "Australian Military Forces" made by Stokes & Sons, Melbourne. The new Turkish government was so poor that they had to buy second hand clothing to use as their military uniforms.

My father started going to Ankara in 1920 before it had become the capital of the new republic. It was just a center of resistance against the advancing Greek army, the occupying forces and the army of the Sultan supported by the British and French. Plus there were rebellions in various parts of the country mainly instigated by the government in Istanbul. These years 1919-1923 were a very dark period in the history of Turkey. In 1923 the Lausanne Treaty finally brought universal acceptance of the Turkish Republic with its present borders.

My father was always away on business trips. We saw him very rarely at home. He was using one room of an old hotel in Ankara called Taş Han (Stone Han) for many years. My uncle was a doctor and went to Ankara to work at the Ministry of Health. So my aunt's house was his family connection in Ankara. There was no telephone in the first years and when it was connected it was too expensive to use freely. My mother corresponded with my father. This correspondence was of course in old Turkish. Then he started coming home on Saturday morning and returning on Sunday evening by train to Ankara. As he left, we would wave at him whenever we could and he would wave back with his white handkerchief and throw some chocolates from the train. After I graduated from Robert College in 1944, he wanted me to work with him. So

I went to Ankara and he showed me a room at his office where he was also living. This was a new apartment house at Yenişehir, the new section of Ankara. The building was made with the stones of the old Taş Han and he would joke by saying, "I moved with the stones to Alemdar apartment" which was the name of the family that bought the stones of this old han.

He never thought of buying land and settling in Ankara. At the early stages, especially when the Greeks were approaching Ankara, land was very cheap.

He wanted me to register to the law school in Ankara, but I wanted to go to Philadelphia to study business administration. However, the war was still going on in Europe and the Far-East, so there was no direct communication with America. Against my will, I enrolled at the law school where I found my old school friend Bülent Ecevit whose father also insisted he attend the same school.

I would try to help with the correspondence in English between my father and companies in England and Switzerland. He was representing G. & A. Baker Ltd. and was trying to sell airplanes to Turkish Airlines. Finally he succeeded in selling them the De Havilland passenger planes. In 1945, he took me with him on a plane from Istanbul to Eskişehir where the headquarters of the airline was located. This was my first experience in flying.

Finally international airlines started coming to Ankara. I found a job with Pan American Airlines, worked for about a year and saved money to go to the States. I obtained a passport and an acceptance from the Wharton School of Business at the University of Pennsylvania. One day I showed my father the acceptance and the passport and the ticket to New York. He looked at me and said, "Don't bring us a Christian girl and do anything you want!"

My father could not attend university, so he wanted his sons to learn as many languages as possible and complete ufiversity. He had heard in Ankara that the foreign primary schools would be closed, so he registered me, age five, and my elder brother to a French school, St.

109

Joseph in Kadıköy. In 1938 when the second world war started he said, "You have learned enough French. The British will win this war and English will be important. So you must go to Robert College and learn English." There you could take French and be exempt from taking a second language. But he insisted that I should take German as a second language at this American school. The Germans were advancing all over Europe and our German class was very crowded, about 40 boys. By the end of the school years in 1944, the Germans were losing the war and our class was reduced to only seven students. My father could read in French and German but his English was very limited. Still he managed to type his own telegrams in English. Sometimes I tried to correct and shorten the telegrams but he did not want me to change a word. Finally he would type and send the cables with his office boy without my having a chance to read them. He had his own way of doing business and correspondence was a big part of it.

He would also read books on economy in French and German and he wrote two books. His aim was to improve the economy of the country and he did not approve of the tight measures taken by İnönü and his government. He wanted a liberal economy and was advocating a moderate inflation to speed up the economy. His books were not for sale but to influence deputies and government officials. His first book called Great Wish was published in 1932 while Atatürk was alive. It is dedicated to Atatürk and other leaders of the country. From childhood days I remember his writing this book at Kızıltoprak. He would fill the ink pot at the small writing set of my mother. He would use a pen to dip in the ink and write quickly in old script.

I would listen to the sound of his hand writing and watch him before falling asleep in my mother's bed. These were among the rare occasions when I would see my father. His second book, National Turkish Bank, was written in 1948. I had come back from my schooling in the States and the Marshall Plan had started. My father wanted to form a new bank to direct investments towards the industrialization of Turkey. This book also was not for sale to the public but tried to influence the leaders of the country. His liberal thoughts were accepted later in 1950 by the Democrat Party.

He was advocating free education for the children of Turkey. He was insisting on the construction of highways and bridges. He wanted to develop agricultural production and increase exports. He was insisting on having a meeting with the principal bureaucrats to discuss his principles of development. Unfortunately, neither Atatürk nor İnönü nor the bureaucrats of the Ministry of Finance gave attention to his wishes.

His end was very tragic. One summer day he was sleeping in the back room which was a little cooler. My mother was sleeping in her regular room. All the doors and windows were open during this hot day. My father woke up to a sound coming from the corridor on the second floor of the house. He jumped out of bed and saw a thief running down the stairs. It was a woman who had sneaked into my mother's bed room, took some jewels and earrings and was running away. She dropped a pair of scissors she had tucked into her belt. My father ran after her bare footed in his nightgown. She was a young woman and ran out of the garden to the railroad in front of the house. He ran after her and caught her. She started punching on my father's chest. The neighbors heard the noise and came and caught the thief and took her to the police station. My father said that he would dress and come to the station. As he reached the garden gate he dropped dead suddenly. It was a heart failure. His body was brought to the house and layed on a sofa. When I heard the news, I rushed to Kızıltoprak but there was nothing to be done. He was covered with a white bed sheet but his white hair was showing. So I touched his hair for the first time to say good-by. This was the end of another Ottoman.

Chapter 12
Anecdotes from Kızıltoprak

Stories were related by elders of the family. They were repeated when an occasion arose. So we almost memorized these stories. But there were also stories by old nannies, the maid, cook, gardener or other servants. We had many visitors who would come and stay a few days at Kızıltoprak. There was no radio (TV was nonexistent) and music was made by members of the family except for a grammophone which could play records of three minutes. My father had brought many records from Vienna and Berlin. So we could listen to operas by Caruso and other famous singers. We had also several Turkish music records of the factory of EMI at Yeşilköy. Most of the records bore the "His Master's Voice" emblem.

There were songs which we did not know how they came to Kızıltoprak. Some came even from Africa, songs by black slaves. One which I could not decipher is: Nana atinigurassa

Nana atinigiliya
Nana atinigurassa - gandu
Nana atinigiliya - gandu

This must originate from Sudan or Ethiopia. Another one is from Kazakhstan and I will not try to translate it, it is as follows:

Bizim Kazan Kal'asında
Satılay bülbül palazı
Zahlat salkan mala gibi
Hürriyata palazı
Sımırık kışının kanadı
Senin gibisini bulsay bulur
Padişahın sanadı

Ey ceyidi cıllama
Cıllap işler bulgama
Senin gibisine bulsay bulur
Padişahın sanadı

No one knew how these songs came to Kızıltoprak but they were
sung at festive times and caused a lot of laughter. One day, I had a secretary who migrated from Sinkian to Japan and somehow came and settled in Istanbul. I recited this poem to her as she knew the Kazak
Turkish. She opened her eyes wide and said "This is a very noble song!"

Another funny song was taught to me by our gardener Mahmut
Ağa. He had worked many years with Leyla Hanım and then with Feride
Hanım, my grandmother. One day he said, "I will teach you a song and
remember me when you grow up." Again I will leave the song as is:

Alma karunun pulunu.
Peşine gelir kununu,
Senden yer, senden içer
Oğluna kızına pulunu.
Tarla alacaksan düz al,
Karı alacaksan kız al,
Boşanmış alma ki, atım teper.

Mahmut Ağa laughed and stopped. When I inquired why he had
stopped, he said, "There is the end of it but I will not tell it to you."
When I inquired further he said that the end is rather shameful.

My father liked this song and was especially intrigued by the last
part. He told this story on many occasions and laughed very much at the
ending which we could never find out. The last news from this gardener Mahmut ağa was a letter from Ardanuç (near the Russian border). He
was asking my grandfather to change the head man of his village. My
randmother laughed very much and said, "He still thinks that your
grandfather is the governor of Trabzon."

113

SECTION II
FROM OTTOMAN LIFE
TO THE REPUBLICAN LIFE

Chapter 13
Kızıltoprak and the Old Way of Life

Through my mother's memoirs we saw the lifestyle in Istanbul between 1914 and 1917. The first world war was going on but Istanbul had not yet been occupied by the Allies. There were difficult times during the Balkan War and the Bulgarian army had come near Istanbul at Çatalca, but they were stopped and pushed back. Before that the Russian army had come to Ayastephanos* and they were stopped. No enemy soldiers had set foot in the capital of the Ottoman Empire.

There was fighting going on all fronts. I had listened to stories of war in Iraq where my father-in-law was wounded. He would tell how the British occupied Mosul after the ceasefire. A bullet had burned the back of his uniform and he escaped death by just one millimeter. We still keep the burnt uniform of this Ottoman major who later became a Liteunant General in the Turkish Republican Army.

He would tell how the Arabs would steal the parts of cannons and sell them to the British. The Turks would offer a little more, so the next night, they would steal the same parts from the British and sell them to the Turks. He was not very talkative so his stories were few. During the first world war the most important enemy was the British. They were the leader of the Allied forces. America had only one ship in the port of Istanbul during the occupation. The American Bristol Hospital in Istanbul was named in its memory. It was later purchased by the Koç Foundation, but it is still referred to as the American hospital.

At Kızıltoprak we grew up listening to war stories. My grandfather was a governor in various parts of the empire so he was not at the front. My father was an Istanbul citizen and they were exempt from

---

(*) Old Greek name of Yeşilköy.

military service. He was drafted only after the disastrous war in the Dardanelles. We had many gardeners and cooks who had been in actual fighting. Süleyman Ağa, the gardener, participated in bayonet fighting in the Dardanelles. He had big wounds on his cheek and his arms. He was a tall and strong man from Anatolia. Many of his friends lost their lives on this front. The cook Idris had to walk all the way to the Suez Canal. He would tell stories of fighting with Arabs supported by the British in the area which is now Syria and Palestine (later Israel). My mother showed me pencil-like darts which were dropped from planes on Turkish soldiers by the British. If one of these hit your head it would go down and come out from your chin. My uncle was a doctor at Beirut hospital and he managed to get on the last train returning to Istanbul.

Our childhood at Kızıltoprak was full of such tales from the wars at various fronts. There were refugees who had come back from the Balkan War. They talked with accents from Albania, Greece, Bosnia or Bulgaria. Each region had its own type of Turkish that had mixed with the local languages. There were also many people who came back from Aleppo, Cairo or Baghdad carrying an Arab accent. People from Azerbaijan spoke a totally different Turkish. Our neighbor named Princess Tevhide had managed to get out of Cairo in time and had an income from Egypt. Her house is still standing at Kızıltoprak and is one of the few surviving mansions.

The old habits and ways of life continued at Kızıltoprak. We had moved from Taksim Square to Kızıltoprak in 1926 or 1927. My grandmother enlarged the house so we had enough room for her two daughters and son. There was no electricity or running water in the house. The house was heated with wooden stoves and lighted with kerosene lamps. Meat and butter would be lowered into a well in the garden to keep cool. We had cupboards with screens to keep away flies and preserve food. During the summer we would buy ice and put it in a special bottle with a compartment for ice which cooled the drinking water; this bottle was called karlık which means "container with snow."

This karlık had disappeared from Kızıltoprak. I found it many years later by a strange coincidence. One day I went to meet my daughter Füsun who was studying at Ankara University. The train was delayed for an hour and I decided to go to Kalamış where my grandmother had built an apartment building of two and a half stories. It had been sold by my mother some time earlier, but I went there to see what had happened. The demolition men were tearing the apartment down. All of a sudden, I saw our karlık among the debris that was taken out of the building. I went and picked it up. It is made of glass but covered with a wicker basket which protected it.

I went inside the half demolished building. They had taken out the courna of my grandmother and left it in the corridor. This is a marble basin used to hold hot water in a Turkish bath. I bargained with the men and bought the courna for twenty liras. I told them that I found our karlık but they did not understand what it was. The demolition men showed me the large iron bars used in the construction and said, "These iron beams saved our life!" I remembered the construction of the building done by architect Vedat Tek, the elder brother of my grandmother. He had used heavy iron bars to hold up the floor and the ceiling of the apartment of his sister. While the demolition men were calculating the money they could get from the scrap iron dealers, I put the courna and karlık in my car and went to meet my daughter at Haydarpasha train station.

These old pieces from Kızıltoprak are now at our house at Levent.

In the 1930's the old way of living continued at Kızıltoprak. We lived four generations together under one roof according to the old family rules and disipline. My granfather had a separate guest room called the selamlık which was reserved only for male visitors. The separation of men and women had ended officially but traditions continued. Lady guests had another room upstairs. We the children could not enter these rooms because they had to be kept clean and ready for guests all the time. These two rooms would be kept closed and locked. When the telephone arrived at Kızıltoprak it was placed in the selamlık and only elder people could use it.

When electricity came we were quite puzzled. At times, when there was nobody around, we would throw a pillow to the lamp dangling on the ceiling. Gas lamps were taken to a storage room where old trunks and so forth was kept. They stayed there for many years, but when the electricity cuts started, they came out again for occasional use.

When running water first came it had a very high pressure. My grandmother had a small pool in her front garden where she would put red fish and it had a fountain. Its jet could reach the third floor balcony of my grandfather.

The kitchen was still in the garden outside the house and food was carried to the dining room in copper serving plates. They had a lid to keep the food hot and shield it from dust or rain drops. The dishes had to be carried back to the kitchen for washing.

There was a turning cupboard between the kitchen and the wash room. The dishes would be placed there and returned to the kitchen. In the same way food platters would be taken from this turning cupboard.

The laundry was washed in a room adjacent to the kitchen outside the house. Water was being boiled in the garden in big cauldrons over a wood fire. A charwoman would come at certain days to do the laundry. There were two marble sinks in this room for the washing process.

When the house was torn down I took these two marble sinks and the turning cupboard and brought them to Levent together with the front door of the house and a lattice which had remained on one of the windows. I also took the windows of my grandfather's study which had small red panes on the upper side. Now people who see these pieces at Levent remember the old house.

The method of shopping was quite different. There was a storage room with a large chest to hold dry vegetables and rice. They were bought in large quantities from a shop in Kadıköy and brought home by a porter in a carriage accompanied by my grandmother.

Most of the vegetables and fruits were grown in the garden. Seedlings would be prepared in the green house or in protected places in the garden and then the transplanting would be made according to the season. All fruit and vegetables would be consumed at the time they were ripe. Out of season fruits and vegetables would be very rare. Chicken and eggs were also available in the garden. In the old days there were cows in the stable for milk but later the horse and cow stables were used for storage.

Carriages, horses and cows were sold after the war ended. Whenever necessary, the gardener would go to the carriage stand at Kızıltoprak and bring a carriage. In winter time a "long carriage" would come every morning to take my brother and me to St. Joseph school.

In 1938 a tram car system was established from Kadıköy boat landing to Bostancı which stopped at Kızıltoprak. The tram was also extended to Üsküdar, Bağlarbaşı and Moda. The only public transport was the train which ran infrequently. The tram eased public transportation.

In those years a Frigidaire refrigerator came to Kızıltoprak. This immediately eliminated the buying of ice and the karlık. City gas also came and eliminated the mangal which was used to prepare tea toast and make coffee after lunch and dinner. The mangal was still used in the summer when breakfast and afternoon tea were taken in the garden. No one liked the electric toaster and the mangal was always preferred to prepare toast.

Kızıltoprak was a musical house with three pianos, one my mother's, one Leyla Hanım's and one my aunt's. My grandmother liked to play her special drum, a darbuka, and would have them made to order in Bursa. She always brought back several darbukas when she visited Bursa to go to the hot baths.

At St. Joseph I joined the brass band and started playing the baritone. In summers I would take piano lessons from Fulya Hanım, a famous teacher of Turkish music. I also started the flute at the Istanbul Conservatory which was at Beşiktaş at that time.

My mother played the piano and the violin. Leyla Hanım had a small harmonium which her father had brought from Paris made by Debain & Co. (Inventeurs de L'Harmonium Hors Concours 1867). She

120

had also a tef* which I still keep at our house in Levent together with the harmonium.

My grandfather M.A. Ayni had a big library divided between his selamlık and his study on the third floor of the house. He had books in old Turkish and Arabic. My grandmother had no books in her room and did not care much about reading.

My mother read a great deal and had a library consisting mostly of English novels and history books. My aunt had a library of English and Turkish books. My uncle had many books in German because he was educated in Frankfurt. My younger brother Ali was an ardent reader and he had many Turkish books which he used to bind and start his own library. My elder brother and I had books in French and Turkish. So altogether the house was full of books of all kinds and there was a lot of reading done. As there was no radio or television, people had more time to read.

The old way of life continued at Kızıltoprak up to the end of the second world war. In 1942 my grandmother died. She was running the house and kept the discipline necessary to oversee four generations together under one roof. My mother's name in the house was küçük hanım which means "young lady." She was not responsible for the chores of the house and that is how she had so much time to read and write. In summer she would take all of us to swim at Kalamış bay or at Fenerbahçe beach. She would rent one or two row boats and we would swim in the clean waters of Marmara Sea. She taught us how to swim and she would bring us back in time for lunch at Kızıltoprak. These were the regimented but happy days of our youth.

My grandfather died three years after my grandmother. Gradually the Ottoman generation was fading away. But my father and mother were still alive and they represented the last generation of the Ottomans.

The republican era started in 1923 but that generation's values, concepts and way of life changed very little. My mother, aunt and uncle

(*) Tef is a round tamburine with small brass cymbals attached to the frame.

had been educated in English and German schools but their living habits were completely according to Ottoman style.

Habits and way of life change very gradually. For instance we, the children, would get up when an elderly person came into the room. The seat of everyone was known so we would not occupy these seats anyway. Only when my grandfather was away would I go up to his library room and study my lessons. I knew when he would be back, so I would come down before his arrival. We could not enter our grandmother's room before taking her permission. My aunt had two rooms which were used only when she came in the summer. No one would enter these rooms during her absence. The house had an interior order which was the Ottoman way of life.

After the death of my grandmother and grandfather the running of the house fell on my mother's shoulders. She did not like this responsibility at all because all her life the house had been run by her parents. Luckily there was Azime "Bacı" who was an old time servant in the house. (Bacı means a woman who is not a relative but a close faithful person.) She took over some of the chores. My parents no longer had the means to keep a cook who stayed permanently. When the last cook left Azime Bacı started cooking in the vestibule next to the dining room. She cooked the meals that she knew. My mother was not very happy with this solution but accepted the situation. The meals of the gardener were taken out to the kitchen which was not functioning any more.

The gardener was doing the shopping and taking care of the front garden which was only for flowers. The back garden which was a vegetable garden could not be tended any more. Vegetables were bought from the nearby retail shop.

Azime would take care of all the chores like carrying wood to the stoves. Coal was kept in the garden and broken in to small pieces by the gardener but Azime would carry it to the stove in the dining room. She would do small repairs and take care of the old house. My father was not travelling any more and moved his office to the Veli Alemdar han in Galata, Istanbul. He was helping my mother in her housework. My mother's name was still "küçük hanım" but the number of people who would call her by this name was diminishing.

Kızıltoprak was getting away from being an Ottoman kiosk. After my aunt's death the house was divided into two sections. My cousin Ismail Arar had a bath and a kitchen added to his part of the house. The division was easily done by locking one door at the lower corridor and another door on the second floor corridor.

It was not possible to keep the gardener any more. So the flower garden dried up and the vegetable garden was full of wild grass. Only the old trees like figs, mulberries and prunes would give fruits in season. The chickens and turkeys were also non-existent. Only the ram that was bought before the sacrifice holiday would stroll in the garden and eat the grass. In the old days the custom was to buy a lamb and feed it in the garden. In the last days of Kızıltoprak a ram was bought just a few days before the holiday.

The Ottoman way of life was gradually turning in to the Republican way of life. Food was cooked in smaller quantities, as much as Azime would cook. My father was getting old and my mother had never cooked in her life. She was a connoisseur of jam and would prepare jams. She never dreamed of buying ready made jam from the market. She would make all kinds of jams from summer and winter fruits. She had a special cupboard to store her jams. The jams would be kept in big jars and she would give a jar to each of her sons.

There was a bell hanging on a tree in the back garden. The back garden gate would be closed always with an iron bar. Anyone who came through that door would pull a handle on the side of the gate which triggered the big bell. The back gate was of three sections large enough to allow a carriage to enter. When this door was closed we had a way of climbing the wall and opening the door from the inside. It was also possible to get our car in. There was no parking problem on the back street but it was done to keep the car safe from the children who would play around it.

After my father died, my mother did not like living there alone with

Azime Bacı. She moved to the apartment she had rented for winter months. After the last Ottomans went away, we could not maintain their large houses. Thieves began to break in and steal the lead pipes. They stole also the "flat ud"* of Leyla Hanım which was in my locked cubboard. We tried to find some people to live in the house. We could not and finally decided to sell it. İsmail Arar, my cousin who owned half of the shares, found a construction company to tear down the house and build an apartment house of six flats, three for him and one for each of us. I tried to stop this quick liquidation but could not find the financing to buy my cousin's share. So the garden and the house were gone.

(*) Ud is a musical instrument like a lute.

Chapter 14
Old Konaks

The Ottoman way of life was quite different from our present-day of life. First the composition of the family was different. It was customary to have a few generations live together in a konak, a large house of 15 to 40 rooms. In the house there would be the elderly people, grandmothers, grandfathers, grand aunts and other elders, younger people, children, servants, maids and ahretlik, the distant relatives or friends. The way of living and means of communication created this togetherness. For instance my grandmother had a kalfa, an experienced maid named Şerif who was in charge of the younger servants. She had a daughter who was married away to a rich man's stupid son. They gave them a farm house outside the city walls at Çırpıcı, Topkapı. Sherif had to walk from her house to Topkapı and take a tram car to Eminönü, then walk to Galata and take the ferryboat to Haydarpaşa to take the train to Kızıltoprak. This would take her more than five hours', travelling and it was impossible to return the same day. She would stay a few days with her old mistress.

In old houses there was always a guest room and bedding for guests. The matresses, pillows and quilts would be kept in the yüklük, a special storage place in the rooms. Guests would stay either in this guest room or, if necessary, matresses would be laid on the floor of another room.

These households were accustomed to receiving guests at any time. There were very few hotels and it would be improper to go to a hotel. You would have someone to stay with when you went to another town. The situation changed when my father started going to Ankara. At first he would stay at inns until later hotels were built and he stayed at a hotel. Then he rented an apartment which was used as an office and had a bedroom at the back. When I started to work with him in Ankara in

1944, he gave me a room next to his at the back of the apartment.

I went to Eskişehir to my uncle who invited me in 1936. I also stayed one night with my nurse who had married and moved to Eskişehir. If I had not stayed with her she would have been very offended. She had prepared her own bedroom with freshly puffed pillows and newly aired cotton mattresses. Her husband was a chemist at the railroads.

My grandmother had guests who would come from Baghdad or Aleppo and stay a few months. We would get used to them. They would have their special place at the table and when they left they would be lamented for a long time. We would talk about them and miss them. We would be very happy when my aunt, uncle and their son Ismail came from Ankara for the summer. Their rooms would be prepared and ornamented with nice smelling flowers. They would come for the whole summer. The house would be more crowded. We would have a very nice time and parties would be arranged.

All weddings, births and circumcision ceremonies would take place at home. No one would think of going to a hospital or a hotel. The hospital was only thought of for a major surgery. Once someone went to the hospital, it was quite rare that he or she would come back. The average age level was below 50. Those that were healthy lived, those that were weak could die. The return of my grandfather from a hospital in France was quite an event. The prostate surgery could not be done in Istanbul, so he went to Paris for this operation. He spent months in the hospital. It seems the doctors lost hope and he was dying. His sheikh from Üsküdar appeared to him in Paris and sat at his bed side. This gave him the will power to survive. Of course this was an imaginary tale which our grandfather told us. Finally we heard that he was coming back by boat from Marseilles. We went to the boat landing at Galata to meet him. The gardener carried his suitcase. He was very weak and walking with a French cane that had a rubber tip which we had never seen before. I still keep that cane as a souvenir of my grandfather.

Kızıltoprak was not a big konak. My grandmother had plans to demolish the house and build a stone mansion. But at the last minute they discarded this plan and decided to enlarge the old house. I remember this renovation in 1927. A big pit was opened in the garden for the slaking of lime. The limestone was placed in a large wooden container and water poured over it. This was a dangerous operation and children were not allowed to approach the pit. The limestone would crack and melt away with the water and the quick lime would flow into the pit. This very white stuff would be left for a few days to become slaked lime. Then it was used to make mortar for the construction. We were very strictly forbidden to approach the pit and they said that if we fell in our skeleton would come out. For this reason we only threw stones into the pit from a distance; the sound of "Lop!" would be heard.

Near the well the carpenters made a working table and started cutting lumber. A very nice smell of wood would come from that part of the garden. At another place piles of sand came in wagons drawn by buffalos. There was also a pile of pebbles that came with horse drawn carts. Finally the back garden became an area of construction. The experienced workers were of Greek origin and they would speak Greek among themselves. The workers were poor boys, shabbily dressed immigrants from Anatolia. The material kept on coming by horse and buffalo wagons and we began to see lots of animals in the garden. Naturally all of this hassle became a reason for play and enjoyment for us the children (we three brothers plus my cousin in the summer).

In Ottoman life there was a garden between the house and the street. For the girls who could not go out in the garden there was a smaller walled garden called the avlu. This was a high walled area between the house and the garden, well protected from foreign eyes. No stranger would be allowed into the house unless accompanied by a known person. Only relatives and acquaintances would visit the house. In order to invite a friend, I had to take permission from my mother or father. When we were to visit a friend's house we had to give information about our friend's family. No permission would be granted before knowing whose house we were going to visit.

127

The gates would be kept locked and at night iron bars would be placed over the gates. The gates of the garden walls had a bell attached so that one could hear that the gate had been opened and send someone to inquire or just look from a window and see the newcomer. The house at Kızıltoprak had five gates, each with a specific use. (See attach. plan).

The front gate was used by the elderly of the house and by guests. This gate had two sections each with an iron knocker. This door is now mounted on the wall at our house in Levent. When electricity was installed at the house an electric bell was placed on the side of the gate. Those who could not find the bell still pounded the knocker. In case of an electric cut the knockers were left in place.

Each one had his own way of ringing the bell. My grandfather would press the bell a long time. The maid who ran to open the gate would run with anxiety. She would also shout "The master has come!" She knew that at the opening of the door he would ask first for his slippers and would direct some other questions that the maid would not be able to answer. For instance he might ask, "What is there tonight for dinner?" Of course the maid who opened the door would not be able to answer and would be scolded.

When our great uncle (Hasan Tahsin Ayni), my grandfather's brother, would visit he would press the bell continously until the gate was opened. So the bell would ring all over the house. Inevitably the door lock would not open and there would be a great commotion. This way the whole house knew that the great uncle had arrived.

Guests would very politely ring twice with a small interval and someone would run and open the gate. The postman would ring once but with a long stretch. He would generally bring a letter from my father.

The balcony on the first floor had a gate which was not very visible from the garden. So very few people came to this door. This gate had neither a knocker nor an electric bell. It had a door bell like a bicycle ring. If that bell rang it was understood that a stranger or a beggar had come to the balcony gate. Sometimes vendors of watermelon or other

128

fruits would end up at this gate. In winter this door was pasted over with paper in order to keep the cold out so it could not be opened. So if someone came in winter to this gate, he or she would be signaled to go to the front gate. The iron stairs leading to this balcony was on the opposite side of the garden gate so we would wonder and ask ourselves, "How come they fail to see the big front gate and come around the garden, climb the stairs, and find this door?"

At the back of the house there were two doors. One was placed there when the house was enlarged and the other was a very small gate of the old part of the house. This gate was only 1 meter and 20 cm high and had no lock. At the back there was an iron bar and a sliding bolt. One had to bend down in order to pass through it. In the old days the doors were made against bandits. It forced them to bend down to come into the house. This door was used mostly by the children of the house and the servants. A repair man or gardener who had to enter the house would also use this gate.

The door that opened to the new pantry leading to the dining room had only a key. It was a tall and wide gate. This door was used by the members of the house to go out to the back garden and by the maids. If someone was going out to the street they would use the front gate. There was another reason for this separation.

No one coming from the street would enter the house with their shoes. Everyone had their slippers in a room on the side of the front entrance. There were also separate slippers for men and women guests ready in this room. People going to the garden from the pantry door would wear wooden sandals on their slippers called "takunya". In this way mud or dirt would not be carried into the house.

When an elderly person left the house from the front gate he or she would be followed until the garden gate to say farewell.

The two back gates were used only by people of the household and had neither a bell nor a knocker. They were opening to the small garden which dates back to the days of separation between men and women when girls were allowed to go out to the small garden without a head cover. It was closed with high walls, one gate leading to the back garden and the other to the front garden. These two gates would be locked and barred at night.

There is a story about the old small gate of the house. One night during the war years some thieves came and tried to break the door. All men were either at the war front or on a trip somewhere. My grandmother took my grandfather's double barreled hunting gun and opened a window overlooking this small gate. She fired two shots in the air and the thieves ran away. I am still keeping this gun at our house in Levent.

There were ways of getting in and out of the house without opening the gates but you had to know your way. I would leave my window open and climb to the veranda roof, then down from the mulberry tree. Late at night I had to climb the mulberry tree and step from the roof by using the dining room window iron bars. In this way I could get in and out without disturbing anybody.

It was not very often that people went out at night. On such rare occasions as a wedding or returning late from the city from a cinema or theater, the big key of the front gate would be carried with us. We would inform the maids not to put the iron bar or chain on the front gate. The garden gate also was not to be locked. If by mistake they forgot and put the chain on the door, we would go around back, knock on the window and wake them up.

There was another door opening to the storage room which was never locked. This was identical to the front gate but had lost its function because the portico to which it opened was closed in at the big repairs and the door was left just where it was.

There was a hidden door from this storage place to the green house adjacent to it. There were so many trunks and things piled up that it was not visible. From the outside, it was at the end of the greenhouse and looked like the wall of the building. It had a lock and wooden bar on the inside and I never saw it opened or used.

There was another aspect connected with the doors of the rooms.

In winter each door was covered with a blanket, rug or kilim from the side of the corridor. In this way when the door was opened this hanging blanket or kilim would keep the cold air from coming into the room. As rooms were big and ceilings high, it was difficult to keep the rooms warm. Each winter these door covers would be taken out of storage and hung on the doors.

Each room had a wood burning ceramic stove except the dining room which had a black iron coal burning store. Only this room was heated constantly in winter.

Each summer 30 to 40 çeki of firewood would be bought and stored in the basement of the house. The wood would come in horse drawn wagons to the spot nearest the entrance of the basement which was under the balcony of the first floor. The gardener would bring a few men to carry and store the firewood. There was another entrance from the small garden to the basement from where the wood was carried into the house.

Coal was stored outside at the back of the kitchen and was burned mostly in the kitchen stove and, in winter, in the dining room iron stove. Charcoal would also be stored in the basement and would come with long carriages drawn by a team of buffaloes. They were coming directly from the forest of Alemdağ where charcoal was prepared.

All this preparation for winter was made during the hot summer months. My grandmother would estimate how much wood, charcoal and coal had to be bought to last through the winter.

The house was mainly heated with the ceramic stoves and "mangals". At the end of the summer these ceramic stoves would be repaired as needed and their pipes tied to the ceiling leading to the appropriate chimneys. Each stove had a wood storage box made of decorative steel. These boxes would store at least two days' requirement of burning wood. This work with the stoves was done by the gardener in close supervision of my grandmother. The maids would light the stoves according to her instructions. The bedroom stoves burned only at night. Some bedrooms would be heated with a "mangal" from fire obtained from other burning stoves.

The bathrooms each had a stove which also heated the water. In general the small bath on the second floor was heated. The large bath room on the first floor was used rarely and only during the summer. This bathroom had an ornate marble kurna that is now decorating our balcony at Levent.

Mangals were of several types. My grandmother had a small mangal made of brass which she used to heat her bedroom in winter. She had a stove too but used it only when she was sick. Otherwise she would just use a hot water bottle to heat her bed and the small mangal to break the cold. My grandfather had a stove in his library and would take a mangal to his room about an hour before going to bed. This would be enough to take the chill off the room.

My mother had a big white stove in her bedroom and would light it whenever she wished. She had also a mangal where she put hot coals from the stove to heat her room better.

The guestroom stoves would be lit only about an hour before the guests came. The guestroom had a big mangal which was inherited from Ismail Pasha, Leyla Hanım's father. Somehow this mangal had come to Kızıltoprak. Now it is one of the prized items at our house in Levent and we fill it with flowers or fruits as decoration.

The black mangal in the dining room was the ugliest but most functional mangal of the house. It was used to boil water, prepare tea and make toast for breakfast. After the arrival of city gas this good old mangal lost its importance. It would heat the room of the maids at night where there was no stove.

Every morning the first task was to light this mangal. Charcoal would be put together with pieces of wood and paper. The paper would be lit and the mangal placed at the small garden door where there was a draft. A pipe would be placed on the charcoal to increase the draft. The mangal would start burning and send sparks all around. It would be left burning in the open to eliminate the poisonous gas, then taken inside the dining room and used to prepare breakfast.

There was a big steel kitchen stove with an oven in the middle and hot water compartment. Coal and wood would be placed together and ignited. This stove had a large chimney. The stove was large enough to hold five or six copper cooking pots. After lunch the cook would retrieve the remaining burning coal into a tin container and take it out to the garden. It would be extinginished by pouring the dishwater over it, creating a fearful sight of crackling coals and steaming water. This coal would be saved for re-use. For dinner the whole process was repeated.

On cold days the cook and the gardener would take a maltız to their room. This heating utensil would be kept in the kitchen and also used for cooking whenever needed.

There were two open-air fireplaces beside the washing room, each with a black cauldron. These cauldrons would be filled with water with buckets and a wood fire started for heating the washing water. The washer woman would boil the laundry in one of the cauldrons. The other cauldron would have fresh boiling water for the rinse. The laundry would be washed in the marble sinks inside the wash room and then hung in the garden to dry.

Each room had one mangal either of copper or brass. Every mangal had to have a maşa and be half filled with ash. The ceramic or iron stoves had a tray to protect the floor or carpets from burning in case small sparks would fall. A linoleum cover would be put in front of these trays for further protection.

Each stove tray would have a pair of tongs and a small pail. With these instruments, burning coals would be taken from the stove and transferred to the mangal. As rooms were quite large the stove would not heat the room very well and the mangal would help distribute the heat in the room. On most of the stoves there would be a container with water which would get hot from the stove. This water was used to wash hands as the tap water was very cold in winter. My father would take a cup of hot water to shave with his razor. I would envy him and wish my beard would grow and I would also shave one day.

Hot water bottles or rubber bags would be used to heat the beds in winter. In spite of the stove the bed linen would be very cold and these heating devices would help. They had to be very tightly closed otherwise they would leak and wet the bed all over. Window panes and some doors would be pasted over with paper for the winter to prevent the cold. No matter what we did it was difficult to heat the old wooden house in winter. Sometimes the cold would penetrate the marrow of our bones.

Chapter 15
From Ottoman Kiosks to Republican Houses

The reason for naming this book "Kızıltoprak Stories" was that I tried to describe life in the last Ottoman period and how the changes that arrived with the Republic affected us in the kiosk of my parents: the way the house was built and renovated to provide room for the family, the relations among family members; the way of living in a large house with a garden; the surroundings of the house and means of communication: the type of furniture used in the house; the living conditions in summer and winter.

The map in this book gives an idea about the area covered by the Ottoman Empire and the effect of this geography on the working and living conditions of our ancestors who lived the last period of the Ottoman Empire. Their travels in Anatolia, the Balkans and the Middle East were practically adventures. We grew up with the tales of these travels and wars in the last period of the empire.

We are the first generation of the Republic but we lived among the last Ottomans. Some of these events were told to us and some were quietly avoided. We understood some of the tales and could not make out others.

During the Ottoman days some administrators were expelled by the sultan to far off places like Fizan now in Libya. Many people were drafted to the army and sent to Yemen but very few came back. There were practically no roads and the railroad was very limited. There was no Turkish passenger boat service and all sea transportation was done by foreign companies. Land communication was by horse drawn carriages, mules, camels and horses. I am still keeping two mule trunks which my grandparents used. These are special trunks with an iron contraption for hanging on the mule packs. They are made of leather and covered with canvas. The lid has two places for hand locks. The lid protrudes to the sides of the trunk in order to keep the rain out. There are handles on both sides to lift the trunk up to the saddle of the mule. They are made of such strong material that in spite of the rigorous travels they are still in quite good condition. These trunks went to Harput and Yanina, from one end of the empire to the other and finally back to Kızıltoprak. My grandmother kept these trunks, then my mother took care of them.

Kızıltoprak was full of such old objects. Gradually they went out of use and were stored in what was called a taşlık. For instance, candlelight lanterns and gas lamps were all placed in storage and later on became antiques. As mentioned before each room had a ceramic stove and a mangal. When a stove could not be repaired it was sent to the old stable which became a secondary storage place. The mangals were placed in the attic along with their tongs and pails. As was the old custom, we used to say, "You never know, maybe it will be needed one day." So nothing was thrown away. The large door covers gradually disappeared, I was able to keep only one. Now we see such curtains at the entrances of the mosques.

The last Ottomans left Kızıltoprak gradually. First Leyla Hanım died in 1936. She was 86 years old so it was a regretted but timely departure. Then Uncle Sırrı died at a very young age in Ankara. He was just going to be married. His fiancee Nevvare remained single for many years but we lost contact with her. I heard years later that she married. The death of her son Sırrı affected my grandmother very badly. She was a very active and joyful person but she gradually faded away and died in 1942. She was taken to the same cemetery as her mother on the European side of Istanbul at Edirnekapı. During that time my father's mother also passed away and she was taken to Karacaahmet which is one of the oldest cemeteries on the Asian shore of Istanbul. These sudden departures one after the other had a sad effect on life at Kızıltoprak. The last one of the old generation was my grandfather who died at a hospital in Istanbul and was buried at the Zincirlikuyu cemetery. So in 1945 we had only two generations left at Kızıltoprak.

My mother, father, aunt and uncle became the old generation. They were born and raised under the sultans so they were the remaining Ottomans in the house. They all wrote the old script very well, knew the Arabic and Persian words used in the Ottoman language and used these terms quite frequently. This generation lasted up to the 1960's. My aunt passed away in 1958 and was buried together with her father at Zincirlikuyu cemetery.

People from the old Ottoman generation visiting Kızıltoprak were also fading away. My grandmother's sister and two brothers would get together with her quite often at each others' homes. During holidays we would go and visit them all. My grandfather had many friends and relatives.

Their children continued to see each other with my mother and father. Customs were gradually changing. Instead of making holiday visits people began to get out of Istanbul for a few days' vacation. Istanbul traffic had become difficult and it was not easy to visit each other. In the old days it was a pleasure to go from Kızıltoprak to the city. There would always be seats available on the boat, which had first and second class and a luxury class with armchairs. Everybody would find a seat and no one would think of remaining standing. There were always empty benches all around the sides of the boat which were covered with red linoleum mats. At the front in second class there were no mats but you could always find a place on the wooden benches.

Once arriving at the Galata bridge you could go anywhere by tram or the small subway. You would get to the nearest station and then walk to your destination. The tramway had first and second class cars. There would be a rush to get seats but you would always offer your seat to the elderly. Istanbul had its own way of living that showed a degree of respect to others. In public places no one would talk loudly, laughing was also controlled and there were no written laws or regulations for these behaviors.

Kızıltoprak had its own type of discipline. For instance lunch was served after the 12:15 train left the station. This was because my uncle who was working at Haydarpasha would come home with this train. In summer we would always return from swimming no later than 12 o'clock. We would go to swim either at Kalamış or Fenerbahçe. After the tramway reached the beaches at Caddebostan or Suadiye we would also go there. Sometimes I would go to Suadiye by bicycle but would always be back at home by 12:00 o'clock.

In the evening everyone would be at home before sunset. If someone was going on a visit and would be returning late, his plate would not be laid on the table and he or she would not be expected for dinner. No one would go anywhere without informing the elders. If a guest was going to arrive everyone would know this in advance. The children would never touch the telephone. My mother would rarely dial to her neighbors or friends.

Water and electricity were also used carefully. Electric lights would be extinguished when leaving a room. In summer each day two kilograms of ice would be bought in a block form. It would be broken to pieces and placed in the karlık, or water cooler. No one could drink from the karlık. Only at lunch the maids would serve cool water. Sometimes when coming back from the sea we would drink a few glasses and add water to the karlık. At lunch my grandmother would understand this and issue a general scolding. No one would utter a word.

Sitting habits when together with elders was observed. You could not cross your legs in front of the elders. You should get up when an older person entered the room and wait until he or she sat down. When sitting you should sit up straight and not figit. You should not talk at the table and answer only when asked a question. During lunch or dinner children would not take part in the conversation.

My grandmother would plan what to cook and how much because about 15 people would be at the table and there were the maids, gardener and cook to think of.

After the old generation died their relatives and friends continued to visit Kızıltoprak. But they too started going to the other world and decreasing in numbers. Only my mother and father remained from the Ottoman generation. Their first children were born in the last part of the empire but I was born in 1923. I consider myself as the first generation of the Republic. The caliph was still in Istanbul but he left a few months later.

After the death of my father, mother was left alone. There was the old maid Azime Bacı who knew my grandfather and other old relatives and was taking care of the house. She was a peasant woman from the Ottoman days. When the Greeks occupied her town, Göynük, she ran to the mountains and saved her life. She started coming as a charwoman first but then stayed permanently. There was another lady who had migrated from Potgorica in Yugoslavia during the Balkan War and was coming for the laundry. Naciye Hanım knew Bosnian and her Turkish was limited. She would start the fire under the cauldrons and wash the laundry in the old style. My mother never thought of buying a washing machine. I had brought her a pressure cooker when returning from my studies in the States, but she never used it because she was afraid it might blow up. They continued to live quietly the Ottoman way of life.

In 1968 when my mother died, the end of Kızıltoprak was evident. Azime Bacı wanted to return to Göynük, her village where she had grandchildren and children. Once I went to Göynük to visit her and we talked of the old people at Kızıltoprak. She considered herself as part of the family. She kept Kızıltoprak going for a while but when she moved to Göynük that was the end of the house. We gave her a truck load of furniture to take to Göynük.

The gradual dismantling of Kızıltoprak had actually started way back. When the horses and cows were sold, the empty stables gradually became dilapidated. First the horse stable was torn down. The cow stable was used as a storage place and, in winter, to keep the lemon trees and other plants that would not stand the cold weather. The room of the gardener and the carriage shack were also torn down after they became untenable.

The kitchen and the wash room fell into disuse and their roofs leaked.

The last repair on the house was made by my cousin when he settled in his section. He changed the bath on the first floor to a kitchen and added a bathroom to the second floor. But he could not live there very long as his was the north side of the house and very difficult to heat in winter. So he moved to town and left Kızıltoprak. He did not touch the house until my mother, his aunt, died. Then he wanted to sell his share and we could not buy it as we also could not live any more in Kızıltoprak. Most of the old kiosks in the area were being torn down and apartment houses built. We were glad that at least the house was not burnt down by thieves as had happened to Leyla Hanım's house at Bostancı.

Like the Ottoman Empire the house at Kızıltoprak was eventually torn down and disappeared.

Chapter 16
From Istanbul to Ankara
(Ankara as the Capital of the Republic)

Istanbul was built in the year 330 by Constantine as the capital of the Eastern Roman Empire. The Eastern Roman Empire gradually fell under the influence of the people from Thrace. In 419 Justinian becames emperor and his dynasty lasted until 602. He was replaced by Heraclius whose family remained in power until 705. In this century the city became known as Byzantium.

Then Justinian II continued to rule Constantinople until 717. After his death the Isaurian Dynasty took over until 867. At this time the Macedonians gained influence over the city. The kingdom started by Basilius continued until 1057 and ended with Theodora. At this time the city fell under the influence of the Venetians and Emperor Isaac Comnene's dynasty lasted until 1185. When the Crusaders invaded Constantinople, the town was sacked and pillaged and Baudouin I was declared king. The Genovese settled on the opposite shore of the Golden Horn. Byzantium was divided into three parts: Nicea in Asia Minor, Constantinople, and Trebizond. In 1261 the Paleologan Dynasty took over Constantinople and maintained power until the 1453 conquest of the city by the Ottomans.

Thus, from 330 to 1453, for more than a thousand years, Constantinople continued to be the center of the Eastern Roman Empire and the seat of the Orthodox Church. During this period many people from France, Holland, Belgium and other parts of Europe came and settled in Istanbul. Around 1100, the Karaide Jews set up a Jewish quarter in Constantinople. Other peoples from the East and Africa settled in Constantinople. So the city had a very mixed population. Some were brought as slaves but lived and died in Constantinople. Turks and Arabs would come to Constantinople as traders or they would graze their sheep outside the walls. The Maltese must have come from the island of

Malta. Right after the first world war hundreds of thousands of White Russians came to Istanbul. All these communities had their schools, temples, hospitals and cemeteries.

When the Turks took over Constantinople, the sultans minted silver and gold coins inscribed, "Printed in Constantinie." This lasted until 1923, a period of 470 years. The population of Istanbul during these years stayed more or less the same but with an increase of the Turkish population. In this cosmopolitan town, all denominations of the Christian churches coexisted with a predominantly Muslim population. The seat of the Greek Orthodox patriarchate is still in Istanbul.

The influence of the European powers increased in Istanbul after the middle of the nineteenth century. British, Russian, French, German and Italian embassies increased their demands on the Sublime Port which was the prime minister's office. The registry of the Istanbul Municipality shows in 1919, at the end of the first world war, a population of 1,200,000. Out of this only half were Muslims and the other half a mixture of Greek Orthodox, Catholic, Jewish, Gregorian and others.

From 1919 to 1923, Istanbul was occupied by the Allies consisting of the British, French, Italian and a contingent of Americans. During this period the ambassadors of these countries acted like the real rulers of Istanbul or Constantinople. The sultan still lived in his palace at Yıldız and the Sublime Port still existed but they had no real power.

Under these conditions Atatürk went to Samsun on the Black Sea as an inspector of the Eastern Armies but his real intention was to save the country from foreign occupation.

The British and French occupied the Middle East section of the empire and formed new dominions like Palestine, Jordan, Lebanon, Iraq and Emirates in the Arabian peninsula. The Italians had occupied the Aegean islands and started moving towards Antalya. The Greeks occupied Izmir and started moving towards central Anatolia. So there was only the Eastern Army left intact who had pushed back the Russians after the revolution in Russia.

Unoccupied areas were only Central Anatolia and the Black Sea coast. With the help of the army on the eastern frontier, Atatürk managed to organize a counter-attack against the invading forces. First the French and Armenians were stopped in Southern and Southeastern Anatolia. It took from 1919 to 1923 to push back the Greeks from Central Anatolia to Izmir. During this time Ankara had become the center of the liberation movement. The only port not under Allied control was Inebolu on the Black Sea, so supplies had to come from this port.

Istanbul remained under occupation during all this period. The population of Istanbul in 1919 was half Turkish Muslims and the other half a mixture of Greeks remaining from Byzantine times, Armenians, Jews, Albanians, Latins remaining from the Genovese enclave at Galata, Maltese, White Russians, Bulgarians, French, British, German, Italian, Arabs and many other ethnic groups. The municipal census showed the figures as follows:

Muslims	600,000
Orthodox	200,000
Catholics	200,000
Gregorians	100,000
Jews	100,000
Total	1,200,000

All these denominations had their private schools and churches. The patriarch was the center of all the Orthodox population in the world. The authority of the caliphate had dwindled to India and the Far East because the Arabs, who had obtained their independence from the Ottoman Empire, were no longer accepting the sultan as their caliph and had joined with the enemy against the empire.

Between 1909 and 1923 the dynasty of the Ottomans had crumbled. The Young Turks and the Union and Progress Party brought down the monarchy and started a parliament made up of deputies. The sultanate had lost its absolute control. Sultan Abdulhamid was dethroned by the army that came from Salonica, was sent to Salonica and replaced by Sultan Reşad. The last Sultan, Vahdettin, escaped from Istanbul on a British battleship in 1922. In 1924, Sultan Abdülmecid, who was the last caliph, departed from Istanbul.

Istanbul had all the public buildings, big mosques, dervish lodges and other religious and pious foundations, ports and railroad centers, foreign embassies and the kiosks and konaks of all the ruling population of the empire.

Ankara on the other hand was a little town in central Anatolia with only a few houses around the old castle. There were farm houses around Çankaya surrounded with vineyards. Wine grapes were still growing in Ankara when I went there in 1944.

Kavaklıdere, Etlik and all the surrounding areas produced grapes and the name of the Kavaklıdere wines dates from this time.

There were no buildings to house the deputies to the new National Assembly who came from the unoccupied parts of the empire. Atatürk was trying to save the country with whatever force he could gather in Ankara. The Istanbul government was on the side of the occupying forces and the sultan gave orders to arrest Mustafa Kemal and bring him to Istanbul. The caliphate organized a new army with the help of the British to bring an end to the resistance that was being organized in and around Ankara.

Deputies had to stay in school dormitories and the National Assembly was a small old building at what is now called Ulus square. The Greek army was approaching Ankara so they made plans to move the new capital to Kayseri. The battles of İnönü in the Aegean area were fought to delay the advancing Greek army. It was only in the last decisive battle of Dumlupınar in August 1922 that the Greek army was surrendered and its commanders were arrested by Mustafa Kemal's army. When the Greek army was retreating to Izmir all the towns and villages on their way were burnt down and the population had to run to the mountains to save their lives. The country was completely devastated. Before its defeat, the Greek army had approached eastward as far as Polatlı, about sixty kilometers from Ankara and cannon sounds were heard in the town of Ankara.

We listened to these stories from our parents who were in Ankara at that time trying to form the new Republic. The only line of communication left was the tiny port of Inebolu on the Black Sea.

After the Greek army was dispersed and before they ran away from Izmir on British and French ships, they set fire to the city of Izmir. Most of Izmir burned down during those tragic days. The Turkish army walked all the way from Ankara to Izmir fighting against the Greek army.

The occupying forces were still in Istanbul and there was a period of anxiety in the whole country, especially in Istanbul. The enemy warships were lined up in front of the Dolmabahçe Palace with all their cannons pointing to the city. The Greek population of Istanbul were making great festivities and hoping that the Greek army would enter Istanbul.

Uncertainty prevailed on all sides. The British and French were asking for new forces from their dominions. No one was in a position to send relief forces. The British high command in London gave orders to fight if the Turkish troops advanced towards the Dardanelles. Mustafa Kemal and his chief of staff decided first to liberate Bursa from the Greek occupying forces. Before the Turkish forces arrived the Greeks retreated to the port of Mudanya and boarded their boats to return to Greece. As the Turkish forces started to approach the Dardanelles, the British tried to stop them. At that time the Turkish cavalry came from another direction and just encircled the British forces. There was no shooting on either side and the Turkish army came to the outskirts of Istanbul.

Finally the Allied army decided to meet with İnönü at Mudanya and discuss the terms of armistice and evacuation of Istanbul. The occupying forces and their ships left Istanbul in 1923.

Ankara was still a poor little Anatolian town. There were no highways connecting it to the cities. Only the Berlin- Baghdad railroad passed through Ankara. There was only one small station building which Mustafa Kemal had made his headquarters. Ankara was full of swamps and malaria was a common disease. There were no paved streets, hotels, regular hospitals, universities or natural resources such as forests or lakes. Why was Ankara chosen as the capital of the new Republic?

We can accept this decision as a start for the reforms to be proposed and implemented by the new Republic of Turkey.

When Mustafa Kemal landed in Samsun on May 19, 1919, the whole country was in turmoil. He could not stay very long in Samsun as it was a vulnerable point and the British could come with their navy. The first thing he did was go to Amasya, then Sivas and assemble meetings with local leaders of Anatolia. Then he went to Erzurum to organize a first get- together with the representatives of unoccupied areas. He also invited the commander of the Eastern army Kazım Karabekir who had made an agreement with the Russians and Armenians to stop the fighting in the Eastern frontier. His was the only army left in the country and he had orders from the sultan to arrest Mustafa Kemal.

Kazım Karabekir came to Ankara with his cavalry. He could have arrested Mustafa Kemal and sent him to Istanbul. Instead he showed him respect and declared that his army was at his disposal. This was the turning point in the formation of the Turkish Republic. Then Mustafa Kemal could come back as far as Ankara to reorganize his forces and wait for the Greeks to approach Ankara. He sent one of his close commanders Kemal Doğan to the front in Adana to stop the French advance. The local forces in Antep were also resisting the advance of the French.

İnönü and Fevzi Çakmak were organizing a regular army in Ankara. They were also stalling the Greek advance as much as possible in Western Anatolia. Ankara was the ideal spot geographically to start the new republic.

The first agreement was reached with the French on the Syrian frontier with the exception of Hatay and Alexandretta. Another agreement was made with the Russians and Armenians on the eastern frontier. Ankara then became a natural center for the new country, unlike Istanbul which was under occupation and had a very cosmopolitan population.

146

Mustafa Kemal did not come to Istanbul when the Allied forces departed. The Istanbul bureaucracy did not accept Ankara as the new capital and many of them did not move to the new capital. Ankara developed as a new and clean city after the swamps were dried and construction of the new city started.

Up to 1950 the highway to Ankara was not usable in winter months because of a lack of bridges on rivers. In 1945, I drove by jeep from Ankara to Istanbul and it took me seventeen hours. The only safe transportation was the railroad. There were also two flights a day of the Turkish Airlines. After the development of the modern highway systems the character of both Istanbul and Ankara changed considerably.

When the road to Ankara was opened up, bus transportation began to develop. This brought the migration of many people to the cities. There was also a great expulsion of Turks from Bulgaria in 1950 and 1980 where there were large Turkish communities. They were settled around Istanbul and Bursa.

The opening up of new roads in Istanbul and the tearing down of the Byzantine walls at two places also caused a big move of population within the city. The gecekondu or "built overnight" houses began to appear on open land in and around the city. The population of Istanbul increased from 2,200,000 to 5,000,000 in a very short time. The Greeks, Jews and Armenians started leaving Istanbul each for their own reasons. The people born in Istanbul began to fall into the minorities group. The Christian population of Istanbul dwindled and fell to less than five percent.

The name of the city was changed to Istanbul during the Ottoman regime but internationally it was still known as Constantinople for many years. It was also called the "City of Felicity" during the sultans' days. With the start of the Republic, money began to be printed at Ankara and the picture of Atatürk was placed on the currency. The second president İnönü also had his picture on the coins and currency. After his death the currency had only Atatürk pictures. While the old script was still in use, letters sent from foreign countries would be writ-

147

ten in old Turkish but "Constantinople" would be added in Latin letters on the envelope. Gradually the number of people using this name for Istanbul dwindled and no one writes this name on their envelopes.

It can be said that the cosmopolitan population of Istanbul lasted until 1950 and then the city changed its character.

Chapter 17
Development of Ankara

In 1923 when Ankara was declared the capital of the new republic it was a very dry city in the middle of the Anatolian plateau. It was just the old castle and some wooden houses around it. There were farm houses all around the vineyards of Çankaya. In 1945 when I moved to Ankara to work with my father and go to law school, Ankara was still a very small town. I would walk to the law school which was a distance of half an hour in the middle of the prairie. In summer, it was customary to have military camps for all university students. These military camps were three-week training programs around Ankara. We were drilling and staying in tents at night outside of Ankara. The second world war was still going on and Turkey had to be ready all the time. The site of the camp was outside Dikmen close to Balgat. In these open fields and prairies, there was no water source and the drilling was under the sun. At night we would see the glittering lights of Ankara. We did not yet know about air pollution.

My father would tell the stories of his going to Ankara in 1920, by boat to İnebolu and then waiting for a caravan of horse carts. The railway had been cut by the advancing Greek army. The return was also the same way by carriage over muddy roads to İnebolu and then waiting for the boat's arrival from Istanbul. The roads inside Ankara were so muddy that people would be afraid to go out at night. The mud was so deep that you might lose your shoes, so people wore boots. There were no electric lights on the streets, so they had to carry a lantern to go from house to house. At coffee houses they would wait for one person who had a lantern and go with him.

When I went to Ankara Atatürk Boulevard was completed up to Çankaya but there were many empty lots between the new embassy buildings. There were still the vineyards of Kavaklıdere and other smaller vineyards. The swamps of Kızılay were dried up and nice gardens and parks were decorating the Red Crescent square at Kızılay. Population was sparse and new houses were being built. Apartment houses were at most five stories high. Atatürk's farm was functioning as a model farm. The new railroad station was completed. The People's House and Exposition buildings were open to the public.

Twice a week I would go to the People's House to practice fencing. Bedri Rahmi the famous painter would exhibit his oil paintings and sell them for 10 to 25 liras. There would also be painting exhibitions in the military guest house. There was also a theater in the People's House and a large library. The hippodrome was completed and each week there would be horse races. President İnönü would come for the event. My cousin Ismail and I would go and bet on some horses.

Çubuk Dam was completed and Ankara had a large reservoir of water. This dam was also a picnic area where people would go weekends. The football stadium was completed and a shooting poligon was available near the railroad station. Ismail and I would go there and have a few pistol and gun shots.

The trees in Ankara had been newly planted and looked very small to us who were coming from Istanbul. Atatürk Boulevard was very well maintained with lines of flowers and evergreen trees. Red Crescent square had a park with a mineral water buffet which was operated by the Afyonkarahisar monopoly belonging to the Red Crescent. We would organize walking tours with our friends up to Çankaya and back to the Red Crescent park. New embassy buildings were being built on Atatürk Boulevard up to Çankaya where the President had his residence.

The Law and the Public Administration faculties were the nucleus of Ankara University. The Conservatory was also set up in the same vicinity. Each Saturday there was a classical concert at the conservatory which president İnönü and his wife would attend. Turkish music was played on the State Radio broadcasting stations. There were also a few night clubs where there was popular singing and music. Ankara had about four or five cinema houses where mostly American films would be shown.

Atatürk had invited the German professors and musicians who were anti-Nazi and could not stay in Germany. Turkey benefited from these professors in the Law and Economics Faculties in Istanbul and Ankara.

German composer Hindemith was among these professors and he insisted on a new building for the Conservatory. Finally this was possible in 1946. There were also young Turkish administrators who were educated in Germany during the Ottoman period. Some of them came to Ankara to work at the state government enterprises or the universities.

Ankara was rapidly developing as a new capital of Turkey. New administration buildings were set up. The War Academy was transferred from Istanbul to Ankara in its new building. A new Faculty of Languages, History and Geography was built for Ankara University. English, German, French, Russian and Chinese languages were taught. It had also a department for sociology and anthropology.

I did not want to go to law school so the next year I took an exam and transferred to the English department. My friend Bülent Ecevit also did not like the law school so we both ended up at the new Languages, History and Geography Faculty. During the summer military camps continued and we met the boys who attended the Village Institutes. This was a new experimental institution where they would draft young boys and girls after primary school and they would build their own buildings and continue their school education. We were invited by Talip Apaydın and Halim (whose family name I forgot) to visit their school. With Bülent Ecevit we took the train from Ankara to Hasanoğlan Institute near Kırıkkale to the east of Ankara. They came and met us at the station, we stayed one night at their dormitory and they showed us their Institute. They had sections for carpentry, machine shops and other labratories besides their regular studies. They were being trained to be leaders and teachers in their home villages after graduation.

No industry was set up in Ankara. Only the Machine and Chemical Plant of the army was built at Kırıkkale to produce weapons and ammunition. The general directorates of the State Economic Enterprises were in Ankara, such as the Sümerbank (for textiles) and Etibank (for minerals). In front of the new General Assembly stood the Ankara Palas which was constructed by my great uncle Vedat Tek. We would go there with friends to have a cup of tea in the garden.

More and more people moved to Ankara between 1923 and the 1940s. Especially during the second world war when the Germans advanced in Russia as far as Stalingrad, Istanbul began to be evacuated. In 1940, schools were closed early and I went by train to my aunt in Ankara. My father rented a farm house at Etlik and moved some "denks" to this house. A "denk" consists of a mattress, quilt, pillows and a few carpets rolled together and tied with a rope. These were rudimentary necessities in case of a move to Ankara. Many families made similar plans to move to central Anatolian towns if Turkey joined the war, especially those that had experienced the occupation of Istanbul and the shortage of food. Luckily we never saw the house rented in Ankara and the "denks" came back after some time.

In 1950 after I got married, we moved to Ankara and settled at my father's office near Kızılay on the Atatürk Boulevard. I worked at the Marshall Plan as an economist. Ankara had not changed very much. It was still a small town in the center of Anatolia but the Ministries, General Directorate of the State Economic Administrations, the Central Bank, Agricultural bank, Sümerbank and Etibank had built larger buildings to house their staff. Ankara University still had only the faculties of Law, Political Sciences; and Languages, History and Geography. There were new hospitals to cover the needs of the population. My first daughter was born at the Mevki military hospital because my wife's father was a retired general and had the right to use this hospital. The charges for the birth of our first baby was only 27 lira and 50 kuruş.

Ankara's air was very clean and bright. We did not yet know air pollution. Turkish Airlines had a station at Etimesgut very near the city, only a fifteen minute drive from town.

The highways had not changed since the Ottoman days, the bus system had not yet started, so transportation was mainly by railroad. Once I went to Esenboğa which was far away from town (site of the present airport) and the road was dusty and windy. This was the plain where Tamerlane had captured Yıldırım Beyazıt around the year 1402, marking the first defeat of the Ottomans. Tamerlane had elephants and hid his army in the forests. Each soldier had a small tree in his hand. So all of a sudden the forest began to move and the elephants appeared on the battlefield. The sultan's men were fightened and ran away and he was captured by Tamerlane. The Ottoman empire suffered a big blow for a period of twenty years. All these wars and cutting of the forests devastated Central Anatolia.

Atatürk had chosen this town because it was not yet occupied by the Allied Forces and it was the nearest and safest place at the time. When we forget today's Ankara and go back about seventy years, we see the difficult decision that Atatürk had to make in choosing this place as the capital of the new republic. This can be looked upon as the first step towards the reforms and developments he had to go through to establish a new republic upon the remains of a crumbling Ottoman Empire.

SECTION III
REFORMS AND THEIR INFLUENCE ON OUR DAILY LIFE

Chapter 18
New Way of Life - Legal and Unseen Effects

The year I was born the Lausanne Treaty was signed, the Ottoman Empire was dissolved and the new Republic of Turkey was accepted by the world.

At Lausanne, Turkey obtained her independence including the resolution of the Ottoman debts. All the capitulations came to an end. The capitulations which had been granted first to France, were a sort of sign of "grandeur" of the sultans, but in latter years they became a great problem for the empire.

It took some time to divide the Ottoman debts between Turkey and the other countries that had been part of the empire. Turkey could have said to the Allies: "These debts were incurred by the Sultans, you have taken all the petroliferous areas and you have carved out much land from the empire and therefore we are not resposible for these debts." But the Turkish Republic proposed to pay the debts that related to its territory. It took up to 1928 to decide on the division of these debts. Some of the railroads and palaces and other buildings built with these debts remained in Turkey. Finally, Turkey agreed to pay 67% percent of the debts.

At the Lausanne conference Lord Curzon, head of the delegation, said: "The Turks will come soon to ask for money." These words have not been forgotten by our generation and we did not want to ask for money from any foreign power. The strict financial policy of İnönü was mainly due to this threat. He had realized that economic development could not be reached with borrowed funds. It would help to understand better the economic conditions of the Republic during the first years.

In Istanbul there was an administration called "Duyunu - Umumiye" which meant Foreign Debts Administration. It was run mainly by French and English representatives. Their office was the impressive building next to the Iranian Consulate in Istanbul which is now used as the Istanbul Lycee. Those working at this office were mostly from the minorities who knew foreign languages, that is Greeks, Armenians and Jews. The Sublime Port, which was the prime minister's office and is now the seat of the governor of Istanbul, is a much more modest, smaller building.

The embassies of the foreign powers during the Ottoman period were all impressive buildings in Istanbul. The palace of England the palace of France, the Russian and German embassy buildings which are now used as consulate general offices, are still representative edifices of these nations. Around these embassies all these powers had their churches and educational institutions. They had hospitals and other philanthropic societies. They had commercial attaches, libraries and associations to promote their ideals. Besides these there was the seat of the Orthodox Church, the Patriarchate which had control of all the Orthodox churches in the world. There were the Armenian and Jewish organizations, churches, synagogues, and schools all over Istanbul.

It is also for these reasons that Atatürk did not want to come to Istanbul and had a fresh start in Ankara.

When the Republic started they were very strict about the government budget. Expenditures never exceeded the revenues in order to have a balanced budget. Imports were regulated and the balance of trade was always positive up to the year 1950.

This approach to the economic life of the country is in itself an important reform and a sound economic policy.

It was accepted by Atatürk and Inönü that complete independence starts with a sound financial system. After obtaining financial independence, the Republic began to organize its industrial institutions. The sultanate had ended and it was replaced by a National Assembly. It could not be said that it was a democratically elected assembly. Leaders from all cities which were not under occupation were invited to Ankara. Those who had the means and the desire to travel came. At that time the world considered Mustafa Kemal a rebel general and the sultan had condemned him to death. He was successful in reorganizing the country and won its independence. In 1925 he addressed the National Assembly and said: "The Turkish Republic cannot be ruled with the old laws and the old way of life. A new order has to be established. We are preparing completely new laws to change the present administration."

My father would tell us about the days when these events took place in Ankara. People were working to translate the Swiss Code of Ethics into Turkish day and night. Of course it was the old Ottoman alphabet that was used. The new law was prepared and ratified in 1926. In this manner both Muslims and non-Muslims were subject to the same law. At that time the lawyers who knew foreign languages worked and prepared a commercial and fiscal law which were also adopted from the German, İtalian, French, and Swiss codes.

The republic started officially in 1923 but of course everything could not be changed immediately. It took about five years to prepare the new laws and have them ratified by the National Assembly. The application of these laws was restricted to the large towns and population centers. In less developed areas the community habits and laws remained in force. It can still be seen in the case of Eastern Anatolia where local landlords have their own internal rules and regulations. There is no law legalizing this situation but the way of life and local habits still continue as they have for centuries.

The land deeds and property law could be applied only after the maps and registers were taken under control. For instance the great state farm Ceylanpınar which was owned by a family was expropriated and run by the state.

Atatürk knew that the Turkish female population was largely uneducated and living under the old system of laws. In 1934, he gave the right to vote to Turkish women. My grandmother used to make great fun of the peasant woman Satı Kadın who was elected as a deputy to the Grand National Assembly. "What does she understand of the Assembly?" she would say. With this law in 1934, Atatürk was taking a step ahead of Switzerland and some other European countries whose women did not yet have the right to vote.

Technically it was not possible to be ahead of the industrial countries but Atatürk could demonstrate his leadership from a social point of view.

There was great enthusiasm in Turkey, a completely new spirit. The days of anxiety under the sultan's rule was gone and there were new laws and new courts. As a nation, however, there were still difficulties. These new laws did not mean anything to the poor peasant at Ağrı on the Russian frontier. The minorities also continued with their own habits and laws. For instance, Jews would get married first at the synagogue and then have an official wedding at the municipality. It is very difficult to change habits and local way of life even in the heart of Istanbul.

The new civil law brought the following concepts to the Turkish community:

1- The new law forbade a man to marry more than one wife. Thus the old system permitting four wives was abolished. The house at Kızıltoprak was originally built for a man with two wives. The doors of the corridors could be closed and the house separated into two. When we were young, people would talk about "his second harem," meaning "his second wife". Then gradually this word harem was turned into "hanım". In 1950, at the time of the first election made in a democratic form, people began to make propaganda and say that it would be possible to have more than one wife. There were simple people who believed this and gave their votes to the Democratic Party instead of the Republican Party.

2- There was a certificate of marriage issued by the municipality. Those who wanted to could also have a religious wedding but the law recognized only the municipal marriage. In order to enforce their religious laws, Christians and Jews had their weddings legally registered at the churches and synagogues.

3- There were limits to the age of marriage; girls must be at least 18 years of age. My grandmother had been married at the age of 14.

4- In divorce men and women had the same rights and were equal in the eyes of the law. In the old days a man could say, "Boş düştü" (you

159

are finished) and he was thus divorced and could take another wife.

5- Inheritance law was also changed and gave the same rights to men and women.

6- New courts were set up to enforce the law and the old religious courts were abolished.

We would see the application of these laws in the society and observe the acceptance of the older generation. We were also following the new reforms started by the Grand National Assembly in Ankara. Of course, we knew that the driving force behind these reforms was Atatürk and his friends.

Chapter 19
Reforms in Education
and the New Alphabet (1928-29)

On March 3, 1924, when I was just one year old, there was a law on unification of education. All schools were taken under control of the Ministry of Education. The schools opened under the capitulation laws were also put under this ministry. A decision was taken that all Turkish children would attend the State primary schools where education would be non-secular and the teaching of religion prohibited.

In all parts of the country there were great numbers of orphans due to long wars. Orphanages, military schools and the schools of the Ministry of Health were all under the Ministry of Education. The same law allowed university education for religious leaders (imam) and preachers (hatib).

In Ankara new faculties of law, literature, commerce and agriculture were opened. The engineering school was kept in Istanbul. New technical schools and agricultural schools were opened but the Faculty of Theology was on the waiting list. The older population was getting worried and wondered who would do the religious functions when the present imams died away. Who would administer the burial ceremonies? Who would read the Koran?

In 1929, all the foreign primary schools were closed down. My father in Ankara had heard that this was going to happen. He wanted us to learn French so he registered my older brother and me to the French School St. Joseph at Kadıköy. I was among the last students to enter this school from the first class. As we passed our class, the class would be closed down so that within a period of five years the primary school would be closed down. I do not know how I learned French. I was very young and the class for me was play at first, but gradually I grew up and mastered this language. We had to attend as boarding students because there was no public transportation from Kızıltoprak to the school. Cars were very rare and the horse carriage would be too expensive. There were no buses or tram cars. There was only a rumor that tramways would start at Kadıköy.

After finishing the primary school I insisted I should be a day student. I was old enough to walk the distance between our house and the school. I could walk it in 20-25 minutes. In the evening in winter months, I would come home in the dark. The education schedule was very heavy and classes would end at 18:00 o'clock every day.

All the powers like England, France, Germany, Austria and Italy and the USA had opened such missionary schools in Turkey and all over the Ottoman Empire. The report of midterm exams in the photo album here shows the curriculum of St. Joseph. It reflects how during the Ottoman Empire education was completely in the hands of these foreign schools. The names of places were all written in the French way of spelling. The new alphabet had been accepted by this time but the family name law had not yet come out. The certificate that the administration of the school is in the hands of the Christian brothers. There is no reference to the Ministry of Education. During these years a Turkish co-director was appointed to foreign schools. It was not clear what he was doing. The administration of the school was completely in the hands of French priests. Only the teaching of religion was no longer obligatory. There was a lesson in morality which was half religious and half habit formation. During this lesson some students disappeared and only the Jews and Muslims would stay in the class. We found out later that Christian boys were taken to the school church for prayers.

I stayed eight years at this French school, five years as a boarding student and three years as a day student. As the Ottoman Empire weakened these schools became training centers for minorities. For instance, pratically all the administrators' of Bulgaria and Greece were trained at Robert College. These were missionary schools and tried to propagate their religion in Turkey.

My mother was the only Turkish girl in her class at the English High School for Girls which was attended by the daughters of minorities such as French, White Russians, British, Greeks and Armenians. My father had wanted to go to the German school but the family opposed him firmly. When we were registered at the French school there was criticism directed at my parents. Because my father had been unable to learn a foreign language he insisted that we attend a foreign school. It was true that most of our friends were from the minorities (Greeks, Armenians and Jews).

The educational reforms of Atatürk are now being criticized. Some say that it did cut our relations with our past. The Ottoman language was based on a mixture of Arabic, Persian and Turkish. It is true that it was a different language but since we grew amongst people that were using this language we never could call it the Ottoman language, we called it old Turkish. Now we have to accept that it was a language of the elite of the empire because only five percent of the country knew how to read and write. It is a difficult language to write and read because the hand writing and the printed languages are different. Plus you have to have a big vocabulary of Arabic and Persian. There are experts in foreign countries who study and learn this language. Centers like the Middle East Institute at Harvard, and Cornell University in the USA and Kiel and Hamburg in Germany have sections on old languages where scholars learn the Ottoman language and study the old documents.

Now we have many people who learn the old script and Arabic in Turkey. They are also re-printing the old books in the new alphabet. I asked some of these people to translate two books of my grandfather and a book of my grandmother and printed them in the Turkish of today. I had to prepare a dictionary and simplify some of the terms used in their language. I hope that this language will be taken up at our universities and bring up enlightened scholars to study our ancient records.

The reform on education closed down the medrese, or theological schools, of Islam, yet the schools of the Orthodox Church were still functioning and the American, French and British had their missionary schools going. By nationalizing the primary schools in the whole of Turkey, Atatürk was trying to unify the Turkish nation and decrease the influence of the foreign powers.

My grandparents were of the old Ottoman school and wanted at least one of the new generation to learn how to read the Koran. The imam at the mosque in Kızıltoprak started coming as a guest to our house. At that time schools were closed on Friday, so every Friday he would come to us with his fez and turban and black tunic. We three boys were supposed to have some religious education.

My brother Ali was too young so he slid under the table and ran away and thus was relieved of the Arabic lessons. My elder brother Ahmet just refused to sit in front of the hoca and his protest was accepted by my mother. So I was the only one left in front of the hoca.

We started learning the old script with the intention of reading the Koran. So gradually I started learing the rules and letters of the Arabic alphabet. In a few years I could read the Koran in Arabic without understanding a word. When my great uncle would come he would examine to see if I could decipher the Koran. This teaching took seven years and I started memorizing the necessary prayers. In the meantime the fez was abolished and the hoca could wear religious costumes only in the mosque or while going to the cemetery for funerals. So the priest started coming with a hat and regular costume. At first he could not wear the hat and put a beret on his head.

Sometimes I would ask the meaning of these prayers and the hoca would say, "Do not ask, memorize!" Years later I found out that the hoca was from the medrese and did not know Arabic, yet he had memorized the whole Koran from beginning to end.

At that time it was forbidden to teach Arabic in the schools which is why the hoca would come as a guest. Leyla Hanım would pay him a salary of five liras per month. The maid who brought his coffee would sometimes give him an envelope and say, "The Hanımefendi sent this." I did not know what this envelope was. Leyla Hanım once said to me, "We will all die and go away one day. On the holy nights our souls will come and wait for prayers. Do not leave us without the proper prayers." Maybe these words made me learn how to read the Koran and I memorized the necessary prayers. Still, after so many years, on the holy nights according to the Koran, I read the chapter of "Tebareke" from the Koran and recite the prayers. I had asked my grandmother what would happen if I did not read the Koran. She had said that the souls would wait at the chimney and be very sorry if they did not hear the prayers. The chimneys of Kızıltoprak are long gone but, I hope the souls have found the chimney at Levent where we live now.

Chapter 20
Alphabet Reform

With the declaration of the republic, reforms started coming one after the other. It looked as if Atatürk was in a hurry. It seemed that if these reforms were not materialized the Sultanate would come back. He had a conviction that once he was gone these reforms would not be possible and there would be a back slide.

The laws for the new way of life materialized. In order to ensure this new way of life the Turkish nation had to be renewed from head to toe. It was not easy to rejuvenate a population that accepted to be servants of the sultan for centuries. All the minorities constituting the Ottoman Empire had preserved their identity and finally broke away from the empire. The attacks of the Western powers and Russia on the Ottomans were aimed at the Turkish part of the population. They were protecting the minorities and helping their development. Finally they used them as their allies to destroy the Ottoman Empire. This was one of the reasons why Atatürk was in a hurry. After the First World War with the Treaty of Sevres the Turkish nation was almost wiped off the world map. Atatürk made a last effort to save Anatolia and he stopped there. He did not get into the dream of saving his own homeland, Salonica.

He knew it would be a futile loss of Turkish blood to try to advance further. The same mentality was followed and accepted by İnönü. Towards the end of the Second World War when the Germans were evacuating Rhodes and the Dodecanese, they wanted to turn them over to Turkey. İnönü did not want to change boundaries set together with Atatürk. There was much more to do than to enter the war. Only on August 2, 1944, were political and commercial relations with Germany cut. Turkey declared war on Germany and Japan to take effect at midnight on February 28, 1945. The Germans were already completely defeated. Actually, this decision was taken in order to participate in the peace conference and the United Nations.

The word "development" was not yet used frequently but in our childhood we would hear the word "construction" a great deal. The country was completely destroyed and needed to be rebuilt. The reforms looked like a part of this picture.

After the legal reforms the most important question was the subject of general education. The regulations concerning clothing followed. The "hat law" sounds funny today but to get rid of the fez Atatürk had to take drastic measures. To reduce the influence of religion on daily life, the various Islamic sects were closed, even the sanctuary of the whirling dervishes at Konya.

The medrese, or theological schools, were also closed. The Arabic calendar was changed and the European calendar accepted. Time which had been set according to sun rise and sun set was changed to the regular 24 hour Greenwich time schedule. The metric system of measures and weights was accepted. The weekly vacation day was changed from Friday to Sunday. The acceptance of erecting statues depicting people or animals was a radical change in our lifestyle. Making such statues was forbidden for religious reasons during the Ottoman days. Erecting statues of Atatürk in all corners of the country was a big novelty.

On top of these reforms the changing of the Arabic alphabet to the Latin letters was a big step towards universal education. Now after about a lapse of seventy years, we can see the effects of this reform in the country. If the old alphabet had not changed all the reforms could have slid backwards. Only after 1980 was it possible to see advertising signs written in Arabic letters in Istanbul. The Libyan Bank, Kuwait Airlines and some Middle Eastern companies began to put up their signs in Arabic letters. Now they are looked upon as any other foreign name like German, English or French companies. Some shops try to appeal to Arab and Japanese tourists in their own languages.

Atatürk declared in Istanbul in August 9, 1928, that we were going to shift to the Latin alphabet. Then on October 1, 1928, the law for the

167

new alphabet was enacted. Through the media of national classrooms, millions of people learned how to read and write. We started to write our language with simplified Latin letters. Once the difficult and incomprehensible rules of the Arabic alphabet were dispensed with, many people learned the new alphabet easily. Still there are some people who are illiterate and the responsibility lies on our generation.

Chapter 21
Reforms Started in the Ottoman Period
Continued during the Republic

Reforms made in the first years of the republic were not made by the imposition of Atatürk alone. These reforms were the end result of a period of change and rejuvenation. It was, of course, necessary to have a person like Atatürk who would insist on the execution of these reforms.

With the declaration of the constitution in 1908 and the first assembly, the Ottoman absolute monarchy regime was beginning to change.

The most spectacular change during the republic was the "Hat Law" which forbid the wearing of the fez. The fez had become the symbol of the Ottoman way of life. No men could go out on the street without his fez. Even in the house the men would sit at the table with their fez. The Western hat was a symbol of the British, in other words, the enemy.

A Koran in Turkish and in the Latin alphabet was inconceivable during the sultans' time. On the other hand, prescriptions of doctors were mostly written in French. The languages used by pharmacists were the old script and French. The record factory at Yeşilköy would print their records in French and old Ottoman Turkish script. The famous photographers during the sultanate would use French and old script Turkish and in some smaller cities they would use Greek or Armenian according to the owner of the photography studio.

Currency used in daily life continued in old Turkish for a long time after the Republic. It was only after the language reform that coins and new paper currency were printed in the Latin alphabet.

In music printed in Istanbul, French and old Turkish were used jointly. The main foreign language was French, then came German, and English was very rare. Now this order has been reversed.

Now we shall dwell on the above changes and give a little more detail on their development.

Chapter 22
The Turkish Koran and the Call to Prayer

When I started taking Koran lessons at home, I would ask the hoca, "What does this mean?" He would reply, "Don't ask, these are the words of our Prophet, no questioning!" At that time there was no translation of the Koran in Turkish. Some time later my grandfather gave me a copy of the Koran in Turkish. The five times call to prayer from the minaret which had been made in Arabic since the beginning of Islam was changed to Turkish. This was a fundamental change which many people could not accept. The Turkish words were chanted in the same intonation as the Arabic call to prayer but it was in Turkish. The idea was that Turks should call each other to pray in their own language.

At the same time, reading of the Koran in the mosques started also in Turkish. These recitations were advertised in newspapers. The following is a news from the **Cumhuriyet** some seventy years ago:

27 December 1928, Cumhuriyet

HAFIZ BURHANETTIN BEY

Yesterday in large and small mosques all over the town, there was a reciting of the Koran in Turkish.

Hafız Burhan bey recited the "Effür Kan" chapter at the Kabataş mosque in Turkish. Hafız Burhan bey is a graduate of the Davutpaşa school. He has a very good voice.

People who heard that he was going to recite the Koran in Turkish filled up the front of the mosque in the early hours. The crowd was such that some people had to listen to the chanting from the door and windows of the mosque.

Besides this event, "hafız" Zeki bey recited the chapter of "Fatiha" at the Ağa mosque of Beyoğlu on İstiklal street.

These hafızs were brought up during the Sultan's regime but had translated the Koran into Turkish and started to perform their prayers in Turkish in the mosques. The choice of the Kabataş mosque must have been meaningful because a few years earlier this mosque had been used by the Sultans from the Dolmabahçe palace for Friday prayers.

There was another ad in the Cumhuriyet on the same date: We are looking for efendis who know how to read Turkish. They will be accepted as soon as they apply to a bank or a commercial company. Why stay idle and be out of work for a long time. We can teach new Turkish in four months and bring you up in the fields of accounting and banking. We'll find employment for you.

Language and Commercial School Beyoğlu

There was such a need for people who could read and write the new Turkish alphabet that private schools began to advertise courses and were securing jobs after a course of four months.

Teaching of the Arabic script continued for centuries in the Ottoman Empire but it took a long time because one had to learn Arabic and Persian at the same time. Modern Turkish with the Latin alphabet was much simpler and could be learned in a few months. Now it looks simple but to change an alphabet was not an easy task. It is very difficult to change habits. In fact, the old generation continued to use the Ottoman script privately until they passed away.

Chapter 23
Doctors, Pharmacies and Presciptions

It took many years for my mother to give away the clothing of my grandmother. She would give it to the old servants and girls that her mother had brought up and married off. The clothing was arranged in neat bundles in her trunks and big cupboard. The trunks also contained her old letters. The big cloth bags contained smaller bags in which there were receipts of paid taxes, telephone receipts and in one small bag there were prescriptions written for my mother, aunt and uncle.

These prescriptions were mostly written in French, the medical language in the Ottoman days. These presciptions were written in Yanina and in Istanbul.

The prescription starts like this: "To Madame the governor 18-4-191 and No 37558." The name and the address of the doctor are printed in Turkish, French and Armenian. For instance there is a doctor in Beirut at the French Hospital named Pierre Tacha. The prescription is also written in French. The envelope that contained this prescription was printed in America, and it is most probable that it came from the States to Beirut. There is another prescription in French by "Dr. J.B. Violi, Maladie des Enfants, Consultation de 2a 6, Rue Ensiz 6, Pres du Tunel." Only there is an incription on the top of the presciption in old script saying "For Nezihe hanım." There is an envelope with an inscription in old Turkish and Armenian which says, "Pharmacie M.G. Marguilegian, Pera Grand Rue de Pangaltı, Pres du Casino Osmanbey". There is a Turkish doctor named Dr. Fehmi H. Medecin de l'Hospital des Enfants "Hamidiye" written in Latin letters and old Turkish script. The date of the prescription is written "Le 28 Avril 318 re No.25655" in Latin letters. For the year the Arabic date 318 was used which is comparable to 1903. There is also an envelope from Yanina on which French and Greek were used. It is by İttihadı Osmani, Mustafa Hidayet, written in old Turkish, French and Greek. The envelope contains a prescription for my grandmother from "Pharmacie Saadet Faik İskender, Kızıltoprak, Ihlamur, Le 17-12-1327" which corresponds to 1912. The envelope from Yanina was printed in Salonica by Divelis, a Greek printer. This envelope went from Salonica to Yanina and then to Kızıltoprak. There is a tax stamp on the envelope and on the back, the seal of the pharmacy over the closure. I also found a prescription written by "Dr. S. Agopian Cadi- Keuy, Sakyz Aghadje;" it is in Turkish but the spelling is in French. The prescription was prepared at the Kızıltoprak Faik İskender pharmacy and signed by the assistant pharmacist, Mustafaoğlu, all in French.

These prescriptions show how French was dominant, coupled with old script Turkish, Greek and Armenian. Medical education at Istanbul University was also taught in French at that time.

The prescriptions also show the cost of the medicines prepared at the pharmacies. The values are in kurush such as 16.5 or 14 kurush. This shows that medication were quite expensive. The medicines were all mixed in the pharmacy and they were very light, like tea, rose oil, linden mixed with a little quinine.

Chapter 24
Phonograph Records

Records first manufactured in Istanbul had French and old Turkish labels. Latin letters were entering Turkey from here and there. For instance, "Blumenthal Record and Talking Machine Co. Ltd. Trade Mark Orfeon" was written in English, then in old script, "Nevatı Bahrie Thifte Telli Gazeli Hanende İbrahim Efendi. No 12755." I knew İbrahim Efendi because he used to come to Kızıltoprak to play with Leyla Hanım. He played the ud (lute) and had a soft voice. There is another record with a white label on which I recognized my mother's hand writing saying, "Leyla Hanım, Suzidil Şarkı" a song recorded by grandmother's mother. I remember her going by carriage from Kızıltoprak to the boat landing at Kadıköy where they would take the boat to Galata, then take another carriage to Sirkeci and the train to the Yeşilköy record factory. It was a whole day trip and she would come back very tired towards sunset.

There is also another record in Latin alphabet. The brand is Parlofon and the music, a Suzidil song "Bu gönül sevmeyecek sandım" by İbrahim Bey, piano by Leyla Hanım, by Carl Lindstörm A.G. There is also a tax stamp of 10 Kuruş on the record. There are other records by Odeon, Columbia, all inscribed in old Turkish and English.

There was also a violin player called İhsan Efendi. İbrahim Efendi and İhsan Efendi would come to Kızıltoprak to Leyla Hanım and they would play the songs over and over again. It seems these musicians could not read the notes and Leyla Hanım would teach them her music by repetition. Leyla Hanım had her notes on the piano. The musicians would catch the tones by ear and memorize the music.

Chapter 25
Photographs and Photography Studios

Photography studios were among the places where the Latin alphabet began to be used during Ottoman days. For instance the picture of my grandfather, M.A. Ayni, in Yanina was taken by Sotir Z. Dabura Samarinfot Photo and the inscription of the studio was written in Latin letters. There are many photographs taken in the studios of Istanbul, Baghdad, Diyarbakır, Salonica and Cairo. The back of each picture gives the name of the studio in old script Turkish and French, Greek or Armenian according to the owner. There is a picture of my grandfather taken in Salonica by Paul Zepdji and on the back the address is written in French as Rue de Vardar No. 90. By coincidence among the old postcards, I found one showing Vardar Street in Salonica. There are horse drawn tramcars and men wearing fezes. There is no old Ottoman script on the postcard and it says "Souvenir de Salonique" Carte Postal N.B. "Ce cliché est reserve exclusivement a l'adresse." The post office was under the capitulation regime.

The most famous of these photographers was "Abdullah Frères, Photographes de S.M. Le Sultan, Pera, Constantinople." They had also a branch in Cairo.

Photographs, prescriptions and records were not the only instances where the Latin alphabet began to be used in daily life during the Ottoman days. At Kızıltoprak, the Latin alphabet was of constant use because my mother and aunt went to the English High School for Girls and my uncle went to Godesberg, Germany for studies. My grandmother was not much of a reader but she would follow the daily paper Cumhuriyet and read the serialized novels that were published each day. She wrote an article for a paper in Trabzon encouraging the ladies to work for the Red Crescent. She was an active member of this philanthropic association.

175

Chapter 26
The Ottoman Coins

When the law on the new Turkish alphabet came out, immediately the printing of books, magazines and newspapers shifted to the new Turkish but the money in circulation remained as it was. During the first days of the republic new paper money was printed, of course, in the old script and French. I remember vividly the new one lira which was of green colour and had an inscription of "Une Livre Turc" which I would read easily because I had learned French. Among the paper currency we would sometimes see the five lira note but the ten, fifty, one hundred, or one thousand notes were not much seen around. The children would manage with 40 para, 100 para or 5 kurush or 10 kurush coins. The 25 kurush coin, called "the bull's eye," was big money. There was 20 para, 10 para and 5 para coins. Even in our youth you would not get anything for 5 para. The saying "He is not worth five paras" must have come from those days. All these coins were printed in the first years of the Republic in old script. The year of printing was also shown according to the Arabic calendar.

The first 1 kurush in new letters came into circulation in 1937. This coin was not called 40 para but it was 1 kurush.* In order to change this one kurush a 10 para coin was issued in 1940. The old coins remained in circulation for a long time so we were quite accustomed to the Arabic letters on these coins.

The one lira in Latin letters came out in 1934 as a silver coin with an inscription of 100 kurush. All the new coins that were printed had Atatürk's profile on them. Gradually the currency with old writing disappeared from circulation. All paper money was printed outside Turkey, and the coins were minted at the old mint in Istanbul. Much later a

---

(*) One kurush was 40 para; one lira was 100 kurush.

paper money printing mill was set up in Ankara. During the İnönü regime currency and coins were minted bearing his picture and profile. After Inönü, currency and coins returned to Atatürk pictures and profiles.

The generation before us were evaluating the money in terms of gold and silver coins. They would say there was only 6 kurush difference between the gold lira and the paper lira. They were accustomed to the 20 kurush silver coin which was called "Mecidiye" and they would always refer to this coin to evaluate a product or a carriage trip.

Still we are using gold coins minted by the Sultans, the Reshad, Hamid and Mecid coins. There are also Ata and İnönü gold coins. They are not used as currency but as gift or ornamental items and a way of hoarding money or for speculative purposes. The two kurush silver coin also lasted a very long time after the Republic as a decorative coin.

On the bayram, or religious holidays, during visits to grandparents, they would give a handkerchief containing a half or a quarter gold coin. Until the 1950's our great uncle Hasan Tahsin Aynı would give us a new two kurush silver coin that he had saved when he was the treasury undersecretary during the last Ottoman government. This was just a souvenir gift.

Thus the Ottoman influence remained on the currency and coins many years after the end of the empire. Only after 1940 did the Ottoman coins cease to be used as currency.

As it can be seen the changing of the alphabet did not take place with just a law. First many courses started to teach the new alphabet to the public while teaching of the Arabic alphabet was stopped in the schools. In 1929 when I was six years old the newspapers were published half in old letters and half in new letters. Official writing also changed to the new Turkish. In government offices, the old Turkish was used privately by the older civil servants. The persons used to this old language could write very quickly and used it as a stenographic device. Gradually those who were educated in the old Turkish started going to the other world. The old script was thus forgotten and now it is generally called the Ottoman language.

There were many attempts to simplify the teaching of the language during the Ottoman days. The military issued a decree and ordered a simple form of Turkish to be used. This attempt was futile as no commander wanted this change. There were also attempts by Turkish scholars to simplify Turkish. They wanted to create a script between the Latin and Arab alphabets. They had in mind to create a simple Turkish alphabet. All these attemps did not come to a practical result. So Atatürk changed the alphabet drastically. I do not know of any nation which has changed its alphabet in such a short period. Now we have to train experts in the old alphabet to read and understand the old documents. The Ottoman language has become a different language and is taught at universities in the same way as Uygur or Çağatay or other old languages are taught.

The Latin alphabet is written from left to right and the Ottoman script was written from right to left. This is a fundamental difference between the two styles of writing.

Chapter 27
Music

The shops selling music notes and records were run mostly by people of Armenian, Greek or Latin origin. They used the Latin alphabet long before the reform was brought about. Some of their people who were born and lived all their lives in Istanbul never learned Turkish.

One of the most famous shops was that of Fernand Commendinger who was also selling pianos, musical instruments and music books imported from France. He supplied the palace and his emblem had "Fournisseur de S.M.I Le Sultan". The Commendinger shop lasted two generations and his son F. Louis Commendinger continued to operate this shop. He also had a branch in Salonica.

Other music shops were owned by Pascal Keller, at Hazzopoulu Passage N. 25 to 31 Constantinople and Karl Koop- Pianos et Instruments Constantinople Grand Rue de Pera N. 220.

There was a shop called Iskender at Beyazıt which was the only one selling Turkish music. Turkish music was mostly not recorded and the instrument players did not know how to read the notes. So the music was learned by the ear and played until it was completely memorized. What we called "alafranga" music was sold and played in homes or it was on records imported from France and other foreign countries. Among families who had mixed education, Turkish and "alafranga," you could find both types of music.

Leyla, the daughter of my great uncle Yusuf Razi and his French wife Marie Bel gave me her mother's music book that reflects the occupation days of Istanbul.

To Marie (Ismet Hanım), French soldiers were not foreigners and she must have been happy to see the French in Istanbul. She has in her book "Les Poilus a Constantinople," which means the French soldiers in Istanbul. Even among our family there were people who were in favour

179

of this occupation. These stories were told to us by our parents but by coincidence I found this music book which is a reminder of these very difficult days.

Among the family papers there are also some music notes printed in French without any Ottoman script. For instance, "Edition S. Christidis 215 Grand Rue de Pera 216 Constantinople," which was printed in Istanbul. There is also one in Greek.

The various populations of Istanbul lived quite apart from each other. Beyoğlu up to Bebek was the quarter of the French, British, Italian and Levantine communities. There were also large Greek and Armenian communities who were close to the other Christian communities.

The Muslim Turkish population lived on the Sultanahmet and Eminönü side of Istanbul and on the Asian shores in Üsküdar and Kadıköy up to Kızıltoprak and Bostancı. The islands were mostly populated by Greeks and Armenians. The Jews lived mostly in Balat on the Golden Horn and near the Galata tower.

This is another aspect of the Ottoman way of life in Istanbul that lasted for centuries. It shows the difficulties of the change from empire to republic. The generation before us experienced most the difficulties resulting from this type of social change.

Chapter 28
Wearing Apparel Reform
and the Hat Law - 1925

The Hat Law was approved by the Grand National Assembly on August 25, 1925. I was only two years old which is why I never wore a fez. There were many fezes at home and I am still keeping some of them.

Resentment toward the fez goes way back. First the military gave up the fez and issued new head gear for the army. As I mentioned before my father had a hat to wear on business trips to Europe. Muslim men did not go into the street without a fez. Those who could not afford a fez wore a turban or a cap.

The western hat was a symbol of Christianity. During our childhood there was a folk saying:

The King of England is sitting on his throne

He has a cane in his hand and a hat on his head

During the long years of fighting with the English, French, Italians, Russians, Bulgarians, Serbs, Greeks and Armenians, they had been accepted as the enemy and the hat was their symbol.

On the other hand, the common people were complaining about the fez as seen in the folk songs collected by my grandmother at Harput. The fez was imported, mainly from Austria. The color of the low quality ones would run under the rain and drip down on the face. It was very difficult to keep the fez in shape and it had to be ironed often. Despite all these difficulties the fez had been accepted as the symbol of Muslims and the hat the symbol of Christians.

It was in this difficult atmosphere that Atatürk decided to wear the hat and appear in public at Kastamonu. There were not enough hats for everybody in the country. Hats had to be imported in place of fezes. Naturally they were expensive. The peaked cap and the beret, also French attire, were replacements for those who could not afford to buy a hat.

There was no specific law on other clothing, but the hat law was in a way a guideline for the type of clothing to wear. The first years the imams and priests continued to wear the fez and special hats according to their denominations. For instance I remember my hoca going to the bakery in Kızıltoprak with his fez, turban and black tunic. The "brothers" at St. Joseph would wear long black tunics and big three cornered hats. All priest teachers would wear their uniforms in class or outside the school. The "sisters" had grey or black tunics and big white headgear they wore all the time.

With a decree in 1936 all religious wearing apparel was forbidden and everybody including the "imam" and all priests and sisters had to wear normal dress.

That year it was very strange for us to find our "brothers" in normal costume and necktie. In general it did not fit them very well but they were, I understand, happy because it was very difficult to walk on the street with the old tunic and cloak and tricornered hat that the wind would blow off.

The sisters showed more resistance to this law. Inside their building they had a special uniform with which they came to the class. I observed the Austrian nuns because my daughters attended this school. They had shaved their hair so they had to wear wigs until their hair grew. It was in 1970 that the Ministry of Education enforced normal dress habits on them. I believe in general they were happy about it because they could wear normal clothing and grow their hair as they pleased.

Concerning my hoca and his attitude towards the hat law and wearing apparel, when he came the first time without his tunic he felt as if he were not wearing anything. On top of that, he had to wear a hat since he would not dream of going out without anything on his head. He did not want the hat to touch his head, so he wore a small cap under it. Coming in to the house to give Koran lessons, he would hang his hat at the marble entrance and enter the selamlık with his cap. Later on he got used to wearing his hat and came with the cap in his pocket. The hat was always awkward on his head. In Kızıltoprak we would see many men with potur and cepken. These people were either fruit sellers or manual workers in the gardens and construction sites. We did not call them laborers but rather called them peasants. These were people from various parts of the country coming to work on a seasonal basis. No industry would hire them as regular workers. They were away from their home for a limited period of time. You could understand from a man's şalvar (baggy pants) the region he was coming from. People from Adana and the Southeast regions wore very baggy pants, from the Aegean area, tighter but with a hanging pant, and from the Black Sea area, very tight and the back part not hanging down. Today we see these wearing apparel at folk dances.

The unification of dress styles gradually eliminated regional separations. The peaked cap became the most common head gear of the peasant population. Now the hat is not used any more. In the whole world the habit of wearing hats disappeared. Now when you take a plane you see very few people wearing hats or peaked caps. The fez began to look funny even to us. The fez is very rarely seen in Egypt and Lebanon, and it is still worn to some extent in Tunisia and other parts of Africa.

The wearing apparel reforms were certainly very important for women. The requirement of peçe and charshaf was eliminated. My mother suffered a great deal from the peçe and charshaf. Because she attended the English high school she did not have to cover up, but during the week ends and at school picnics she had to wear a charshaf. After walking to the picnic grounds she would throw off her charshaf and start running with her friends.

Wearing a scarf to cover her hair must be a remnant of the charshaf and peçe days. It was a shame to show your hair in public. Now again there are women who cover up their head and wear a long overcoat. When we were small the maids at the house would wear a yemeni when going out to the garden. There are now political parties who favor covering up women as in Iran. It seems even men there have to wear long sleeved shirts in the hot summer months. Atatürk's hat law and wearing apparel regulations must have been issued with an understanding that one day these reforms would have some reactions.

183

Chapter 29
Tombstones

After the change in the alphabet the tombstones also began to change. The old type tombstones would be carved to symbolize the rank of the deceased men and for women there was a different style. These old tombstones still remain as important historical relics for those who want to study Ottoman art and manners.

I once went to visit Split in Yougoslavia to talk with the Trogir shipyard for the construction of a ship. During this trip I had the chance to visit the old Ottoman castle of the city. That was the last castle on the Balkan peninsula and had been taken over by the Austrian Empire. The Austrians preserved the Ottoman relics instead of destroying the castle and its contents. There were still standing some tombstones with the old writing. From the type of fez and turbans on the tombstones you could tell the rank of these men. The women's tombstones were also very delicately carved and ornate.

In that vicinity, I also visited the town of Mostar. Seventeen mosques still were standing at Mostar and the bridge was intact. There were also many Bosnians who could speak Turkish. Some of the old people had been educated in Bursa, Turkey. Going around the town, I saw some tombstones in a field of wheat. It seems in the old days this place was a cemetery. I tried to read the inscriptions on the stones, which were half buried in the ground. On one of them was written "Hasan" and I recited the Fatiha for his soul. This field was planted each year with wheat. Gradually this cemetery will disappear, yet 70 years after the Balkan War these tombstones were still standing.

The Mostar bridge has an interesting legend. It is very narrow and made of stone. At one point the stone bridge is 17 meters high over the river. As with all stone bridges, there is a balcony at the middle of the bridge bearing the inscription of the person who built it. When the

Germans occupied the town, in the Second World War, they transported their tanks over this bridge. The bridge swayed a little but did not collapse. People who live in this area believe that boys when reaching the age of 17 have to jump from this bridge to prove their puberty. The Mostar river is very narrow and when you look from the top you wonder if you could make it. This custom was still being observed and I have a picture of young men diving from the bridge.

During the clashes between Bosnians, Croats and Serbs, this bridge and many of the mosques were destroyed. There are plans to rebuild them but I doubt if financing can be found. Also the workmanship of the stone bridge was a masterpiece of Ottoman architecture. All around the Ottoman Empire the tombstones are very similar. The tomb of Gül Baba at Budapest is still a place of pilgrimage for Muslims and Christians. The Hungarian government maintains this tomb as it was in the old days. It belonged to a Bektashi dervish who had his lodge at Buda.

In 1960 in Kozani, northern Greece, I saw an old mosque and tombstones in the garden still standing. I do not know in what situation they are today.

After the change in the alphabet and due to economic conditions, tombstones went through a transformation. On some they place a picture of the deceased. There are also large ornamental tombstones. Now they are also inscribing some prayers in Arabic. There is a return to the old ways. After the new alphabet came out there was not a single stone with Arabic letters. No one says anything about this development, as religion is looked upon as something between the individual and God.

There is a great assault on old tombstones that have no family left to take care of them. Each time I go to Karacaahmet cemetery where my parents are, I see one or two old stones destroyed. They are trying to open new space in the cemetery. Some tombstones have been collected by an association in an area as a museum of tombstones. As new roads are developed sometimes old marble tombstones are removed.

When the Barbaros Boulevard was opened up from Beşiktaş to

Levent, I saw an old cemetery being dismantled. These were Turkish and Armenian tombstones. They piled them in an area and there was mud all over the place. I took a picture of this pile and sent it to the papers. We had heard that in Bulgaria and Greece they were tearing down the Ottoman cemeteries in order to open roads.

I saw many tombstones in Tripoli, Libya, where the mosques and their burial grounds are still preserved. They were tombstones of people who were there on assignment. There are many such cemeteries outside Turkey. It would be interesting to study and collect information on them. I saw the United Nations Cemetery in Pusan, South Korea, and when looking at the register, I found the name of our captain who did not come back from Korea.

There are other cemeteries at Galiçya and in Syria and Iraq which I have not seen, but the cemetery at the Dardanelles is very interesting. The British cemetery is like a garden with tombstones for all the fallen soldiers. There is one great tombstone for the thousands of Turkish soldiers that died in those battles.

Tombstones could be an interesting approach to study the development and fall of the Ottoman Empire. They stand as frozen historical remnants.

Chapter 30
Tuğra and Epitaph Stones

A tuğra was an ornamented monogram of the sultans. Each sultan had his own seal or tuğra which was used on official documents, decrees and on the gates of palaces or other monumental buildings built by the sultans such as mosques, fountains, bridges, and castles. For instance on the gate of Istanbul University there is a very nice tuğra put as decoration when the building was the Ministry of War.

After the Republic and specially after the change in the alphabet, there was a period when these tuğras were covered up or replaced by the letters T.C. (Republic of Turkey). This was a way to show to the public that the sultanate was finished and the Republican period had started. Now after some years everybody accepts that these monuments belong to the nation and the name or insignia of the person who constructed the building is a national heritage. It is accepted that these tuğras have historical value.

On the main post office in Istanbul there is an inscription of the architect Vedat Tek (my uncle): "Ministry of Post and Telgraph" written in Arabic "Kufi" script. It is a very decorative inscription.

There are many mosques in Istanbul built by the sultans, their mothers, or the grand vezirs. Each of these buildings has an epitaph written in the old script. It is difficult to read these signs because a very decorative form of the old script was used. They usually give the date of the construction and the person who built the monument. There are of course prayers and praises to the builders.

Street names and numbers had to he changed to the new Turkish. But in some old buildings the old names and numbers are written in Arabic or Greek or Armenian according to the owner of the building. They stay as souvenirs of old times.

I found a number on the building of the general directorate of the

Maritime Bank. It was an old sign written in Arabic and bore the number 105. It was forgotten and took the color of the building. I had it removed and still keep it as a souvenir.

Chapter 31
Closing of Convents, Chapels, Mausoleums and Tombs

In 1925, just two years after the declaration of the Republic, the convents of dervishes and tombs of the saints or sultans were closed down. I was only two years old and cannot remember this event. This topic, however, was discussed many times at Kızıltoprak.

My grandfather had a sheikh. He lived in Üsküdar. Sometimes my grandfather would visit him or he would come to Kızıltoprak. Naturally he was received at the "selamlık" of the house. No one else than my grandfather would go to the room except the maid who would take coffee or food. She would have a scarf on her head. Sometimes many bearded people would come and visit my grandfather. I could not understand what they were talking about. We would not enter the "selamlık" but look from the garden to see what they were doing. We would see them eating. Years later, I found in my mother's trunks a Bektashi head dress. Then I realized that my grandfather was a member of the order of Bektashi. Nothing was told to us in this respect.

The convents were set up as religious foundations. My father would tell us how some convents would help the poor and distribute food. The name of this food was "fodla" and many people benefited from these convents or benevolent foundations. It was difficult to differentiate between the needy and the idle beggars. These places degenerated and became places of exploitation. By closing these convents the different orders of the Muslim religion were officially eliminated. During holidays various sects or orders used to have their demonstrations. My mother would tell us how members of these sects would strike iron chains to their backs or stick big needles to their cheeks while demonstrating in public. Our generation did not see such demonstrations and they were almost forgotten. In Iran and other Muslim countries these sects continue their demonstrations. Unfortunately there are people who want to revive them in Turkey.

It is accepted that people want to believe in some supernatural powers and enjoy such meetings. Again today the convents are reopening here and there. The Mevlevi order of the whirling dervishes is officially reopened and they perform their rituals as before. This has now a folkloric atmosphere and they go abroad to give concerts and perform their dances.

During the first years of the "hat law" and the wearing apparel regulations, folkloric dances were made in normal clothing. My grandmother had made zeybek clothing at home. She would dance the "harmandalı" and other zeybek dances very well. She taught these dances to my mother and to us. She also made suits of the Laz (people of the Black Sea), Albanians and others. She would organize parties where such clothing was worn and have a nice time. The Janissary military band in their original uniform was revided only after 1950. Thus the Janissary clothing came out of the military museum to the streets in a folkloric way. It is very nice to revive the past but it should not bring back the old way of living. One should preserve one's culture and folklore. The study of the old customs and music is the best way of keeping the traditions alive.

The mausoleums are another question to be discussed. At the time the convents were closed, so were the mausoleums. These places had become centers of exploitation and a source of resistance to the reforms of the Republic. These mausoleums provided income to some people who had claims on them and who were exploiting the poor and ignorant population. They had hereditary titles passed down from father to son or to the nearest male descendant. To be a dervish, sheikh, dede, seyit, çelebi, or mürit one had to belong to a hierarchic organization. This was connected with fortune telling, witchcraft, healing, writing of "muscas", all of which exploited ignorant people. There are still people who write "sacred" prayers on a scroll and hang it on their necks or they sell beads for the evil eye. Now the evil eye beads have become touristic items. No one can eliminate these things by law. People believe such things as evil

190

eye, or ill omen, or knocking on wood, etc. But when these habits are in relation with the sheikhs or sects or the sultan the matter takes a different aspect. The mausoleums or tombs of sultans, saints or other important people had caretakers who lived off the donation boxes. Some of them were used and are still used as wishing places for relief of pains, wishes for marriage, children and other things. These places could become easily resistance points against the young Republic.

One has to visualize the situation and mentality of the people in Turkey in those days, especially in Istanbul. There was a great tension between Istanbul and Ankara.

After the declaration of the Republic, the sultan was still in Istanbul. He had issued orders to arrest and hang Mustafa Kemal and his supporters. Ankara was approaching Istanbul which was under the occupation of the Allies (British, French, Italian and American). There were talks of accepting an American mandate under a special agreement. The Treaty of Sevres was signed and the empire reduced to a small area in Northeastern Anatolia. Our allies Germany and Austria also lost their empires and no help would come from that side. Russia was in a turmoil. Our old friends the Arabs set up their states under the protectorate of British or French governments. The Greek army had advanced to Polatlı near Ankara, but they were pushed back to the Aegean Sea. We had lost all the islands in the Aegean and practically all the territory in the Balkans. Turks who lived there were prosecuted and had to run away for their lives. In this atmosphere who is going to take care of the mausoleums and tombs. There was no time to think of the convents or religious sects. The palaces were nationalized. The property of the sultans all around the empire was lost. All the land had belonged to the sultan; now the whole mentality had to be changed. We are still suffering from this turmoil. What we call government land can not be controlled unless there is a registry and land ownership deeds. The gecekondu problem arose from this vacuum of ownership.

The closing of the tombs and convents of Istanbul and Bursa had a bad effect on my grandfather. He did not say anything to us but during

191

holidays (bayram) he felt uneasy. He would take me to the Kızıltoprak mosque to the morning prayers and to bayram prayers. Then we would visit the graves of our ancestors. Some of these tombs were at the closed graveyards of the sultans which had all been closed. He would insist to the guard and have the Cağaloğlu türbe opened although no one had been allowed to enter for years. It belonged to the viziers and other high ranking officials next to the tombs of sultans. When we entered he said the prayers to Sırrı Pasha and Ismail Pasha and pointed out the tombs to me. He also read their inscription and I wrote in my notebook where these tombs are located. Very few people went to the mosques and especially during morning prayers they were almost empty. During bayram days the morning prayers would be crowded but there was no question of not finding a place.

Years later these tombs were again opened and now people can visit them as they wish. They are taken care of by the religious administration.

Chapter 32
Calendar Reforms, 1926

When I started at the St. Joseph primary school, we would get out on Friday morning and walk to Kızıltoprak. Friday was the official week end. Only once a month we would leave school on Thursday afternoon and stay at home that night and return to school on Friday night.

Saturday and Sunday were regular working days. Because ours was a Christian school, we had a different Sunday. In the morning the Muslim and Jewish boys would go to the study hall and some students would go somewhere else. We found out later that these boys were Catholic and Protestant. They were going to the school church for Sunday prayers. In the afternoon we would all go on a walk. The destination would be either Fenerbahçe or Kuyubaşı where we would play football and return to school. No religious teaching was allowed in the first years of the Republic. The Muslim children did not attend religious courses but they had found a way for Christian children. Our school was a missionary school and naturally they were here to propagate their religion. After the Republic these schools became cultural centers representing the country they came from.

In 1926, the Arabic calendar was changed to the European calendar. The year I was born was 1340 according to the Arabic calendar. My birth certificate is still registered as 1340. When the certificates were renewed, I asked the registry to change it to the new calendar but they said it was not possible. Now very few people can make out the meaning of this date. In Turkish families there was no habit of having birthday parties. Therefore the date of birth was not very important, only the year would be registered to the last page of the Koran. The oldest person, usually the grandfather of the house would inscribe this date. Then he would chant the call to prayer to the ear of the newborn baby. The child would thus be a part of the family and there would be a record of his name and record of birth in a safe place. The birth certificate would be obtained after a few years. Especially in villages this was a difficult formality. The boys would be registered because they have to join their military service but the girls would not be registered. There were many girls born in the villages who never had a birth certificate.

The Arabic calendar is used in special situations like religious holidays, which are set according to the old calendar.

Today, birth certificates are issued on the basis of the new calendar. Only those who are 70 years and over are still registered according to the Arabic calendar.

The three dates of the cemre (the fires that warm the air, water and earth leading up to spring) and the arrival of winter and summer are still recorded according to the old calendar. It is difficult to change a calendar that has been used for centuries.

In 1945, seven years after the death of Atatürk, the Foundation of Language and History changed the names of four months, October, November, December and January.

The previous names and the present names are:

Old Name	New Name	English equivalent
Teşrini-evvel	Ekim	October
Teşrini-sani	Kasım	November
Kanunu-evvel	Aralık	December
Kanunu-sani	Ocak	January

The new names were not accepted easily and there was a reaction to this change. "Ekim" and "Kasım" were used colloqually so they were accepted easily. But Aralık and Ocak were awkward at first.

Because Ekim connotes planting season it was easily accepted. Kasım also was easily used because it has a connotation of beginning of winter. But Aralık sounded funny, especially to the older generation. Even the youngsters of those days had difficulty to place these months. We would count them and say "Oh, the third one was Aralık!" Now everybody is used to these new names of the months. Anyway the age group that complained is no more around.

This shows that the reform of the calendar lasted from 1926 to 1945. Those who were against the Language Institute and the History Institute continued their subversive activities. Their attacks on these two institutions gave fruit in 1983. When you consider the reforms from a bird's eye view, you begin to see a movement like the waves of the sea. Each wave leaves an impression on the sand. The next wave that comes seems to try to erase this impression but leaves a new impression. When you go higher than a bird's eye view and look at the world with an astronaut's eye, you see just a small bead in the universe. At that point you begin to wonder and think in a different manner.

Chapter 33
Reform in Time Keeping, 1926

When we were young we would hear quite often the phrases "the old time" or "the new time". Now there are very few people who use "the old time". Only those who are very religious keep time in the old way.

There was an Akif Efendi at my mother-in-law's house. He was a devout Muslim and never changed his clock. You had to adjust the clock according to the rising of the sun. He was a good cook and was taking care of the chores of the house. There were not too many people left using the old time.

In 1926 the prayer time adjusted clock was changed to the standard 24 hour clock. Only prayer time, religious holidays and fasting rules stayed with the old time. In business life and normal daily life we think of the 24 hour clock. The old time had to be adjusted according to the sun. This of course was a cumbersome way of keeping time. People got used to the new time quickly and nobody said, "Oh how nice the old time system was!"

Now it looks simple but when you think of the days when these reforms were made, you begin to realize how hard it was to change the habits of the people.

Chapter 34
First Statue 1926

There were no statues in Turkey up to 1926 because it was contrary to religion. Up to that time there was not a single statue erected in the Ottoman Empire. The first statue was the one made for Atatürk and stands now on the point below Topkapı Palace on the shores of the Marmara Sea. It was erected on October 3, 1926.

At the same time there were preparations at Taksim Square for a larger statue to commemorate the independence of Turkey. I remember this statue when it was in construction. The place was surrounded by a wooden curtain. From our house we could see the construction going on inside.

The Taksim monument was unveiled on August 8, 1929. We had no sculptor at the time to build a statue so the Italian artist Pietro Canonica was invited at a cost of 16,500 English pound sterling. The first project proposal had a big pool around it, but the cost was too high so they decided on the statue we have now. It stands eleven meters high and depicts on the four sides the victory of August 30, 1922, with Atatürk on the Kocatepe front. The side of the monument facing Beyoğlu represents the new Republic of Turkey and the two sides represent war and peace. The statue has been repaired lately and fallen marbles were replaced. When it was built it looked inpressive because there were no tall buildings around. Taksim square is a spacious area so the momunent is not squeezed in. The statue of Atatürk at Ulus square in Ankara is almost lost amid big buildings.

In general a person's statue is erected after his death but the situation was different with Atatürk. The making of statues had been forbidden for centuries and to complete the reforms Atatürk had to have a start during his lifetime. Each town of Anatolia was almost in a race to put up an Atatürk statue at its main square. A report from Cumhuriyet newspaper dated May 25, 1934, is interesting: First Statue of the "Gazi" on the Mediterranean Coast

In the town of Silifke on the south coast of Turkey a statue of the Gazi was inaugurated on May 19th. This is the date when the Gazi set foot in Samsun in 1919.

In this statue he is dressed in his military uniform and is facing the Mediterranean sea with his sword in hand. It was built by the sculptor Kenan Ali and was manufactured in his foundry.

There was a great ceremony for the opening of the statue and Kenan Ali Bey was present but Atatürk did not go for the opening.

At that time the family name reform was not yet enforced. When the paper talks about "Gazi" everyone understands who they refer to. The word "bey" is still used after the name of the sculptor. The important change is that a Turkish sculptor can produce a statue in his foundry instead of an Italian artist. This is a big change in the history of Turkey. Statues forbidden by the religion can be produced and erected. Also interesting is the fact that Atatürk is not present at the unveiling ceremony.

Attacks against statues can be regarded as the first sign of reaction to the reforms of Atatürk. After the 1950 election when the Democratic party obtained a majority, the first attack on a statue was made at Yenişehir in the new section of Ankara. Someone attacked the Atatürk statue with a hammer and damaged the monument. I do not remember if the insurgent was identified or not, but the main point is that it was an attack on Atatürk's reforms. It shows that after the 1950 elections these reactionary elements dared to show their teeth.

The statue of Ismet İnönü had a sad story. In 1960 the Municipality erected a pedestal at Taksim square with a dedication of Atatürk praising İnönü. It was right in the middle of the square on the top of the stairs. The statue of İnönü on a horse was completed at the time of the 1950 elections but was never placed on the pedestal. The Republican People's Party had lost power and İnönü could not obtain a majority after this election. He later came to power after a military coup d'etat but stayed mostly in the opposition. The statue was forgotten in a warehouse of the municipality. Very few people remembered where the statue was. Finally, in 1983, the pedestal was moved from Taksim Square, set up at Maçka in front of İnönü's house and the statue brought out erected on the pedestal. This was a nice place overlooking the Marmara Sea but a little apart from the main center of the city.

The fate of statues in Istanbul started to change with the İnönü monument. In 1974 attacks were made on statues erected by the Istanbul municipality. A statue called "Beautiful Istanbul" was placed at Galata near the port and a monument for workers was set up at Tophane in its vicinity. There was a big uproar by the fundamentalist circles. The press supporting the religious parties made a big noise on the ugliness of these statues and Beautiful Istanbul was found obscene. There were attacks on these statues with paint and hammering.

Finally the municipality moved Beautiful Istanbul to an unseen corner at Yıldız Park and the worker statue stayed in a broken shape where it was set up. In 1984, the moment Anavatan (Motherland) Party came to power, there was a strange movement in Ankara. The Hittite Sun monument at Lozan Square was going to be removed and the square renamed Malazgirt. The name of the Abdi İpekçi park was also going to be changed in front of the Ministry of Health. The Hittite Sun is an enlarged replica of a Hittite statue in the Ankara Museum. When it was built and placed on the Atatürk Boulevard at the Health Square, there was a lot of criticism from the religious press. Many people would not accept this monument which is a relic of the past of Anatolia. The discussion on this monument continues and was aggravated after the religious Refah Party won the municipal elections in 1994.

Chapter 35
The Metric System Reform

On March 26, 1931 the metric system was accepted. In Turkey there were various types of measures of weight, length and surface. For water there was a unit called masura. For instance in Kanlıca we had two masura of water allocation. When the water distribution was made during the Ottoman days each yalı had an allocation of continuous flow of water measured by the masura which corresponded to the diameter of a string. This water was coming free of charge from the source in the mountains. It was not easy to charge from the Ottoman measurement units used for 500 years. There were not enough scales and meters in the country. For this reason the application of this law was prolonged until December 31, 1933. The vendors suffered some difficulties. For instance we would take a cup and go to the back door of the garden to buy tahin (sesame paste) and pekmez (molasses). He had a hand scale with two trays. He would place the cup on one tray and take the balance with some stones. Then we would say "5 kurush of tahin and 5 kurush of pekmez". He would place the correct dirhem on one scale and fill the cup with tahin and pekmez. When the weight system changed to grams this measurement was complicated. The government issued conversion tables but it took some time to shift from the okka which was 400 dirhems to the kilogram which was 1,000 grams.

These units were used for so many years that these terms entered our language and expressions. For instance we still ask about the size of a garden as "how many dönüm?" or we say that he has travelled many fersah of distance.

The equivalent of the Ottoman measures to the new metric system were as follows:

Units of Weight
Okka (also called kiyye)	1282 grams
Şinik	500 grams
Dirhem	3.2 grams
Balya	205 kilograms
Çeki (for wood)	250 kilograms

Units of distance
Arşın (Used in textiles)	68 centimeters
Ayak	34 centimeters
Fersah	5,685 meters
Kadem	37.5 centimeters

Units of surface
Dönüm (specified as Cedid Dönüm)	2,500 meter square
Büyük dönüm	2,720 meter square
Atik dönüm	916.6 meter square

There were many other old systems of measurement used for weighing of gold and silver and land units. These measures and their conversion to the new units caused a great many law suits and it is still not completely settled down. When we were young these reforms came one after the other and we thought they were all prepared by Atatürk himself. There was no discussion when a new reform was proclaimed and it was an event for rejoice and happiness. They were taken as a new development and advancement for the nation.

Chapter 36
From the Okka to the Kilogram

Atatürk one day decided to shift from the okka to the kilogram. All okka and its smaller denomination the dirhem were eliminated. We were being westernized. The decimal system must be much better and no one objected to this reform. It suited very well the retail people and street vendors. For instance the price of fresh grapes was 10 kurush an okka, became 12 kurush a kilogram. One okka was equal to 1,200 grams, an increase of 20 percent which was not bad for the retailer.

One okka was equal to 400 dirhems. A bread loaf of one okka was a substantial bread and was a staple item of the family food. The old people would lament the "Okka" and say that the Okka is gone and "abundance" is no more. For instance my nurse, Hediye, had just learned that one okka was 400 dirhems. My aunt was teaching her how to read and write. The shift from okka to the kilogram was quite confusing for her. She had just memorized that one okka was 400 dirhem, now she had to shift to one kilogram which was equal to one thousand grams, yet the kilogram was lighter than the okka. She was confused because 1000 was much more than 400 yet it was lighter. Her explanation was "Well, this is a new foreign invention".

Gradually people began to get used to the kilogram. The old scales and the round copper dirhems became antiques. Some old weights remained in use, for instance, the "çeki" is still used for weighing wood.

People talk about the price of a ton of fire wood, but in practice people buy and sell fire wood by the çeki which is 250 kilograms.

Some old weights are still used in villages. For instance one batman of wheat is one kerosene tin can full of wheat.

Anglo-Saxon countries could not shift totally to the decimal system in their weights and measures. The United Kingdom adjusted the British pound to the decimal system. Neither the US nor the UK could do away with the pound as a weighting unit. It must be very difficult to change all the scales from the pound to the decimal system. In spite of the ease of the decimal system they still have not changed to the kilometer and use the mile as the measurement of distance.

Chapter 37
Rights of Women, 1934

One of Atatürk's mottos was a booster to the Turkish nation: "We shall go above the present level of civilization". What he really meant was that he wished Turkey to reach the level of civilization of industrially advanced countries. He was wondering how we could reach this goal. We were very retarded in agriculture and industry. We had a very limited number of specialists in these fields. The country was barely meeting her food requirements. The scattered villages in the countryside had difficulty feeding the cities. Diseases like tuberculosis, malaria, syphilis, trachoma and other maladies were spread all over the country. In such a situation it required a very courageous leader to set a goal like the one he was aspiring to.

On the question of the rights of women, Atatürk was able to provide these freedoms to women much sooner than did many countries in the world. At that time women in Switzerland did not have the right to vote. Atatürk had a special clause added to the constitution of December 6, 1934. "All Turkish citizens (men or women) who are above the age of 22 have the right to vote and also have the right to be elected after the age of 30."

In the 1935 elections, 18 women deputies were elected to the Grand National Assembly. Never in any future elections were so many women delegates elected to the assembly. Democracy was in a way imposed by the Ankara government on the whole country. Women's rights were also obtained in this manner.

The rights of women were not obtained by a united struggle. Atatürk saw the difficult situation of women in Turkish society. In the old days, women had to live behind veils and the houses had lattices on the windows to keep them separate from society. Women had second-class status under the Islamic laws. We have experienced this in our family.

My grandmother was married to my grandfather at the age of 14. There was a strange reason for this decision. Her father, Sırrı Pasha, was the governor of Diyarbakır while her mother, Leyla Hanım, had remained in Istanbul. They had two daughters who also remained in Istanbul. Sırrı Pasha wanted his older daughter Nezihe to marry Mehmet Ali Ayni who was his secretary at Diyarbakır. At that time, a "mektupçu" was a male secretary or assistant to the governor. However, there were Istanbul families who were asking Leyla Hanım for the hand of her older daughter. She consented to the marriage by herself. When Sırrı Pasha heard this he decided to marry his younger daughter to the man of his choice. As a result my grandmother was married off while she was still a child.

My nurse Hediye was sold at the age of three to my grandmother at Yanina under the custom called "ahretlik" or "evlatlık". I found her paper of sale in my grandmother's bag of old documents. There is another girl that my grandmother bought while she was in Trabzon. The two documents have more or less the same formula. This was a system of adoption of a child and an agreement to take her with her where ever she went and marry her when she came to age. Hediye was given away to my grandmother for eight lira and twenty kurush in the presence of such and such persons. This was the social standing of girls in Ottoman society.

My mother would relate how this small Albanian girl was brought to their house in Yanina by her father who had ten or twelve children and was happy to give one to the house of the governor. My grandmother took good care of her and gave her to my mother as a wedding present. So she moved with my mother to our house and helped with the children. We all liked her very much as an older sister.

After we moved to Kızıltoprak she was always with us. Of course, her lady was my grandmother but she was at the service of my mother. One day in the '30s my grandmother took me on the train to a house at Bakırköy, then a small village. This was a visit to the house of the future husband of my nurse. We walked from narrow streets and reached a

205

small house. My grandmother talked something with the ladies of the house. They offered a cup of coffee to her and a "lokum" and water to me. Then we returned home. Some days before two ladies whom I did not recognize had come to Kızıltoprak. They had come to have a look at my nurse Hediye and my grandmother was returning their visit. I do not know why she took me with her to this family. She would never take a grandchild to visit a family that we did not know. Maybe because I was very close with my nurse and she wanted me to see the future husband of Hediye. She was an adopted child of my grandparents and according to the customs she was married off with her trousseau and there was a check on the family that she was going to join. Hikmet bey the husband, was the only son of this family and we felt they were good people. There was a big wedding at Kızıltoprak for Hediye and Hikmet Bey. He was a chemist at the railroad administration. They lived happily at Eskişehir and had a daughter called Şermin. I kept in touch with them until they passed away. Their grave is very near to my mother's and father's grave at Karacaahmet.

If we look at this episode from a social point of view, of course, we realize the inferior position of women in the Ottoman society. Atatürk wanted to give equal status to women and did not have much time to achieve it. All these reforms were realized between 1925 and 1938. Of course, there had been a social build up since the first constitution in 1908 which broke down the absolute rule of the Sultan. Together with the Republic in 1923 a new era had started. It was only in 1934 that the University reform was made and civics lessons were introduced to schools under the title "The History of Turkish Innovation". These lessons were prepared by the Ministry of Education. They were added to the curriculum of the senior class of the high school and university as an obligatory course. There were strict instructions issued that they should be taught as science lessons. This can be looked upon as brainwashing. There was no other possible way to instruct all the social changes mentioned in this short summary of reforms. Women's rights was one of these reforms.

Atatürk had introduced a reform in religion by accepting the Civil Code and made a revolution by imposing the Commercial Code. The question of women's rights is an extension of the reforms made in the religious laws which governed the Ottoman society. The opposition to Atatürk's reforms stems basically from these changes in the social life of Turkey. Half of the population, that is the women of Turkey, were coming out of practically a slave status to normal citizenship.

In 1984 when the 50th anniversary of women's rights was celebrated, these reforms were still being criticized by religious circles. In 50 years two new generations have come to life but concepts inbedded in a society are very difficult to change. Especially the poorer classes and the village population have a tendency to cling to old habits. The sudden movement of population from rural areas to the larger towns and the creation of shanty town areas "gecekondu" also had an effect on this tendency. There are many people for whom the meaning of women's rights is still very foreign. With the further spread of communications, these rights will be disseminated further and gradually spread throughout the society.

Economic freedom of women has also an influence in this change of attitude. Economic freedom is closely related to political freedom. There are, of course, circles that are opposing such freedoms and want to keep the women folk under the veil and economically dependent on men.

My uncle Sırrı was working at the new State Sugar Factory at Eskişehir where my former nurse Hediye lived. He invited me during the summer vacation. I went to Eskişehir by train and he came to meet me at the station. I stayed a few days with my uncle and visited the sugar factory. He lived at a house on the shore of the Porsuk river and we made a tour of the river by row boat. During this visit I also went and stayed one night at my nurse's home. The little girl brought from Albania had become part of our family and she remained so all her life.

All the other girls that had been purchased as "evlatlık" were also married off as their turn came. They had no salary. They were fed and clothed and they did all the chores of the house. When the lady of the house would go out, they would carry her bag and umbrella. This habit gradually changed and my mother and aunt did not take a maid when they went out but my grandmother would never go out on the street alone. If she was going to take the train, the gardener would accompany her to the station, buy her ticket and wait until the train departed. At her return, they would know with which train she was coming and someone would meet her at the station.

The veil was not worn any more but when the girls went out to the garden they would wear a scarf. My mother was the last generation to wear the charshaf. When she was young she had to have a veil to go out on the street. My father would tease us and say, "My mother brought me to this world too early" because we could visit the neighbors' daughters and they would come to us. God bless them all.

Chapter 38
Family Name Law, 1934

There was no family name during the Ottoman days. Everybody had a first name which was followed by his father's or grandfather's name. My name at St. Joseph was Nezih Halim and my younger brother was Ali Muzaffer.

The Christian and Jewish children had family names. Muslims had an umbelical name given at birth by the midwife or grandmother. My birth name is Mehmet. So I was Mehmet Nezih Halim.

Even the telephone directory was published on the first name basis. My mother was Nezihe Mehmet Ali until her marriage and then became Nezihe Muzaffer. This created a great deal of confusion and the family name law gave the Turkish people a chance to take one name for the family. There was the "lakap", a common name adopted by families in smaller cities which derived mostly from the occupation of the family. But these lakap were not used in the official registers. In general only the first name was considered necessary such as, for instance, "Ismet, Chief of the Eastern Front."

In order to put an end to this confusing situation the family name law was accepted. This was looked upon as a process of westernization. On June 21, 1934, a law was enacted making it obligatory to chose a family name. Those that abstained were fined from 10 to 50 liras. There were restrictions on the names that could be taken; obscene words, foreign names and derogatory terms were not acceptable.

On the birth certificates of our generation there was an additional name shown as the accepted family surname. My mother and father discussed what name to take, both offered to take their nick name as our family name. My father was Muzaffer and my mother called him Meyzi and my mother was Nezihe and my father called her Neyzi as a diminutive and affectionate nick name.

209

Finally my father went to the registry and asked to take Halim as the family name. The registry man objected and said that this was an Arabic name and could not be taken as family name. So my father went the next day and said that he decided on "Neyzi". The registry man asked what this name meant to which my father replied with a serious attitude, "It is the grandfather of Atilla". "Ahhh" said the registry man, "your father-in-law must have found this name."

The registry man at Kızıltoprak must have known Mehmet Ali Ayni my grandfather, from Kızıltoprak. My father told this story many times at home and whenever there was a strange new family name that we heard, we used to say, "Mehmet Ali bey must have found it"!

To take a family name was naturally not a joke but at that time there were very funny stories about family names. Many people could not find a suitable name and the registry persons would assign them a name. Then of course there were the question of the leaders of the country like Gazi Mustafa Kemal and İsmet Pasha. What family name were they going to take? It was the topic of the day.

The Republican Party was looking for a suitable name for Gazi Mustafa Kemal. The secretary general Recep Peker and the head of the Turkish Language Foundation Saffet Arıkan were looking for a suitable name for the founders of the Republic. One of the psychological reasons for this family name law was to create a new image for the nation and get away from the Arab influence.

In a conversation between Recep Peker, secretary general of the Republican Party, and the head of the Turkish Language Foundation Arıkan suggested the name "Atatürk" for the founder of the Republic. Gazi Mustafa Kemal Pasha accepted this name as a gesture made to him. It means the father of the Turks. No one else would be allowed to use this family name. Even his sister took her name as Atadan. The law passed on October 25, 1934, states no one else can use this family name.

Atatürk found the surname İnönü for İsmet Pasha. He was taking as a family name the place where he had won two battles against the Greeks which changed the fate of the Turkish nation.

My father would have several tales each time he returned from Ankara. I do not know who invented this story but it was very funny and we all laughed very much. Atatürk gave the surname of İşer to the general manager of the İş Bank. In this form the name İşer has a different meaning and it can be understood as someone who is urinating. This situation was explained to Atatürk and he changed the name to Eriş.

At this time of accepting a new family name, brothers and sisters from the same family took separate names. For instance Leyla hanım, took her name as Saz. Which was appropriate for her as it means music. Her sons took different names. Vedat the architect took Tek and his brother Yusuf took Bel. The registry man at Kızıltoprak accepted Ayni as the family name of my grandfather. So there were many different family names in the same family. It took some time until everyone could get used to these new names. Everyone continued to use the name they knew. For instance my old friends from St. Joseph still call me Halim because our teachers, the monks, used to call us by our family names and not the first name. Now I use "H" as a middle name initial as a souvenir of old times. Many people do not understand what this H. stands for. On the other hand, those that call me Halim are gradually fading away.

The process of going from the Ottoman Empire to the Republic of Turkey is still going on.

Chapter 39
New National Days:
July 1, 1934, Cabotage Day

One of the advantages obtained at the Lausanne treaty was the right to navigate between Turkish ports. What is now looked upon as a normal right of Turkish ship owners had been given as a capitulation to all foreign flag vessels. Now this day is only celebrated by the navy and the schools of navigation. Life goes on as usual, the day is not an official holiday so not many people know what this celebration is about or even realize that there is a celebration. There is a ceremony at Taksim square and at Beşiktaş in front of the Barbaros mausoleum. The towns of Izmir, Mersin and Samsun also have an official celebration. No one writes to each other or congratulates each other on this occasion.

During the Ottoman days foreign ships would carry goods and passengers between Turkish ports and foreign lands. As a result the Turkish merchant fleet could not develop and this was one of the reasons for the loss of the empire. The ports also were governed and operated by foreign powers. For instance port of Istanbul was built and operated by the French. Haydarpaşa was built and operated by the Germans. Practically no customs duties were collected at the ports. The buildings of the Turkish Shipping Company and the customs building at the port of Istanbul were built by the French. Due to the capitulations, the Ottoman Empire had lost control of the seas.

My mother had a sad story about this situation which I never forgot. When her father was appointed to Yanina as governor they took her along on a trip from Istanbul to Preveze which was our port on the Adriatic Sea. The boat they took was a Greek passenger ship. During the voyage a Greek person got up at the dining room and gave a derogatory talk against the Turks. No one could intervene. This story impressed me very much. Imagine an empire who sends his governor to a province in the Balkans and does not have one passenger ship of its own. The ports of the Black Sea, Mediterranean and the Red Sea were all serviced by Italian, Austrian, Greek, English or French ships. Ports like Beirut, Hodeida and Basra were all linked to Istanbul by foreign shipping companies. No one can imagine an empire who does not have her own means of communication. As a results these far flung parts of the empire disintegrated and got lost.

The seas are not controlled only through shipping; the ports and lighthouses are also important assets and sources of revenue. For example, the navigation rights of the Bosphorus were in the hands of a British company called Waford. They had an administration based at Kilyos on the European side of the Bosphorus right on the Black Sea. They had a lighthouse just outside the Bosphorus to indicate the entrance to the straits. If there was a fog, ships that would miss this lighthouse would run aground at Kilyos or Yönburnu point on the Asian shore of the Bosphorus. At these two points the British, which also had the concession of salvaging, had a salvage and coast guard service to save the people on the grounded and damaged ships. The British would collect the lighthouse fees and profit from the salvaging operations. They would give a small percentage to the Ottoman government and their colonial people lived very comfortably in Istanbul.

This Cabotage day that we celebrate represents the nation's right to control its seas and develop its merchant shipping.

Chapter 40
Youth and Sports Day
May 19, 1936

During the Ottoman days, the only holidays that were observed were the two religious bayrams, the Sugar and the Sacrifice days.

The 19th of May is the day when Atatürk landed at Samsun on the Black Sea to start the war of independence. This day was not celebrated until the last days of Atatürk. The other events like the declaration of the republic, the various victory days were more important.

May 19th began to be celebrated as a sports day. We could see the preparations from the top floor of our house. The stadium of the Fenerbahçe football team was a place where all the schools would get together and prepare for the 19th of May events. The stadium did not have the facilities they have today, it was just a football field with seating facilities on one side. All the other sides of the field were just fenced in and you could see the players if you climbed a tree in the vicinity. All the students of the Kadıköy area came to this stadium on the 19th of May 1936 for the sports festival. I could follow the activities from the third floor of our house with binoculars. The military band could be easily heard at a distance. There were no apartment houses obstructing the view and there were no traffic noises.

A law was passed on June 20, 1938, to change the name of the sports day to Youth and Sports Holiday, thus placing it among the official holidays. Offices and schools were to be closed for that day. This law came right before the death of Atatürk. It looks as if Atatürk wanted to leave a souvenir to the Turkish Youth. Now each year May 19 is celebrated as a sports festival all around the country.

Like all reforms of Atatürk, this remembrance day became a target for the religious and fundamentalist groups. They did not want the girls to parade in shorts. The uniforms of the schools were changed to long sleeves and long skirts. During the anarchic days they even sabotaged the events. All these reactions were to harrass the spirit of modernization.

It is interesting to watch these festivities on the TV. You can notice the difference of attitude in various cities. In Ankara the uniforms of the students are more solemn and covered up as much as possible. Then Istanbul is a little more relaxed and the Izmir ceremonies are in a normal atmosphere. In Lefkoşe (Nicosia) Cyprus you can see girls in short sleeves and shorts as it was in the early days of the Republic.

This day that started as a Sports day is like a barometer of the mentality in the administrative apparatus. Political attitudes of the government are reflected in the demonstration by the students at government middle and high schools as well as the military schools and the police college. When you look at all these small reflections of attitude you begin to see the reactions to the reforms started after the Republic.

Chapter 41
Other Celebration Days

After the Republic there were some days and events that had to be commemorated or at least remembered. For instance 30th of August became Victory day. It was the day when the Greek army was defeated. The final offensive was planned by Atatürk and İnönü at Dumlupınar and was completed by August 30, 1922. This date was also declared Aviation Day. Later on these dates were separated and aviation day was not celebrated any more but spread thoughout the year at many occasions when money was collected to buy and build airplanes. Each letter that was posted had a one kurush aviation stamp added. Besides the airplane stamps the state lottery administration, called "Tayyare Piyangosu" allocated its revenues to the aviation industry. During the sacrifice holidays all the skins of sheep sacrificed were donated to the Turkish Air League. An airplane factory was built near Etimesgut airport in Ankara. I visited this factory in 1938 when I went to Ankara. There was also a private airplane builder at Kalamış near Kızıltoprak named Vecihi Hürkuş. He had built several planes and in later years started a company under the name of Hürkuş and was carrying newspapers from Istanbul to Ankara.

There was also a Language Day which is now quite forgotten. The alphabet had changed from Arabic letters to Latin letters but the language was not changed. When we were young in the early forties, it was a fad to use Arabic and Persian words which was a sign of being well read. Even the speech that Mustafa Kemal gave at the Grand National Assembly in 1927 was completely in the Ottoman language full of Arabic and Persian idioms.

To understand this old language one needed to learn Arabic and Persian words. I had a special notebook to register and memorize these idioms. It was fashionable to use this flowery language. The "Language

Day" was set up on September 1932 as a symbol of purifying the language from these foreign words. The announcement given in the daily **Cumhuriyet** two years after the inauguration of the language day is a good example of the attitude of people in those years.

LANGUAGE DAY

"If we were to celebrate all the reforms made after the establishment of the national government all the days of the year would not be sufficient. However, there are such reforms that set a basis for our nationalism and extend towards the future. For this reason at the first general assembly of the Republican Party on September 26, Language Day was inaugurated. This festive day is now having its first anniversary. Our advancement on the path of our leader will lead us to a bright future. Our ancestors' language will be the language of the Turks and will make possible the propagation of science and technology which was hindered by this complicated mixture of Arabic and Persian language. We have a great past of thousands of years. We belittled it, we did not use it and it became rusted. The star that emerged from the mist started sending its rays and illuminated our path, recreated the forgotten language, and offered it to us for use. Our continued usage of this language will help us in future developments. Today there will be a meeting at 16:00 o'clock at the Istanbul People's Party to celebrate Language Day. There will be an opening talk by the head of the People's Party followed by singing of our national anthem and party marches. This will be followed by a speech given by Refik Ahmet bey. There will be readings of poetry and prose in the old and new languages.

"Besides these activities the President of the Language Association will give a talk on the radio by using a pure clean language."

It is interesting to see this announcement in the form that was presented in those years. The family name law was not yet accepted. New Turkish is just emerging but Arabic and Persian words are still dominating. It is specified that the speech of the president on the radio will be in a "clean" language.

I remember my younger brother coming from his primary school and say "I like my country more than myself" or such phraseology. My grandmother would laugh very much and say, "Let the bees sting your tongue," meaning what you say is utterly rubbish.

To see the great change in the language, a look at Atatürk's original speech and the simplified version by Prof. Hıfzı Veldet is very revealing. It is very interesting that the Language Reform was suggested and implemented by a person who was brought up in the Ottoman language and culture. There had been attempts before Atatürk to simplify the language and the alphabet but a radical change was made possible by Atatürk himself.

As you see in various sections of this book of memoirs, French was the dominant foreign language during the Ottoman Empire. Medical and Engineering schools used French as their teaching language. German was common in the railroad administration. There were very few people who knew English. The minorities used their own proper languages or used French as a mutual language. There were Greeks and Jews born in Istanbul who never spoke Turkish. The Jews use the Catalan dialect of the Spanish language.

The Albanians tried to propagate their language. The Arabs never learned Turkish. The Ottoman Empire did not propagate their own language as the British and French did in their empires. Africa is now divided between Anglo-phone and Franco-phone areas. Wherever the Ottoman Empire went, they let the people use their own language. They took Arabic and Persian and mixed it with Turkish and created an elite language used in the palace and among the administrators. Turkish was spoken in villages in Anatolia with various dialects according to the regions. We had seen in the memoirs of the governor of Diyarbakır that the Arab and Kurdish languages were used among the local population.

All these show the importance of the language reform started after the Republic. The Turkish History and Language Institute is still working on the development of the present Turkish language.

Chapter 42
Republic Day, October 29

The Republic Day is the most important of new celebration days. All the means of communication like the TV, radio and the press emphasize the importance of this day. There are official celebrations at Ankara and all goverment offices. Parades are organized by the military and schools.

During the first years of the Republic, there was only the People's Party and all celebrations of the Republic Day were dominated by the party flag of six white arrows on a red banner. During these celebrations it was customary to praise the Republic and remember the drudgery of the past. On the streets they would set up wooden archs of triumph covered with laurel leaves and the Turkish flag with the banners of the People's Party. There would be a picture of Atatürk on top of these decorations. At night these stands would be illuminated and each house would put up at least one flag. Large mansions would decorate their balconies with flags and electric lights. In main squares of Istanbul where there were fountains, illuminated water cascades would be set up. There would be one at Taksim, Beyazıt and Üsküdar squares. The people would come out and have a nice time.

When the two party system started, the People's Party and the Democratic Party would have their own decorations on their party buildings. They organized folkloric music in front of the main buildings and play music and dance in the streets. This was a way of demonstration for the parties and each of them would have a nice time. In Ankara, there would be an official ball attended by the president and all cabinet members. Foreign diplomats would come with their special attire. There would be receptions at the military guest houses in other towns around the country. Republic Day parties were the most important social functions of the year.

Now the holidays have changed their character. People look at the calendars to see which day of the week is a national holiday. They make plans as to where to go during this period. Whether national or religious the holidays are a means of running away from town for a vacation at a touristic place. Only the officials congratulate each other on Republic days as a matter of routine formality. The number of flags displayed at houses is decreasing.

The decoration of houses is almost forgotten. The street decorations are gone. Military parades are made at Ankara, Istanbul and other towns. In the old days the infantry and cavalary would march from Beyazıt square to Taksim square. People would watch the soldiers all along the roads. Now the parades are made at a place where the municipal and other members of the protocol watch the parade from a stand. The parade is broadcast on the TV so everybody can watch from their homes.

Chapter 43
Elimination of Titles
and the New "Bay-Bayan"

In 1934, all titles given by the sultans were abolished. There were official and social titles and ranks according to the position of the person. The term "pasha" was given to army generals. There were also civilian high officials or governors who would be called "pasha." Terms like "Aga", "Hacı", "Molla" were gradually forgotten but now the "Hacı" or pilgrim has again begun to be used more often. The term "Sheikh" was also forbidden to be used as all convents and chapels were closed. Now they have reopened unofficially and the term sheikh is used for leaders of Kurdish landlords in eastern Anatolia. This was not an official title but came from the feudal days. Each family or clan was run by the eldest member of the family which might extend to several thousand people. The title goes from father to the eldest son. It has now political ramifications. All the family votes according to the inclination of the sheikh. The chief of the family is the "postnişin" which means the one who sits on the sheep skin. He does not collect a tax but as all the land belongs to him he owns all the crops and the herds of animals. He also owns several villages including all houses. This is an unofficial continuation of the centuries-old feudal system. The peasants work as sharecroppers.

Some of these tribes are still nomads. They live in tents and roam around according to climatic conditions. The roaming tribes are gradually disappearing due to the mechanization of agriculture and opening of new highways. This dates back to the conquest of the area by Selim III in the Middle Ages. The feudal sheikhs were annexed to the empire with the condition that they would supply men and horses during campaigns. Their lands and villages were left to their possession. After the Republic and the new borders with Syria and Iraq were drawn, the nature of these migrating tribes and land ownership changed. The chiefs are elected as deputies from their regions so they have a political representation at the national assembly. The men are required to serve their military service. Laws and regulations change but many habits imbedded for centuries cannot be altered.

To replace the titles bey for men and hanım for women two new words were accepted: bay and bayan, bey and hanım were used for people who had means and an esteem in the society. A lesser degree for men was efendi. All these terms were replaced by bay and bayan. These words began to be used on envelopes in the mail and other official functions. In some cases they were used to reprimand people. For instance if someone stepped on your toe in the boat or tramway, you would say "Bayım, be careful" meaning you are not a bey but just an ordinary bay.

Chapter 44
Buy Turkish Products

During the Ottoman Empire there was no industry in Turkey. It was a completely agricultural country exporting tobacco, grapes, figs and other agricultural and mineral products. All the required consumer goods and even textiles were imported. The villages had a self sufficient economy and they would trade for such products as kerosene, salt, sugar and such things as nails for horseshoes, etc. They would barter their produce for such products at the market place. All consumer goods were imported to cities like Istanbul, Izmir and Salonica and sold in shops run by foreigners or the non-Muslim minorities.

My mother would tell us how they bought biscuits coming in tin boxes from England. There were famous shops like Horozdibak, Pigmalion, Karlman and others who sold all kinds of imported products. The world was still on the gold standard. My father would tell us how he would place gold coins in his pocket, go to Vienna and buy goods. Only after the First World War did paper money begin to circulate and customs administrations become established. Then import restrictions started.

Cotton textiles were called American cloth; tiles that came from Marseille in France were called Marseille tiles; rope would come from England. After the start of hostilites in the First World War all imports stopped. People could not find products used in daily life like pots and pans, plates and forks and knives, kerosene, sugar, thread, window pane and glassware as all these products were imported. Flour for bread was imported from Canada, USA and Russia. The stopping of flour imports created a shortage of bread in Istanbul.

My mother would tell us how difficult it was to find decent bread. Flour, sugar and everything else were on the black market.

After the world war ended, war continued in Turkey from 1919 to

1923. This situation made the shortages even worse. The boundaries were not set clearly. The first clear-cut boundary was the one with Russia and Iran. The boundaries of southern Anatolia were undecided. The question of Mosul oil and the Hatay remained unsettled even in 1923 at the signing of the Lausanne treaty. Finally in 1936 agreement was reached on Mosul oil, Turkey would receive 10% of the oil that had been obtained at Mosul for 25 years. However, this field was not exploited by Britain for many years and Turkey could only get a little from it in 1936.

The border of Thrace was uncertain. There were discussions about Dedeağaç (Alexandropolis) which remained west of the Nigris river which later became the frontier with Greece. Turks living in Greece held Balkan land and the Greeks living in Anatolia were exchanged. The Turkish people who lived on the Aegean islands returned to Turkey. All of the Turks living in Crete came back. Only a small number remained in Rhodes because it was occupied by Italians. They came to Turkey after the Italians left the island during the Second World War. The Turkish people in Cyprus which had been turned over to England after the Crimean War, were also forced to migrate under the British rule.

Because of the fact that our parents' generation suffered all these troubles at the end of the Ottoman Empire, we grew up with tales of the wars in the Balkans, uprisings in the island of Crete, the invasion of Tripoli by the Italians, the Russian wars and the continous endless struggles in the Arabian peninsula. The Russians came to Ayastefanos (Yeşilköy) and almost took Istanbul. At the time of the arrival of the Bulgarian soldiers in Çatalca, my grandmother's mother wrote to her daughter in Trabzon, "If necessary I will take the girls and go to Bostancı". My mother and aunt remained in school in Istanbul when their parents went to Trabzon.

The people who started the Republic had suffered greatly from the lack of textiles, sugar, bread and other needs, which is why they wanted these products to be produced locally. There was a lack of technical knowledge so they went into partnership with non-belligerent countries like Belgium to produce cement. Later new partnerships were set up with French and English companies. Tiles and bricks began to be produced locally but all this development was very slow and the Ankara administration began to be uneasy. Furthermore, in 1936 there was a rumor that the Italians were going to attack Antalya. Atatürk had a new road built from Burdur to Antalya and this attack never materialized.

The development of the public economic enterprises came during this period. That is why Sümerbank was set up to start the textile industry, Etibank for the mines and, Denizbank for the maritime lines. In order to obtain technical knowledge, young engineers were sent to Russia to learn about the textile industry. The western countries did not want to lose their market and therefore abstained from supplying machinery and expertise. The same situation was faced in the glass industry. The Paşabahçe plant at Beykoz could not produce window panes because of lack of know-how. The İş Bank took this project seriously and approached the Belgian, French and American industries to obtain know-how. They all said "You do not need a glass industry, we will sell to you all your requirements." Finally Paşabahçe had to go to Russia. A new glass industry was set up at Çayırova together with Russian experts and finally Turkey began to export glassware and window panes to the west and even to the United States.

Locally made textiles were very rough and not nice to wear. When we were children we would get cloth from Sümerbank factories and shoes from the Beykoz factory which also belonged to the same state bank. A Beykoz shoe would cost 5 liras and if you gave an addional 50 Kurush a steel heel would be added. You needed strong shoes as we did a lot of walking.

New sewing houses were set up to produce military uniforms and Sümerbank was providing the material necessary to produce these uniforms. During the war of independence the government had great difficulty finding uniforms for the army. My father would tell us how they collected stockings from the houses to be given to the soldiers. In the first days of the resistance movement everybody would wear what they had. The army was practically non-existent except for the one army left on the Eastern front. The others were irregular groups of the old Ottoman army. İsmet İnönü's first job was to put order to this situation. Çerkez Ethem, who had a strong force, was opposed to this organization and left and joined the Greek army.

There was a law to encourage the use of locally produced products but there was not a penalty for non-users. As a result it was government offices and enterprises who started to apply the law. For instance the Railroad Administration, the PTT, and the Maritime Bank. This bank had its own sewing house and produced the uniforms necessary for the personnel on the ships and on the ground. This little factory came very handy when new student uniforms were needed at the maritime school in Ordu on the Black Sea. The minister of transportation was going to visit the new school on July 1 which is the Maritime Day and the students would make a parade. But there was very limited time. So instructions were given to the sewing house to set aside everything else and produce these uniforms. Cloth was obtained from Sümerbank and the uniforms were ready in time for the minister's visit.

There were weeks organized to inform the people about what was available from the state factories and other local production. At the primary schools children were taught songs on the consumption of local products. It was the tenth aniversary of the Republic. I went to my younger brother's school performance. They had prepared plays and songs. One of them was "I have apricots ...." this was a song praising locally produced goods. Thus they were teaching children to prefer local products. You could call it brainwashing.

The question of local products is still discussed. If a local product is good and satisfies our needs, we use it gladly. But if the local products break down then we are very dissatisfied. Once I was in New York with my wife and noticed a glass piece by Paşabahçe in a store at Times Square. First we could not believe it because this place was a very competitive store. Therefore, if the product is good it can be sold in the most competitive place in the world. We were glad because about 30 years ago, the same circles had said that we should not produce glass products!

What I want to say is that these results cannot be obtained by laws or decrees. It is the capacity to produce and maintain a quality that is competitive with the world industry.

Chapter 45
Ayasofya and Kariye Become Museums

No one else than Atatürk could dare transform the Ayasofya (St. Sophia) mosque into a museum. This was followed by the Kariye (Chora) museum which was materialized at the time of İsmet İnönü administration.

On February 1, 1935, upon Atatürk's orders, the mosque of Ayasofya became a museum. This was a very risky and important decision. The Kubilay incident was very recent. There was an atmosphere of uprising of religious and fundamentalist circles. People in general were stunned and did not know what to say. We, as children educated during the first years of Atatürk's, could not understand this decision. The first time I went to Ayasofya after it became a museum I saw the great shields of Allah, Muhammed and the prophet Ali on the ground standing against the wall. Later on they were again hung in their original places. They were so big that there was no other place for them so they too had become museum pieces.

There were many mosques destroyed in the Balkans and many people remembered these incidents. Some mosques were converted into churches. In 1935 the population of Istanbul was about 600,000 and the number of mosques was enough for the population. From a religious point of view the conversion of Ayasofya into a museum did not have an adverse effect on religious requirements. On the contrary it had become a subject of pride to have preserved for 500 years the Byzantine mosaics on its walls. If as a church Ayasofya had been torn down at the time of the conquest, no one would be saying anything about it now.

Lately the Aya İrini church was restored as a concert hall. It had been used as a military museum for some years. When I was about 15 years old we went with my uncle to visit this military museum. In its garden there was an entrance opening to an underground cistern. They had made a wooden gangway to walk around the cistern. This cistern has been closed down and the entrance is completely lost. There was even electricity in this cistern to have a view of the columns which are similar to the present day cistern museum of Yerebatan. I hope one day an enterprising manager will reopen this cistern and put it at the disposal of tourists.

The conversion of Ayasofya and Kariye from mosque to museum are two landmarks for the republican mentality. İsmet İnönü also gave importance to the secularist, non-sectarian point of view of the government. In 1940, we started hearing that there were very valuable mosaics in the mosque of Kariye. Prof. Whittemore had discovered Byzantine mosaics under the plaster which covered the inside of the building. It is natural that religious circles were opposed to converting a mosque into a museum. The governor of Istanbul, Lütfi Kırdar, without making any alterations to the mosque started cleaning up the plaster and bringing out the mosaics dating from the Byzantine period. We were proudly watching this operation which showed to the world that the Turks who conquered Constantinople had a high regard for the art of that time. Of course there were people who thought differently, but at that time they did not dare to voice their criticism.

SECTION IV
REACTIONS TO THE REFORMS

It must be in human nature to resist any new idea. History, proves that initially many new ideas met with opposition and sometimes fierce reactions. Therefore it is natural that not everybody approved of the new ideas or reforms that came during the Atatürk period. I tried to show how some of these reforms developed in the Turkish society. For instance; the fez. No one dared to say, "Let us not wear the fez", but Atatürk went to Kastamonu from Ankara and said, "This is a hat gentlemen!" and put the hat on his head.

Before this, demonstration there were many developments. The Sultanate was abolished, new laws replaced the old laws derived from the Koran, but the appearance of the society remained the same. Before the hat there was a sheep skin Kalpak worn by many people, especially in winter. This had came from the Kazaks or Caucasus Turks. The military had replaced the fez for the ordinary soldier with a Kabalak which was made of cloth and much cheaper than a fez. For the officers they had made a hat without a brim. The public in general continued to wear the fez or turban as they were accustomed until the hat law was passed.

I am sure that Atatürk knew there were not enough hats in Turkey for everyone. He did not declare and say "Let us wait and import enough hats and then we will have a hat law". As we see from old pictures taken in Istanbul streets there are many people wearing hats and there were shops selling hats. Even my father had a hat he called the "European hat".

My father would relate how everybody in Ankara was busy trying to obtain a hat. Besides hats they started selling peaked caps and berets in the shops. Now after about seventy years, most people do not wear any type of hat. The regular felt hat became quite expensive and is now out of fashion. Religious people put on a scull cap in the mosque for prayers. This cap is usually made at home and can be carried in the pocket. The "kasket" (peaked cap) has become fashionable among peasants.

There were reactions to all the reforms introduced during the Atatürk period of the Republic, 1923-1938. The most important of these are the revolt of Sheikh Sait and the Menemen incident.

Chapter 46
The Revolt of Sheikh Sait

During the Ottoman period revolts were common in some parts of the empire, especially in the last years when the influence of Istanbul and the Sublime Port had deteriorated. In the period covered in this book of memoirs, which is about two centuries, we see constant uprisings, revolts, wars and separation of various areas to form a new kingdom.

On the other hand Russia, Austria-Hungarian Empire, England, France and Italy were constantly trying to take some parts of the Ottoman Empire. Or if they would not take an area they would try to set up a state under their contol like in Egypt, Greece, Bulgaria or Bosnia-Herzegovina. The empire survived in its last years only because of the balance of powers and the competition between these expanding empires.

In order to gain control of the world's trade routes, these great empires of the last century were especially competing to take the petroluferous areas and the straits that were under Ottoman domination. When we consider history we see that all empires have a start, a growing period, a declining era and final dissolution.

In 1923 with the international Lausanne agreement, the boundaries of the new Turkey were set up by Atatürk. The term Misaki Milli or National Union was a term that was used often when we were young. It had a connotation that the Ottoman era which was made up of several nations must be confined to national borders. After the First World War the following nations emerged from the Ottoman Empire:

In Europe: Yugoslavia, Albania, Romania, Bulgaria, Greece and Cyprus to be a dominion of Britain. All these countries except Albania had separated from the Ottoman Empire and set up their own kingdoms and had their own flags. They all had ties with the Ottoman Empire and the great powers of the world. These relations were put in a clear cut form at the Lausanne agreement. At that time they found out that there was an island on the Danube which still belonged to the Ottoman Empire. It was annexed to Romania.

In the Middle East, the following new countries were set up: Syria, Lebanon, Iraq, Jordan, Saudi Arabia, Palestine, Kuwait, Qatar, Yemen, Bahrain and the Emirates of the Persian Gulf. These countries were connected to the following empires:

Syria under French mandate
Lebanon under French mandate
Iraq (a Kingdom) under British mandate
Jordan (a Kingdom) under British mandate
Saudi Arabia (a Kingdom) under the influence of England, USA and France through petroleum companies
Kuwait (an Emirate) under British mandate
Yemen (a Kingdom) under British control
Bahrain and Palestine under British protectorate
Emirates of the Persian Gulf under British and American control
In Africa: Libya (a Kingdom) under Italian control
Egypt (a Kingdom) under British control

In summary we can say there were sixteen kingdoms, emirates, principalities and protectorates that emerged out of the Ottoman dissolution. Turkey came out as a republic after a four-year independence war fought from 1919 to 1923. The area accepted as the borders at Lausanne was declared as the National Union area and Atatürk declared that not one foot of land would be given and no claims would be made over the land given to the new countries. For the Ottomans this meant the loss of three-fourths of their territory as a result of the 1911 Libyan War, the 1912-13 Balkan wars and the First World War 1914-1918.

During this time the Ottoman sultan remained in his palace in Istanbul then under French, Italian and British occupation. These three powers intended to divide the land between them and give a part to the Greek kingdom. The Greeks would occupy the area from Izmir to about half the Anatolian peninsula. The resistance movement started on May 19, 1919, led by Atatürk with a protest against this partition of the empire. When we look at the situation of the world in those years this was a natural continuation of the First World War. The victorious Allies were free to carve out as many new dominions, kingdoms and protectorates as they wished.

Asia and Africa was divided up into colonies and protectorates. Why should there be any change and who was Mustafa Kemal? He was just a general of the crumbling Ottoman Empire.

For us the situation was just the contrary. Millions of Turks had died in the Balkans, the Arabian deserts, the Dardanelles and the Russian front. At some fronts such as Iraq they had lost the war and had to retreat. There was a cease fire declared by the British and the Ottomans at Mosul. Then the British took Mosul after the cease fire. At Suez our army lost the battle and retreated to Damascus, then Aleppo. In Beirut they fought the French and the local Arab sheikhs supported by the English. On the Russian front we had won the war and advanced as far as Batum and Bakü, Azerbaijan. The Russian army and their allies the Armenians could not stop the Ottoman army. From a geopolitical point of view, the Ottomans had an advantage. They lost great territories but they could retrograde and make a counter attack. The start of communism in Russia gave us this chance because the Russian army just disintegrated. It had advanced to Erzincan in the north and lake Van in the south together with the Armenians. But after the start of communism the Russian army was disbanded and the soldiers did not obey their officers. They started to retreat to their own country. This gave the Ottoman army a chance to push back and take over Batum and Bakü. But the British army which was still in Iran did not want the Ottomans to take this land and we were obliged to retreat to our present frontier with the Soviet Republic which is now Georgia, Armenia and Azerbaijan. There is a special area called Nahcıvan which is separated by a special treaty

236

that no one can enter this area without Turkey's consent. During the last phase of the Ottoman Empire at least the Russian front was not under attack.

Many years after these events, we can look at history and comprehend the situation more clearly. The Russians also lost great territories to the French who came to Moscow under Napoleon and to the Germans who almost took Petrograd and were stopped at Stalingrad. The Russians retrograded and then pushed back their enemies. During the Second World War the Germans went even as for as Egypt in Africa and occupied practically all of Europe. Then they lost the war and were completely occupied by the Allies. The Russians took arms and ammunition from America and advanced into Central Europe and occupied Berlin.

The Ottomans lost their territory in Europe, the Middle East and Africa, after many disastrous battles. In Anatolia and especially in the Aegean, they could not fight but resisted to the advancing Greeks, French, Italian and British. They went back almost to Ankara and prepared a new army. The armistice obtained with Russia made it possible to regroup the remaining forces from the Eastern frontier and then push back the Greek army supported by the Allies. Atatürk also was successful against the French and Armenian armies who had occupied the Adana and Gaziantep areas in the South. He made the first treaty with the French after capturing a thousand French soldiers who were advancing towards Ankara. These victories in the Aegean and southern Anatolia created breathing time for the government in Ankara. The sultan was still in Istanbul where the British were in occupation. After the fighting ended in the Aegean, the nationalist forces took over Bursa and came nose to nose with the British army which was holding the Dardanelles.

The Ankara government declared the frontiers of the new Republic of Turkey as it is today and asked the sultan and his family to leave Istanbul. London ordered the British to fight against the nationalist army as it approached the Dardanelles, but the commander in Istanbul saw the situation and decided to withdraw his forces by sea to Istanbul.

237

The balance of power had changed and a local defeat would be very alarming to the British. No one wanted to fight any more. The French and the Italians had made special agreements with the Ankara government. So finally the British and the occupation armies of France and Italy left Istanbul and returned to their own countries. Istanbul was in a way reconquered by the Turks in 1923.

During the Ottoman Empire the area between the Danube River down to the Indian Ocean was under one loose administration. The Ottomans who conquered this area over the centuries granted a type of internal autonomy to the nations that lived in this large area. So the Arabs who were five centuries under Ottoman rule did not loose their identity. The various emirs were always semi-independent in their own territories. Petroleum had not yet been found and therefore they were very poor. Every year the sultan would send gifts and money to the Emir of Mecca to maintain the religious buildings for pilgrimmage. The last sultans built a railway from Istanbul to Jiddah to facilitate the pilgrimmage voyage. Only in Egypt there was a presence of the Ottomans more than any other Arab region. The language of the Egyptian palace was Turkish. They were closely related to the sultan's family in Istanbul. They had their palaces and summer residences in Istanbul. In a way Egypt became semi-independent after the opening of the Suez canal and the English and French took over the administration of the ports and the canal under the regime of the capitulations.

The other Emirates were so poor that no one ever thought of going to Kuwait, for instance. Iraq also was very poor area without petroleum. There was some seepage of oil at Mosul and it was used locally in very small quantities for lighting only. It is after the development of the automobile and the car industry that petroleum gained importance in the world. The big powers wanted to have small Kingdoms or Emirates under their control to exploit the oil as they wished. This was the main reason for taking this area away from the Ottoman Empire.

After the declaration of the Turkish Republic in 1923 the question of minorities had to be solved. Within the national boundries there were many Greek, Armenian and Arab people left. There were also many Turkish people left in the Balkans. In Istanbul there was a mixed population of Greeks, Armenians and Jews together with a Muslim population left since the Byzantine days. During the Ottoman Empire, nationalism was not accepted and all the subjects of the sultans were Ottomans. In reality only the Turks could not proclaim their nationality but all the other minorities would call themselves Greeks, Armenians, Arabs, Jews, etc. The Turks could only say, "We are Muslims. In Anatolia also there was a mixed population of Greeks, Armenians and Jews.

Atatürk had saved Anatolia from the occupation of the Allies and declared the national boundaries which had been accepted by the Allies and practically all countries of the world. It was agreed to exchange the Turkish population left in Greece with the Greek population left in Anatolia.

There was also another agreement with Yugoslavia to bring back the Turks left in Yugoslav towns and villages. This was followed by another agreement with Bulgaria in 1950 to accept the Turks who wanted to migrate from Bulgaria. The Turks in Greece up to the river Nigro in Western Thrace were left in their places as were the Greeks who lived in Istanbul. A few years ago there was a big expulsion of Turks from Bulgaria to Turkey. This is the continuation of the dissolution of the Ottoman Empire which took five centuries to build. It takes time for people to settle down but movement of population still continues around the world. These migrating minorities from both sides were victims of the dissolution of the Ottoman Empire.

There was no question of exchange of population for the Arabs and Kurds who stayed within the national boundaries of Turkey. First there was no official differentiation between Kurd and Turk. They had fought side by side against the Armenians, Greeks, Russians, French and British. Fighting with the Arabs was strange to the Ottomans. In reality the Ottoman armies did not fight against the Arabs, as the main enemy were the French and especially the British who had helped the Arab sheikhs to gain their independence from the Ottomans. As we see in the memoirs of my grandfather and his father-in-law Sırrı Pasha, the Kurdish and Arab tribes had a certain degree of autonomy and they would sometimes kill an Ottoman administrator to prove this self-administration. The Ottoman army had to fight with the British and French forces, these two imperial powers had brought soldiers from India and Africa to fight the Ottomans. The Arabs were doing mostly guerilla warfare and acting as guides to the British and French forces. They still suffer the consequences of this defection.

The Kurds also wanted to set up their own independent government. There is still fighting going on for this cause. The Barzani tribe managed to get a semi-autonomous state in northern Iraq. We do not exactly now how the Sheikh Sait uprising started during the first years of the Turkish republic. What we know is that Kurdish tribes got together and occupied Diyarbakır and Elazığ and took the risk of fighting against Atatürk.

The following passage is from my grandfather's book Milliyet (Nationalism) published in 1943. He and his father-in-law had lived many years as administrators of the Ottoman Empire in Eastern Anatolia especially in Diyarbakır and Elazığ. We as the first generation of the republic do not have much knowledge and experience in the Kurdish and Arab lands. During our childhood, these subjects were not discussed or written about. Now scholars are beginning to analyze the social developments during the empire and the republic.

"In 1910 I was the governor of Mamuretul-Aziz (the old name of Elazığ). I travelled all over Dersim (now called Tunceli). When I went to the Ovacık township of Dersim, I wanted to see the source of the river flowing through this area. We went by horse to find the source of the river. About ten minutes before we arrived at our destination the twenty gendarmes that were with me dismounted from their horses. I was astonished and asked the reason why they had dismounted their horses. These people were from the Dersim area and according to their belief the saint, Munzur Baba, had disappeared at a place in Munzur mountain and this river emanated from that spot.

"For this reason in honor of this saint I also dismounted and walked the remaining distance to the source of the river.

"A few years ago (It must be 1936 or 37), an agitator called Seyyit Rıza, a leader of the region, started a rebellion in this area against which the Turkish army started an operation. The leaders of this rebellion retreated to Kutudağ which was a very difficult terrain to penetrate. To get them out of this area was a very difficult operation. Sabiha Gökçen who was an adopted child of Atatürk flew over this area and dropped bombs on the caves where they were hiding and they were obliged to surrender. I was wondering where the Saint Munzur was at that time and why he did not come to rescue them. For centuries the Dersim area was famous for these rebellions and the army of the Republic went to the area and deported them to various places in Turkey. Now new construction and development activities have started at Dersim.*"

This is an example of an Ottoman adminstrator writing during the republican period and referring to the Kurds as intriguing agitators without saying who was instigating this intrigue. In the same text he also notes that the people of this area were making a living from robbery and brigandage.

The Arabs wanted to break away from the Ottomans and were looking for an appropriate time. They were following the developments in the Balkans. Nations who lived in the Balkans were helped by the Russians, the Austrians and the French to rebel against the Ottoman administration. The Arabs also followed the same system and broke away from the Ottomans and set up many semi-independent states or sheikhdoms under the protectorate of new powers.

There are various rumors about the Kurdish rebellion during the first years of the Republic. During the Erzurum convention that was set up by Atatürk to unite and fight against the invading forces, Kurdish leaders joined this congress and were promised autonomy at the end of the fighting. It is said that the first uprising came because this promise was not fulfilled.

(*) Milliyetçilik, Mehmet Ali Ayni, Istanbul Maarif Matbaası, 1943, Pages 227 and 228.

241

After this revolt, the Kurds divided into two main groups. The ones in the North sided with Atatürk and those in the South insisted on an autonomous area. Finally the republican forces including the Nothern Kurdish tribes dominated the situation. I remember the days when Sabiha Gökçen as the first woman pilot participated in this operation. The newspapers were full of her accomplishments.

The rebellious Kurdish tribes were settled in towns in the western part of Anatolia. For instance, Kamuran İnan's family was settled in Bursa. So he was educated in Bursa and later went to Switzerland for further education. We heard that many insurgents in the east were hanged by Salih Omurtağ, the head of the army in that area, and some people were put to death by firing squads. All the atrocities were related by word of mouth and left many bitter memories in the minds of people. It is the inevitable result of civil war. In 1952 I went to Diyarbakır to conduct a market survey for the petroleum industry. The Batman refinery, the first Turkish refinery, was just completed. The Turkish Mining Institute had found oil at Raman and vicinity. This petroleum was refined at the new refinery and distributed to the area. This was a big success for Turkey as the known oil resources of the Ottoman Empire had been taken away by the Allies.

The southern frontier was not completely agreed upon at the Lausanne conference in 1923. This border was drawn up by French and British geologists with the aim of taking over all petroliferous areas. In fact there is an oilfield just outside the Turkish border on Syrian soil. This was specially planned by the French because they were taking control of Syria. England was taking the oil fields left in Iraq.

When the Turkish geologists discovered oil in Raman, the international petroleum companies were very upset. Their geologists had made a mistake and there was oil left on the Turkish side. All the known reserves were taken by the victorious countries and Russia. These victorious countries are always interested in Eastern Turkey and keep an eye on it. Now this area has become a big source of energy obtained from dams on the Euphrates river. What I saw at Diyarbakır

242

in 1952 astonished me. Everybody on the street were talking Kurdish. Men had an understanding of Turkish because they had learned some at the military service, but women did not understand Turkish at all. I visited the museum of Ziya Gökalp who was a famous writer during the Ottoman period. The writings of Sırrı Pasha, my grandmother's father, explains in his memoirs that everybody speaks Kurdish or Arabic in this part of the empire. He also reports that Kurds outside the city walls of Diyarbakır live in tents and migrate according to the seasons. The arrival of the rural people to the town increased the intensity of the Kurdish language. At that time Ankara radio could not reach the Diyarbakır area. In general the shopkeepers talked among themselves in Kurdish but knew enough Turkish to speak to their clients. The children were playing in Kurdish and women spoke Kurdish among themselves. Men who had served in the military could converse in a rough Turkish.

The Turkish Republic had failed to improve the language in these areas. The hopes of my grandfather about the construction and development activities in Dersim had not yet materialized.

My second visit to the Lake Van area was in 1974. I was in charge of the Maritime Bank which had an operation at Lake Van. We had built a ferryboat to carry the train from Tatvan to Van to make a link with the Iranian railroad. We went together with the Minister of Communications Ferda Güley and his entourage. This was an official visit so I could not get in touch with the people as much as I would like to. I observed the backward situation of the area and the lack of development. Each year we had to send 75 workers to the shipyard at Tatvan to build new ships and to repair those in operation. This was a difficult task because the workers in Istanbul did not want to go and stay in this area for about three months. I made a plan to improve the hotel at Tatvan which was run by the Bank and open a branch of the Bank in that city. The only bank was a branch of the Agricultural Bank.

We held an exam to pick 50 students who had completed middle (Orta) school and entered the high school at Tatvan. When the boys

243

reached Istanbul we had a dormitory ready and they started attending the technical school of the Haliç shipyard in Istanbul. There was a big row when it was understood that the buys from Tatvan could not follow the lessons in Turkish. Thereupon we started a Turkish course and in a short period the boys learned Turkish and continued their schooling.

In 1983 I visited the lake Van area for another market survey. I stayed at the hotel at Tatvan that I had had repaired several years ago. Some young men came to visit me. They were from among the boys that I had invited to the Haliç technical school. They had become electricians, mechanics and welders and were working at the Tatvan shipyard. They were talking fluent Turkish and had brought me some honey as a gift. If since the beginning of the republic, government economic enterprises had trained some 50-60 young people and sent back to these areas, economic development could have started rapidly.

During the years 1978 and 1979, Kurdish propaganda was intensified in Eastern Anatolia. Listening to the radio, I could hear a language that I could not understand. The station was Radio Free Europe (The American station). Then radio Israel, BBC and Radio Moscow were giving news in the same language. I found out that this language was Kurdish and it was clear that all these countries were concentrating their propaganda on this area. I also saw that there was agitation in the labor unions and they were making excessive demands. One of them went to complain to Kamuran İnan, who was a deputy from Bitlis.

All the deported families came back because their land was not confiscated. He took this complaint to the minister of communications under whom I was working. I talked to the labor union man who made this complaint. I said jokingly "Why do you give your votes to the Democratic Party? They have not done anything for this area." The reply was just silence. This meant, "You are right but what can we do!". I also knew they could not do otherwise. You have to know the conditions of the area. You must obey the chief of the area. It was the same situation for centuries as reported in the memoirs of my grandfather and Sırrı Pasha, his father-in-law.

The reason for my citing the Dersim revolt as an example of the reaction to Atatürk's reforms is to illustrate the social environment and customs. Atatürk's reforms did not change the religion of the Turkish Republic. What he did was to put to a formal shape the reforms that were started with the declaration of 1908 during the sultan's regime and the formation of the first Assembly. The reforms and laws brought by the Republic upset the way of life of the Ottomans and brought about the Republic of Turkey. It is evident that some circles did not accept these changes. The Sultanate and the laws derived from the Koran were eliminated. The incident of Kubilay is just one of them. In order to be able to maintain the present borders and to continue with the republic, we have to study our social and anthropological development and prepare long-range plans.

Chapter 47
The Menemen Revolt and Kubilay Incident

When the Turkish Republic was declared there was an embarrasing situation. The sultanate was abolished but Sultan Vahdettin was succeeded as Caliph by Abdülmecid Efendi. If Mustafa Kemal had not been successful there would have been a Sultan - caliph residing in the occupied capital of the Ottomans. It is not known how the situation would have developed but it is seen that there were forces that wanted the sultanate to stay in one form or another. There was also a large number of persons whose interest was with the continuation of the sultanate. They had come to an agreement with the occupying forces and did not want to change their status of living. There were religious leaders, the hocas who did not want even to mention the name of the Republic. How could they, the servants of the sultans for generations, accept a totally unknown form of government? They did not know what would happen to them when the sultanate was abolished. The Grand National Assembly had set the boundaries of the Republic but the situation was still not definite especially the border with Iraq. The Ankara government insisted that Mosul should stay within the Turkish borders. The town of İskenderun was debated with the French. There were British forces in Mosul and French and Italian soldiers in İskenderun (Alexandretta). The occupying forces and the sultanate were trying to do away with the Ankara government. On the other hand the reforms made by the Republic were decisive steps, not something that had been seen in other countries. The reforms were coming one after the other. The events from 1923 to 1938 are breathtaking. The Ottoman Empire had been decimated but a new Turkish Republic had emerged from its remnants. When we look at the events of this period from a geopolitical point of view, we see an empire which ceases practically, all its territories are occupied almost completely by foreign powers, but comes back to life with a rejection of this occupation by forces coming from the middle of Anatolia. There is only one point to bear in mind. This pushing force that liberated the country was not coming from the Ottoman sultanate, which had joined the First World War together with Germany and Austria. These empires also lost the war and their territories but their mainland was not occupied by the Allies. On the contrary the Allies wanted to occupy almost all of the Ottoman lands. Then an Ottoman general decided to fight back the invading forces.

He had to fight also with the Sultan's remaining forces. Only the Turkish part of the invaded country took part in the war of liberation and sacrificed the people remaining in the Balkans, Syria, Iraq, the Aegean islands and Cyprus by accepting the present frontiers as the Republic. Unfortunately, this situation is even discussed today in 1997 and the Treaty of Sevres is taken into consideration. Many people confuse the Ottoman Empire with the Republic of Turkey. There have been disastrous wars with great loss of life and millions of people left homeless. These events are not forgotten and they still talk of the Armenian genocide. The atrocities against the Turks in all parts of the empire are rendered irrelevant because we do not make propaganda in this respect. The recent events in former Yugoslavia showed to the world once more the atrocities made during ethnic persecutions.

Now let us explain the Menemen incident. There was a reaction in Bursa to the call to prayer from the mosques being made in Turkish. Mustafa Kemal went to Bursa and gave a talk to explain why we were changing the call to prayer from Arabic to Turkish. The event was calmed down. The Aegean area is always the leader in political activities. During the Republic the opposition usually develops from Izmir and finally there is a change of government.

Manisa was one of the old capitals of the Ottoman Empire therefore the religions and pious foundations of the area go back into history. Atatürk had stopped all the religious sects, chapters, medrese (theological schools), sheikh and dervish organizations, writing of charms, sorcery and witch-craft; descendants of Mohammed, "dede, "baba" and

247

such titles were abolished. But these people were still living and they were faithful to their sultan. They had benefited from these titles and now they had lost their source of income. The new regime did not try to collect these people and punish them. The descendants of the Nakshibendi sect Sheikh Esat lived at Erenköy near our house in Kızıltoprak. My mother and grandmother always advised us not to go to that area by bicycle. They did not tell us the reason why but they wanted us not to go to their vicinity.

I was curious and one day I ventured to go in that direction from Kuyubaşı. I crossed the cemetery of Sahrayıcedid and came to another cemetery. I climbed up the wall and looked to this forbidden area. It was full of big tombstones with turbans. I sensed that this was not a place to be involved with and jumped on my bicycle and came back to the Kuyubaşı fountain in one stretch. There I had a drink of fresh Kayışdağı water which flowed free from a fountain and returned safely home.

There were supporters of the sultan who were helping this Nakshibendi sheikh at the mansion of Şevki Paşa. Still residing in Istanbul were many circles in favor of an American mandate or friends of the British or French occupying forces. There are not too many analyses of this period but what is known is that the reforms instigated by Ankara were accepted with a grain of salt. When Atatürk was alive not many people dared to come up directly against the reforms. But this Nakshibendi sheikh with the support of royalist circles sent his son Mehmet Ali as Şehzade to Manisa. This was an old Ottoman custom. My grandfather, M.A. Ayni, has analyzed this habit in his book **Türk Azizleri** (Turkish Saints) and he explains how a hoca named Osman Fazlı sent one of his followers Ismail Hakkı as molla to Üsküp (Scopie).* We can compare this situation with the molla organization in Iran and religious groups that supported Khomeini. The Ottoman Empire had a similar organization of mollas who were a state within a state. The reforms during the Republic separated the state from religion and put an

---

(*) Türk Azizleri N.1- by Prof. M.A.Ayni, Marifat Basımevi, Istanbul 1944, Pages 18-20.

248

order to religious affairs. Naturally the people who lost their power did not like these reforms and they wanted to try and continue their old ways.

When Mehmet Ali went to Manisa he was greeted as Şehzade, that is the son of the sheikh. The Ottoman ways and habits had not changed in Manisa far away from Ankara. Manisa was a very rural area; the roads were the same as the Ottoman days. They had a Greek invasion and now they were free again. Sheikh Esat had also appointed the retired imam of the military hospital of Menemen as chief of this region. For those days this was a customary thing to do. For centuries these appointments were made by the various religious sects. This is a good example of a state within a state.

The Nakshibendi followers were having meetings in private homes as usual. The last meeting was held on December 6, 1930, at the house of Mutaf Hüseyin, the maker of praying caps (takkeci). At this meeting they made plans to get arms and munitions to start an uprising. There were young candidates who were newly introduced to the order of Nakshibendi and they were very eager to act. Among them there were criminals who had 24 year prison sentences and had escaped. There were not many people in the backward villages of Menemen who understood what the republic meant. The Nakshibendi followers went to the villages of Paşaköy and Bozalan to recruit forces and found new people to join their cause. After gathering some more people they returned to Menemen and occupied the mosque. They informed the public that they had declared the religious government with acceptance of all Muslim laws (the sharia). Naturally the people present did not know what to do. Not so long before the Greek army had occupied the town and only the "efe" had shown some resistance. The Nakshibendi opened up the green banner of Islam and invited people to declare the sharia. They started shooting in the air and spread rumors that an army of 70,000 Muslims were coming to town.

Upon this noise and commotion the gendarmes present in Menemen came to the mosque headed by a Captain Fahri. They could not disperse the armed crowd because they were outnumbered and had only maneuvers ammunition.

The insurgents opened fire and the reserve officer Kubilay was wounded. The fire of the gendarmes was ineffective because their bullets were just blanks making a noise and having no effect. The insurgents made the people of Menemen believe that they had super powers and were bullet proof. Only when help came from the gendarmerie armed with real bullets did they run away. But during this interval they killed the reserve officer and the two night watchmen.

This was how the first bloody reaction to the reforms took place 67 years ago. What was their aim? It was clear that just by taking Menemen religious law would not come back. Maybe they had other plans which they could not implement. Maybe they had ties with the Sheikh Sait uprising in the East. One party from the East and the other party from the West would put pressure on Atatürk. The people supporting the caliph in Istanbul would join them and put an end to the reforms which came with the Republic. Maybe they would go further and ask the help of France and England. This would start another civil war in Turkey.

In later years a statue was erected in the name of Kubilay at Menemen. Each year there are annoucements in the press on his death anniversary. Time heals all wounds. Like the gradual forgetting of the cabotage day. These two events are, of course, very different from each other but they are important keystones of the formation of the Republic. These events should not be forgotten by future generations.

Chapter 48
Changing the Call to Prayer
from Turkish to Arabic

Many people forgot that the ezan, the call to prayer, was changed to Turkish during Atatürk's regime. Atatürk's idea was that Turks should invite each other to prayer from the minaret in a language that they understood. Each day we are inviting each other to pray in Arabic.

There were long discussions on whether it was possible to change the prayer chant to Turkish. Upon this conversation Gazi Mustafa Kemal went to Bursa in 1932 and gave a speech explaining why we should change the call to prayer to Turkish. Finally in July 1932 the Pious Administration made a declaration that the müezzin would chant the call to prayer from the minaret in Turkish. The Turkish text was as follows:

God is great
God is great
There is no other god than God
There is no other god than God
Come to the namaz
Come to the namaz

Of course many people objected to this simple call to prayer. There were some incidents in reaction to this call. Atatürk explained that the question is not just a religious issue. He emphasized that we should accept our national language to form our national identity in all aspects of life.

The Latin alphabet was accepted, religious schools (medrese) were closed, teaching of Arabic was forbidden. After all of these transformations the call to prayer in Turkish was quite difficult to accept by religious people. The Turkish chant was in the same rhythm as the Arabic prayer, so not much had changed but as a child I had a "nostalgic" attitude and did not know what to say. For hundreds of years the call from the minaret had been in Arabic and now it was changed to Turkish. I could not understand the meaning of this change. Most probably Atatürk felt that the religious people would one day try to abolish all the reforms and for this reason he decided that we should call each other in Turkish rather than Arabic. Unlike Christianity there has been no reform in Islam. Atatürk brought a completely new concept by separating the religion from the government. These were the preparations for a secular society.

The stopping of Arabic teaching, calling to prayer in Turkish and the municipal wedding were all new developments for Turkey. The "hoca" could wear his fez and white turban only in the mosque and to take the dead to the cemetery. These were symbols which meant that religion was something between the human being and God and that the State had nothing to do with this relationship.

The first reaction to the reforms was to bring back the Arabic chant after the Democratic Party came to power in 1950. It became the fashion to place loud speakers on the minarets to increase the volume of the call to prayer. Maybe the growth of towns and the noise of traffic made this necessary. After 1950 attending mosques increased. Friday prayers became crowded. Fasting during the month of Ramazan became more popular. No one is arrested because of eating openly but there are many restaurants that close at lunch time. During the Ottoman days those that did not fast or ate in public were taken to the police station and punished.

The backward trend increased after the 1950 elections and coming to power of the Democratic party. Those circles that did not want to come out openly during the Atatürk period were also careful during the İnönü period. After the Menderes government, religious demonstrations increased in general. They even benefited from the funeral of Field Marshal Fevzi Çakmak. He was a religious person and in his later days they tried to draw him into politics. They made a big demonstration at his funeral at Beyazıt square. During the Democrat Party regime the meaning of democracy was misused and attempts to go back to the old system were encouraged. The meaning of democracy was accepted as an unlimited freedom to do what you wished. The visit to Mecca for pilgrimage was reduced as much as possible during Atatürk's regime. They started to encourage pilgrimage, arguing that since people are spending foreign exchange for touristic tours to Europe, they should also have a chance to go to Mecca.

More and more women began to wear the old charshaf and to tie scarves to cover their hair. During the Atatürk regime no one wore the charshaf anymore or covered their hair. Only the very old and the poorer people would have a scarf on the head. The question of covering up women was followed by the religious groups and today some young girls attend the university in this type of attire. This was encouraged mostly by the National Salvation Party (MSP). This shows that people had an inclination for this type of clothing but during the Atatürk period this would be unacceptable. The İnönü period was a continuation of the reforms of Atatürk. When Bayar and Menderes came to power they gave leeway and concessions to the religious circles to obtain more votes at the next election.

Religious education was also encouraged during the Democratic Party period. The Koran courses started first secretly and then came out in the open. This resulted in the deterioration of the national education system. The Peoples Houses of the Republican Party were closed down. The Village Institutes were accused of instigating communism and closed down. Religious teaching also was added to the curriculum of the universities. Now they are propagating the teaching of Arabic. I have no objection to the teaching of Arabic as a foreign language. We have to learn the language of our neighbors and do trade with them. Powers that aim to divide Turkey and bring back the Sevres agreement have always used religion as their base. For this reason we have to develop our education policy and try to keep up with the advancement of the world.

Reforms are not realized upon the wish of one person alone. There has to be a leader to realize these reforms but the time and the climate has to be ripe. Religion during the Ottoman rule had taken an obligatory form. For instance the question of fasting in the Ramazan. The fasting period which was part of the Muslim religion became an official formality. According to the sharia, it is a sin to break the Ramazan fast once it is started, but the decision to fast is an individual one. For this reason those that did not want to fast began to eat secretly or smoke in secret. Those who fast eat more than normally at the special meals prepared for the Ramazan. Those who were seen eating during the day were taken to the police station for the falaka punishment, beating the feet with a long stick. This was a degeneration of the humble habit of fasting.

My father would tell us how they were obliged to go to the mosque while they were in school. Naturally young boys would show their reaction by creating mischief during prayer time. Those who were in the front row would put out their tongues at the hoca all together at the same time. The hoca could not do anything until the prayers ended but was very mad. After the prayers there would be a lot of running around in the mosque.

When we were young there was no obligation to fast in Istanbul. The elderly people would fast because it was a habit to fast during Ramazan. Now I see that many young people who have nothing to do with religion start fasting during Ramazan. Some do this in order to stop smoking, or stop drinking or just to reduce weight. Like old Bayrams fasting also changed its character.

Now during Bayrams plans are made to get away from the big cities to recreation areas. Visits to the graves of the ancestors and visits to relatives are evaded. To go to the mosque and put a cap on one's head is supposedly a religious act. There are many people selling caps for prayers. To be religious has begun to be synonymous with reverting to the past. To grow a beard has become a sign of piety. Those who lose their hair grow small beards and whiskers. This has become a new fashion. It is also a fad to carry prayer beads in public.

Starting with the reversal of the call to prayer from Turkish to Arabic, social pressure has been increasing on the religious front. It is, of course, in the interests of those who benefited from the religious foundations and institutions. Religion has been used as a means of oppression in all parts of the world. The Muslim religion did not have a capitalist class. There was no institution like the Vatican to govern the wealth of the mosques. The institution of the caliphate ended with the Ottoman Empire. Naturally there will be interested parties to revive this institution. We should never forget that the capitalist powers sided with the sultan and obtained a decree to condemn Atatürk to death. Atatürk succeeded under all these adverse conditions. He separated the state and religious affairs.

He did not close the mosques as it happened in Albania, China, Russia and Bulgaria where all the churches and shrines were confiscated. He left the individual free to practice his own religion. The best way to get an idea about the reforms of Atatürk is to read the speech that he delivered in the Grand National Assembly in 1926.

SECTION V
THE END OF THE OTTOMANS

Chapter 49
The Story of Kızıltoprak

No one mentioned the sale of the house in Kızıltoprak until my mother passed away. Half of the house belonged to my aunt, and half to my mother. After the death of my aunt, my cousin Ismail Arar divided the house and had some repairs made to his section. The partition was easy. The house was originally built by a man who had two wives. By locking a door on the first floor and another door at the second floor the house was divided into two equal parts. The kitchen and the laundry place were in the garden outside the house. To us there was no change because we were very close with my cousin and his wife. They would come in the summers from Ankara and we would live together. They did not stay very long in Kızıltoprak and moved to the city, then to Ankara. So the two locked doors were again opened but their part was not used by my mother. My mother's section was large enough for my parents.

After the death of my father, my mother remained with her old maid Azime bacı at Kızıltoprak. When my cousin lived there it was much better; at least there were some people going and coming to the house. After they moved to Ankara loneliness and sadness set into Kızıltoprak. The garden could not be tended and started growing wild. The vegetable garden completely dried up. Only in the front garden there were evergreen trees and plants, acacias, box-trees, lilacs, pine trees, horse chestnuts and linden trees still bearing their fruits according to the season.

The stables in the back garden were either dismantled or run down. Only the cow stable remained but the roof was falling apart. The kitchen and the wash room could not be used anymore. The white paint on the house was gone and the roof was leaking in several places. Kızıltoprak was gradually running down.

After the death of my mother in 1968, Ismail and his wife Güher decided to sell their share. Right at that time I had gone into debt to buy our present house at Levent and could not take an additional credit because of high interest rates. İsmail owned half of the house and we three brothers owned the other half. The old faithful Azime remained alone in the house. Sometimes she would go to visit her daughter at Üsküdar or go to Göynük to her son. Thieves started breaking into the house. They would open the door at the back small garden or cut a window bar and break a window and come in. They would cut the old lead water pipes or steal a few things. None of us could leave our present homes and go and stay at Kızıltoprak. All we could do was to repair the damages caused by the thieves, find Azime bacı or ask my nurse's husband Hikmet bey to stay at Kızıltoprak a few nights. In this way at least there was a light at night and the thieves could not break in again. It was clear that the end of Kızıltoprak had come.

One day we had a get-together on my cousin's side. We were very friendly with my sister-in-law Güher and we used to tease each other a lot. İsmail had found a builder and proposed that we turn the house over to him. He would build a new building and give us six flats: Three of the flats would go to Ismail and the other three to us. At that time most of the old mansions in Kızıltoprak were still standing, many of them in the condition of ours. The construction companies were working mostly in the Kadıköy and Moda areas. I made a suggestion of not selling the property and turning it into a touristic area. The house could be a folklore museum with all the old clothing, fezes and other objects remaining in it. I knew no one would accept this idea and it was my sister-in-law who protested first. She said this was a crazy idea and was very mad at me. I did not want at all to see the house demolished. My brothers were not in a hurry to tear the house down either. If I paid his share, Ismail would consent not to give the house to the construction company. However, since I would not be able to find the financing, I had to consent to the demolishing of the house.

We were also losing the whole garden. This was our last meeting at Kızıltoprak and my cousin made the agreement with the construction company.

Then there was the problem of dividing all the furniture, antiques, books and what not. There was a century-long accumulation of household goods. Each of us would take some things and carry them away. We gave Azime bacı a truck load of wardrobes, chairs, armchairs, copper utensils and rugs to take to her son at Göynük. I asked my nurse's husband to dismantle some parts of the house that I wanted to keep. One was the revolving cupboard between the laundry and the kitchen. I would fit into this closet and turn around to the kitchen which was locked. I would collect whatever I could find left like börek, pastries, etc., put them in a copper container (sahan) and turn it over to my brothers, get back in the revolving cupboard and come out again in the laundry.

Naturally my grandmother would find the empty sahan somewhere in the garden and she would understand where the börek had disappeared to. There was plenty of food at the table in Kızıltoprak. But to pass to the locked kitchen from the turning cupboard, take some things and eat them on the top of a tree was quite an excitement. I also had the two big marble laundry tubs in the wash room removed. My grandfather's library had windows that had red panes in the top part. When the sun would go down it would reflect to the wall as a red light. I liked these windows, so I had them removed. The door of my aunt's room had glass windows which I liked very much. I took the double door of the main entrance door with its hinges and door knobs and the door opening to the small garden and its iron bar.

After my brothers took what they wanted, there were still many wooden chests, big cupboards of the dining room, the antique bed room which was bought by my father from Yıldız Palace when the sultans went away, all the old clothing kept by my grandmother in old wooden chests, an old coffee grinder, a big clock with a statue, big mirrors, and other old furniture that nobody wanted to take.

I was able to store these things at my brother-in-law's farm in Yalova which had a cold storage house with an empty attic. Ahmet İsvan was my school friend and later we married two sisters and became relatives.

He sent his truck and two of his men to Kızıltoprak and we loaded all these objects. I used to go there twice a year and put rat poison all around the furniture and put moth balls into the trunks and the mattresses and rugs. That way I would store all these souvenirs for about twenty years. Then the Maritime Bank allocated me a guest house at İstinye when I was the general manager of this bank. It was a nice place but I did not want to move there because I did not know how long I would stay in that position. This gave me a chance to move the old furniture of Kızıltoprak to this guest house.

Thus I had a chance to sort these old items and do repairs. The old wooden trunks were repaired and varnished. They looked very nice and my daughters took one each. One of the trunks is now in Hamburg at the house of my older daughter Furuğ. The other one is at Füsun's house who lives next door to us at Levent.

The marble sinks are decorating our garden and they have become very nice flower pots. I have two kurna from the house in Kızıltoprak. One that was bought by my grandfather when Marko Pasha's mansion was demolished. It is a very old piece. The other is the one I found and bought at my grandmother's apartment in Kalamış.

After we distributed the furniture and I saved whatever I could save as souvenir, we completely abandoned the place. One evening when I was going by train to Ankara, according to our custom, I looked to the side where our house was. The night was dark and rainy. The house was torn down to the first floor and looked like a pile of lumber. The wet lumber was shining like marble tombstones. This site was very depressing for me and I decided never to go and see the place. The old pine trees in the garden were cut down, the chestnut, linden, acasias, all of them were gone. There was only one tiny pine tree that had grown by itself. This was the only tree saved from the axe of these strange people.

In spite of very hard feelings, I had to go to take over the flat that was allocated to me. These people had made an office at the cow stable and used the decorated ceiling of my aunt's room and a door from my grandfather's library. I had no sayso but could not prevent myself and asked the men why they cut down the trees. They were startled by my question, as most probably they sold the trees as fire wood. One of them pulled himself together and said, "Mister, the apartment house has to be seen in order to sell."

The Kızıltoprak area has changed completely. After they built the first apartment flats on the site of the cow stable, they built another building in the vegetable garden. We were living in that garden as one large family; now there are more than forty families living one on top of the other.

In Kızıltoprak the only things that are left from the old house is the garden gate of the front garden with its red brick supports and the iron railings. The only tree that survived is the little pine tree that grew by itself.

The end

Appendix 1

In order to give an idea about the atmosphere of life during the last years of the Ottoman Empire, I took as an example the letter of the mayor of Istanbul, Yousuf Razi, to the occupying forces. The answer of A. Defrance is also interesting. The letters are in their original French, they represent the attitude of the occupying forces and reflect the state of the Ottoman administration in 1921.

Reponse de M. Defrance, Haut-Commissaire de France, a la protestation de Yousuf Razi bey, Prefet de la Ville, contre l'occupation de l'Hotel de Ville.

Constantinople, le 28 Janvier 1921

Monsieur le Prefet ,
Par votre lettre du 14 de ce mois vous m'avez adresse une protestation contre la decision prise par M. le General commandant le Corps Français d'Occupation de Constantinople au sujet de l'installation de son Quartier General a l'Hotel de Ville de Constantinople.

J'ai l'honneur de vous faire savoir que je me suis empresse de donner connaissance a M. le general Charpy des observations formulees dans votre lettre.

M. le general Charpy m'a fait savoir que, des le mois d'octobre dernier, le Gouvernement Ottoman avait offert, pour etre mis a la disposition du Commandement français, plusieurs immeubles parmi lesquels figurait l'Hotel de Ville.

Lors de son arrivee, M. le general Charpy, poursuivant l'etude de cette question entreprise par son predecesseur, se livra a un examen approfondi des propositions qui avaient ete faites, visita personnellement les immeubles presentes et decida d'accepter les offres du Gouvernement ottoman en istallent a l'Hotel de Ville les bureaux de l'Etat-Major du Corps d'occupation de Constantinople.

M. le general Charpy a ajoute, qu'en vue de faciliter a l'Administration prefectorale le transfert de ses bureaux, il evait accorde un delai pour l'evacuation des batiments dont il s'agit et avait offert des moyens de transport.

Enfin M. le general Charpy m'a fait savoir que, connaissant vos sentiments, il lui est penible de vous causer quelque ennui, mais il est convaincu qu'apres les entretiens qui'il a eus avec vous, vous comprendrez qu'il est dans l'obligation de maintenir les ordres qu'il a donnes pour pourvoir le Corps français d'Occupation d'une installation definitive et convenable.

A. Defrance

Lettre personnelle adressee par Youssouf Razi bey, Prefet de la Ville, a M. le general Charpy, avan la remise de sa protestation officielle, pour eviter l'occupation de l'Hotel de Ville.

Chichli, le 12 Janvier 1921

Mon General,

Ce n'est plus comme Prefet de La Ville que je m'adresse a vous c'est simplement comme un particulier qui a toujours trouve au Quartier General français un accueil cordial et bienveillant et qui vous est specialement reconnaissant de la façon dont vous l'avez reçu tout dernierement. L'occupation de la Prefecture, qui entrainera fatalement le bouleversement de tous les services municipaux qui y sont fortement centralises, produirait une impression des plus penibles sur la population de Stamboul, au milieu de laquelle vous allez vous installer et dont vous ne tenez certainement pas a blesser les sentiments.

L'occupation d'un ministere serait une atteinte directe a un gouvernement, dont l'existence est officiellement reconnue, bien que actuellement son pouvoir effectif soit bien reduit. Je ne crois pas qu'il entre dans les vues de la Republique française de lui porter un coup aussi sensible.

A cote de ces considerations, il y a evidemment les besoins du Quartier General qu'il faut assurer pour son installation a Stamboul. Je crois que les deux immeubles que j'ai fait visiter hier au capitaine Bichon, sur la grand'rue du tramway, peuvent y donner satisfaction jusqu'a un certain points.

En effet, la Prefecture est une construction mixte en briques et en bois et disparate dans sa forme, les deux immeubles en question sont en pierre, en excellent etat et tres bien distribues a l'interieur. Ils ont bel aspect sur la rue principale de la ville, l'une d'elles a une entree monumentale en marbre, les pieces sont belles et bien eclairees. De ces deux immeubles, l'un est occupe par des refugies russes que l'on pourrait caser au Musee d'hygiene et l'Ecole des Beaux-Arts. Ces deux institutions officielles, si interressantes qu'elles souent, ne peuvent supporter la comparaison avec les services municipaux; elles pourront donc chercher a se loger ailleurs, ou meme fermer provisoi rement leurs portes.

Si ces deux immeubles sont insuffisants comme capacite de logement, on pourrait en chercher un toisieme a proximite pour les completer.

Veuillez m'excuser, mon general, d'etre encore revenu sur cette question. J'ai l'intime conviction que je ne m'ecarte pas de vos vues en cherchant a trouver une solution qui satisfasse aux besoins legitimes du Quartier General sans apporter une trop grande perturbation dans les affaires publiques et sans alterer les sentiments de notre population si sincerement sympathiques a la France.

Yousuf Razi

Protestation adressee par Yousuf Razi bey, Prefet de la Ville de Constantinople, aux Hauts-commissaires de France. d'Angleterre et d'Italie, contre la decision prise par le general Charpy d'occuper l'Hotel de Ville.*

Constantinople, le 14 Janvier 1921

Monsieur le Haut-Commissaire,

Au nom de la population de Constantinople, que j'ai l'honneur de representer en l'absence du Conseil Municipal, je proteste contre la deci-

---

(*) Correspondance between the Mayor of Istanbul Yusuf Razi and the occupying French forces about the take over of the municipal building by the French.

sion prise par M. le General Charpy, commandant du Corps français d'occupation de Constantinople, d'occuper l'Hotel de Ville pour y installer son Quartier General.

A l'exception des edifices religieux, l'occupation de n'importe quel local public ou prive ne peut affecter la population de Constantinople autant que celle de l'Hotel de Ville. Le Gouvernement ottoman lui-meme ne pourrait disposer du siege de la municipalite sans commettre un abus de pouvoir, distincte de celle de l'Etat et les ressources de la Ville - si precaires - proviennent exclusivement de taxes directes ou indirectes prelevees sur la population locale.

Cette occupation serait d'autant plus sensible a la population de Stamboul, qu'elle n'a cesse de conserver le calme le plus complet depuis le commencement de l'armistice, malgre les provocations de certains elements locaux; elle n'a jamais temoigne aucune hostilite aux troupes alliees et les autorites municipales, de leur cote, ont ete correctes et deferentes envers les autorities interalliees.

En outres, tous les services municipaux etant fortement centralises a l'Hotel de ville, leur demenagement entrainera fatalement une desorganisation de l'administration municipale, ainsi qu'un arret de ses services, quel'on a tant de peine a assurer aujourd'hui, tant bien que mal, avec les moyens insuffisants dont on dispose.

La bonne execution des services municipaux interesse l'enseble des habitants de la ville, les militaires comme les civils, les etrangers comme les Turcs. Aussi suis-je oblige de decliner toute responsabilite pour la perturbation qui pourra se produire dans ces services.

Mais j'aime a esperer, Monsieur le Haut-Commissaire, qu'une demarche amicale des hautes autorites interalliess, aupres de M. le general Charpy, pourra le faire consentir a modifier sa decision en ce qui concerne l'Hotel de Ville; je l'espere d'autant plus que les santiments de haute bienveillance de M. le general Charpy sont bien connus de notre population, qui avait accueilli avec confiance la nouvelle de sa nomination a Constantinople.

Yousuf Razi

Appendix 2

In order to give an idea about the dissolution of the Ottoman Empire, the book of David Fromkin, **A Peace to End All Peace**, is an execellent reference point. This book analyses the developments in Great Britain and gives details about personalities in the Ministry of War in London. The book describes how Sir Mark Sykes drew the map of the Middle East without having much knowledge about the area.

Passages from this book are very revealing:

"Lloyd George persuaded Lord Milner and his associates of the strategic importance of the war in the East in the winter of 1917, when it was by no means clear that the Allies would be able to win a decisive victory there or anywhere else. Even after the United States entered the war in the spring, it seemed entirely possible that the Americans might not arrive in time to stave off a negotiated peace agreement that would leave the belligerent countries more or less in their existing positions. There were also those who were worried about allowing the Germans and Turks to retain control of an area whose vital importance had been underscored by the Prime Minister.

"The assistant secretaries of the War Cabinet, Leo Amery and Mark Sykes, worried that in the postwar world the Ottoman Empire might fall completely into the clutches of Germany. Were that to happen, the road to India would be in enemy hands, a threat that the British Empire could avert only by ejecting the Turks and Germans, and taking into British hands the southern perimeter of the Ottoman domains. The Cabinet, from the beginning, had thought of annexing Mesopotamia. As for Arabia, arrangements had been made with the local rulers who had asserted their independence: they were subsidized and could be relied upon to remain pro-British. That left Palestine as the only point of vulnerability. As the bridge between Africa and Asia, it blocked the land road from Egypt to India and, by its proximity, it threatened the Suez Canal and hence the sea road as well.

"Amery, the leading figure among Milner's associates in the government, discussed the matter in a memorandum to the Cabinet dated 11 April 1917. Warning against allowing Germany to strike again at Britain through domination of Europe or the Middle East after the war, he argued that "German control of Palestine" was one of "the greatest of all dangers which can confront the British Empire in the future."

"Amery, along with Mark Sykes and, later, William Ormsby-Gore, had been appointed assistant to Maurice Hankey in heading the secretariat of the War Cabinet. A Member of Parliament and an army officer who had been serving in the War Office, Amery had become one of the inner band directing the war effort in the division of responsibilities within that of Sykes. Yet Amery had already involved himself in a matter affecting Middle Eastern policy by lending a hand to an old friend.

"An army officer whom Amery had known in South Africa, Lieutenant-Colonel John Henry Patterson, had commanded a Jewish corps in the Gallipoli campaign, and asked Amery to help get permission from the War Office to create a regiment of non-British Jews to fight under British command. This regiment would then be sent to fight in Palestine if and when Britain invaded the Ottoman Empire from Egypt and the Sinai. Patterson was an Irish Protestant, a student of the Bible, a professional army officer and amateur lion hunter, known for his bestselling book The Man-Eaters of Tsavo and for his buccaneering spirit. The idea of a Jewish regiment had come from Vladimir Jabotinsky, a fiery Russian Jewish journalist who believed that Englishmen resented the presence in Britain of a large immigrant population of able-bodied Russian Jews who were not yet British subjects and who did not undertake military service. While he did not at first say so, Jabotinsky was inspired by the thought that a Jewish military unit helping to liberate Palestine would go far toward making the Zionist dream a reality. Patterson was enthusiastic; the Jewish corps he had commanded at Gallipoli had been created in large part through the efforts of

Jabotinsky's associate, Captain Joseph Trumpeldor, and Patterson had enjoyed commanding it. On 11 December 1917 General Sir Edmund Allenby and his officers entered the Holy City of Jerusalem at the Jaffa Gate, on foot. At the Citadel, Allenby read out a proclamation placing the city under martial law. To the French representative, Picot, Allenby explained that the city fell within the military zone, so that authority in the area was vested solely in the commanding general. As commanding general, Allenby would decide how long the area would remain under an exclusively military administration. Only when he deemed that the military situation permitted him to do so, said Allenby, would he allow civil administration to be instituted. Until then, the question of the Sykes-Picot Agreement and the ultimate disposition of Palestine would be deferred.

"The liberation of what he called "the most famous city in the world" was what the Prime Minister had wanted for Christmas; with it, he later wrote, Christendom had been able "to regain possession of its sacred shrines." The capture of Baghdad and Jerusalem had produced a tremendous psychological effect, he claimed, but also a material one. "The calling of the Turkish bluff was not only the beginning of the cracking-up of that military impostership which the incompetence of our war direction had permitted to intimidate us for years; it was itself a real contribution to ultimate victory."

"After the capture of Jerusalem, Feisal's Arab forces, under various Arab and British officers, showed their worth. Campaigning in Transjordan, the raiding parties continued their hit-and-run attacks, while the regulars, trained by Joyce and transported by his colleague Hubert Young, disproved the contention - frequently advanced by British intelligence officers in the past - that they could not stand up to the Turkish army. A significant role was planned for them in the next phase of the campaign by Allenby, who intended them to spread disorder among the Turks on his right flank.

"Allenby was now in position to march on Damascus, and then on Constantinople to deliver the knock-out blow to the Ottoman Empire, but just at that moment his hand was stayed. The Germans were preparing an offensive against western Europe, made possible by Russia's surrender, which allowed Ludendorff to bring back Germany's armies from the eastern front. Suddenly Allenby was obliged to send back to Europe almost all of his British troops. On the first day of spring 1918, German troops launched a surprise attack that smashed through Allied lines in northern France and threatened to win the war before American reinforcements could arrive. It was not until the summer that the fury of Ludendorff's offensive was spent. Meanwhile Allenby remained in Palestine, rebuilding his forces for the future.

"From Christmas until summer's end, as Allenby awaited a chance to resume his offensive, political battle lines were forming within the British government and the Allied camp as to the ultimate disposition of the lands composing the Ottoman Empire. Meanwhile Enver Pasha was starting on a sort of Ludendorff offensive of his own in the north, designed to capture the Turkish-speaking lands of the Czarist Empire - Azerbaijan and Turkestan- and perhaps then to descend on Persia, Afghanistan, and India to destroy Britain's eastern empire while all of her British troops were away in Europe.

"In retrospect, Enver's offensive, like Ludendorff's, looks like having been a last desperate throw of the dice. But at the time the Ottoman Empire's capabilities and intentions were less easy to assess; and the Ottoman offensive brought vast areas of the northern Middle East hitherto uncontested in the war, into the spotlight of world war and polities.

"While Enver was attacking north and east, Allenby was at last able to resume his attack on Enver's forces in the west.

THE ROAD TO DAMASCUS

"Between Christmas of 1917 and the summer of 1918, Allenby laid the foundation for resuming his campaign against the Turks. In Januaary and February he restored and extended Jerusalem's railway connections to the coast, so as to relieve his army's dependence upon pack animals and ruined roads. He raided enemy forces to keep them off balance. Meanwhile he trained his raw Indian troops for the coming campaign.

"Damascus was the next objective on his line of march. Even more than Baghdad and Jerusalem, it was an important city for all historical ages. Believed to be the oldest continuously inhabited urban center in the world, its origins were lost in the mists of time. Damascus was a flourishing oasis town before there were Jews or Arabs, Moslems or Christians, Englishmen or Germans. The capture of Damascus would symbolically complete not merely the British occupation of the Arabic-speaking Ottoman Empire, but also assure Britain's place in the line of legitimate succession from the ancient world conquerors who had sealed their triumphs by achieving mastery of the oases of Syria.

"Britain claimed to be something other than a traditional conqueror, for she was acting on behalf of an array of associated powers and causes. Allenby was an Allied commander, and his armies were prepared to advance under many flags. Among their banners was one designed by Sir Mark Sykes for Hussein and the Arab cause. Its colors -black, white, green, and red- were meant to symbolize the past glory of Moslem Arab empires and to suggest that Hussein was their contemporary champion. Hussein's only modification of the design was to change the hue of the red. Sykes had ordered flags to be made up by the British military supply offices in Egypt, and then had them delivered to the Hejaz forces.

"The British-designed, British-produced flag of Arab nationalism signaled a critical issue as Allenby's armies prepared to march on Damascus: the extent to which the particular British officials who mattered most in shaping Middle Eastern policy were sincere or cynical in their espousal of the various causes to which they had supposedly been converted along the way. Sir Mark Sykes, who before 1914 had admired the Turks as a ruling people, had become converted during the war to the cause of liberating the subject peoples from Ottoman tyranny. An outspoken anti- Semite, he had come to express his concern for the Jews, as did Meinertzhagen, also an avowed anti-Semite. Colonial officials such as Storrs and Clayton, who had always maintained that

Arabic-speaking natives were incapable of self-government, appeared to support Sykes as he hailed the renaissance of Arab independence. Not all of these conversions were genuine.

"At one end of the spectrum was Sykes, who believed in honoring the pledges of which, in large part, he was the author. At the other end were operational officers who deplored the pledges, and at times deprecated the causes in whose names they had been made. At the beginning of 1918 Sykes, in London, moved into a Foreign Office position in charge of the politics of the Ottoman theater of war. Those in charge of the politics of the Ottoman theater of war in the field -Clayton in Palestine, Wingate in Egypt, and the Government of India in Baghdad- were skeptical of the politics of idealism that Sykes had come to espouse, though they did not tell him so openly. Beneath the surface civility of British government interchanges in 1918 there ran a hidden line on which the Foreign Office and officers in the field pulled in opposite directions. Baghdad, Jerusalem, and, beyond Allied lines, Damascus, awaited word of their eventual fate, unaware that a tug of war within the British bureaucracy might decide it.

"When William Ormsby-Gore joined Amery and Sykes as one of the three assistant secretaries of the War Cabinet, he brought with him a more concrete interest in the immediate prospects of the Zionist idea. Ormsby-Gore, a Member of Parliament and secretary to Lord Milner, had gone out to the Middle East to work with the Arab Bureau. Under his personal command was Aaron Aaronsohn, leader of a highly effective, intelligence- gathering group operation working behind Ottoman lines in Jewish Palestine to provide information about Turkish troop movements. Like Jabotinsky, Aaronsohn was attacked by fellow Jews for identifying Zionistinterests with those of the Allies -and thus endangering the Palestinian Jewish community, which Djemal Pasha was tempted to treat as his colleagues had treated the Armenians. Aaronsohn's information about Turkish defenses and military dispositions proved to be of great value to the British military command in Egypt, however, and was appreciated by Ormsby- Gore."

Bibliography

Aksüt, Ali Kemali   Profesör Mehmet Ali Ayni: Hayatı ve Eserleri, Istanbul 1944

Altar, Cevat Memduh   Paul Hindemith ile Karşılaşma

Ancien Diplomate   Le Regime des Capitulations, par un Ancien Diplomate Droit International, Paris 1898

Andonyan, Aram   Balkan Harbi Tarihi

Arar, Asım (Dr.)   Son günlerinde Atatürk

Arar, İsmail   Atatürk'ün Halkçılık Programı

Ayni, Mehmet Ali   Türk Azizleri: İsmail Hakkı

Ayni, Mehmet Ali   Şeyh-i Ekberi Niçin Severim

Ayni, Mehmet Ali   Milliyetçilik

Ayni, Mehmet Ali   Tasavvuf Tarihi (Yeni basılan bölümü) İslam Tasavvuf Tarihi

Bardakçı, İlhan   Balkan Bozgunu ve I. Dünya Harbi

Fromkin, David   A Peace to End All Peace, Avon Books, N.Y. 1990

Gates, Caleb Frank   Not to me Only

Gardey, L.   Voyage du Sultan Abd-ul-Aziz de Stanboul au Caire

Hauser, M. Henri   Histoire Diplomatique de l'Europe

Irmak, Sadi   Atatürk Devrimleri Tarihi

Imece, M.Selim   Atatürk'ün Şapka Devriminde Kastamonu ve İnebolu Seyahatleri

İpşiroğlu N. and M.   Kök Atatürkçülük

Kemalettin Şükrü   Mütareke Acıları, İstanbul 1930

Ministry of the Interior	Türkiye'de Yunan Fecayiyi, İkinci Kitab 1338 - Istanbul
Neyzi, Ali	Hüseyin Paşa Çıkmazı No.4
Neyzi, Ali	Meyzi ile Neyzi
Neyzi, Muzaffer	Büyük İstirham
Neyzi, Muzaffer	Türkiye Ulus Bankası
Saner, Necat	Atatürk Dönemi
Saz, Leyla,	Haremin İç Yüzü
Saz, Leyla,	Le Harem Imperial (French translation)
Saz, Leyla,	Solmuş Çiçekler
Shaw Stanford	Osmanlı İmparatorluğu ve Modern Türkiye
Tunaya, Tarık Ziya	Türkiye'de Siyasal Partiler Vol. 1 İkinci Meşrutiyet Dönemi
Woodham-Smith, Cecil	The Reason Why
Young, George	Constantinople

List of Names

279

PICTURE
ALBUM

The note on the photograph above reads: "To my grandson Sırrı, a souvenir of Kızıltoprak. October 5, 1928. Leyla".
On the right, Leyla Hanım, in her youth.

Leyla Hanım in her middle age (above). Leyla Hanım and myself at Kızıltoprak (left). She wrote, "A withered, tattered rose and her tiny rosebud", at the back of this photo dated 1927.

283

مفتق دوسوبم

هندم زبا هام افنده كوروشترك عاف...

The letterhead of Leyla Hanım's private stationery (left) and the Albanian gardener at the Bostancı house which burned down in a fire (far left). Above, Leyla Hanım's handwriting: "My loyal, my dear little neighbor - so you mailed me a letter on your way and received mine in Yanina. Two days after your departure, little Yusuf was sick again. I was ill, I had my tooth pulled out. See what has befallen us, sweet little Feride, my dear neighbor. One evening we went to Bostancı with Esat Pasha's wife and spent the evening there. They are all very well. Vedia is playing some pleasant tunes in the other room now. You write that you are bored at Yanina. That is what happens when you are abroad, away from home".

Sırrı Pasha's residence in Beşiktaş just before being torn down (above). On the left, the Doctor Ismail Pasha (1806-1879).

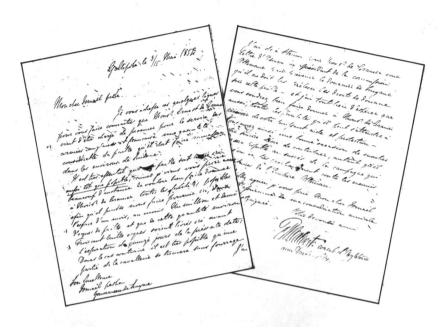

Letter of the British Consul at the
Dardanelles (1854) addressed to
Ismail Pasha (above). Sırrı Pasha's
younger brother (right).

Captain Fuat bey, son of the Doctor Ismail Pasha and Leyla Hanım's brother (above). Mehmet Efendi, Sırrı Pasha's elder brother, in the Cretan costume.

Sırrı Pasha, his son Yusuf Razi Bey and his son-in-law Mehmet Ali Ayni Bey (1894).

The imperial document conferring a medal awarded to Sırrı Pasha by the Czar of Russia (above). "The Medal of Sveto Stanislav. St. Petersburg, January 29, 1881. We, the Czar Alexander Ftoroy II, the Czar of Russia by the grace of God, the Czar of Poland, the great King of Finland, et cetera, et cetera have presented Sırrı Pasha, the Governor General of Roumeli, The Stanislav II medal which is dispatched under cover of the present".
On the left, Sırrı Pasha at Ruschuk, 1875, Chief Secretary of the Danubian Province. His fez is in the style of the period of Sultan Abdülaziz.

289

Above, Sırrı Pasha in his study with the Mufti of Diyarbekir. The boy sitting on the floor is Kamuran (Kandiyeli), Sırrı Pasha's son by his second wife.
Sırrı Efendi in 1869 (right).

حوبه اربكرك تشكيله ما سپلوه دياربكرده ايا اسلام حربه
بوندن شبر اعله

The Governor General of Diyarbekir, Sırrı Pasha, at a ceremony with Field Marshall Zeki Pasha and Kurdish Chieftains (above).
Sırrı Pasha in Baghdad with his sons Vedat (Tek), standing, and Kamuran.

JOURNAL ILLUSTRÉ TURC "MALUMAT,,

منافع ملك ودولته خادم هفتالق مصور ترك جريده سيدر

Direction et Administration 52 Avenue de la S. Porte   مطبعه واداره سنه سود اب عالی جاده سنده ۵۲ نومرولی دائره در

Le numéro 100 para s   اسعه سی ۱۰۰ پاره در

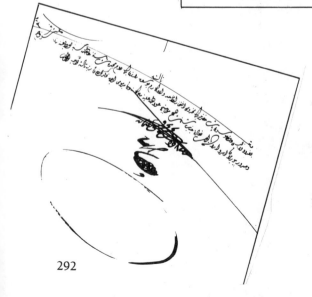

Cover of the magazine "Malumat" (Information) dated December 12, 1895 both in Ottoman Turkish script and in French. The photo is one of the last pictures of Sırrı Pasha. The price of the magazine is 100 paras which is the equivalent of two and a half kurush. At the time it probably was an expensive magazine. On the left, the imperial document awarding the medal of the Third Rank to Sırrı Pasha.

292

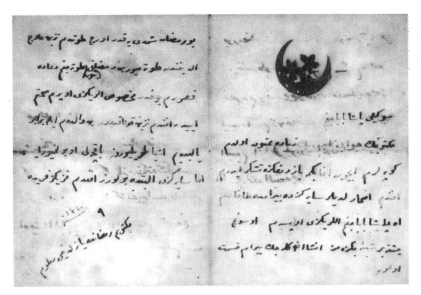

Letter written by Feride to her father, Sırrı Pasha, in Baghdad (above).
Photograph of Mehmet Ali Bey, the new Governor met by wellwishers upon arrival in Yanina (below). The gentleman carrying a walking stick and wearing a fez, seated in the first carriage is my grandfather Mehmet Ali Ayni; next to him, Yahya Bey, the Mayor. November 26, 1911.

Visiting cards of
Mehmet Ali Ayni
the Ottoman and
Latin scripts.
Ottoman script, t
to bottom: Distric
Governor of Cara
Province, Provinc
Governor of Yanin
Governor of the
Province of Yanin

PROFESÖR MEHMED ALI AYNİ
Kitab Sarayları Tasnif Komisyonu Başkanı

KIZILTOPRAK - İSTANBUL

TELEFON : 60228

Mehmed Ali Aini
Gouverneur de Carassi

Feride Hanım with her grandson Ali
(Neyzi) at Kızıltoprak (1929).

294

Mehmet Ali Ayni in Edirne with his father Necip Efendi and his sister Fatma (1877).

District Governor of Latakia, M. Ali Ayni, 1908 (left). Governor General of Trabzon, M. Ali Ayni, 1912 (below).

Manifestation des Francs-Maçons sur les quais de Salonique

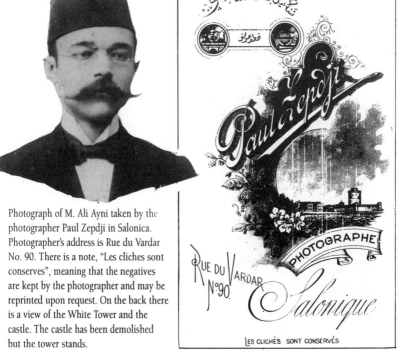

Photograph of M. Ali Ayni taken by the photographer Paul Zepdji in Salonica. Photographer's address is Rue du Vardar No. 90. There is a note, "Les cliches sont conserves", meaning that the negatives are kept by the photographer and may be reprinted upon request. On the back there is a view of the White Tower and the castle. The castle has been demolished but the tower stands.

M. Ali Ayni and Süleyman Nazif, the poet, in Diyarbekir in 1894 (above). Grandfather Necip Efendi, M. Ali Bey and my mother Nezihe at Scopje, February 19, 1898 (left).

Leyla Saz's grandchildren Nezihe, Selime, Sırrı, Refika. At the back of the photo: 359 Grand Rue de Pera. En face du Bon Marche-Phebus, Constantinople.

Leyla Hanım in 1900 (?). Uncle Sırrı on his nanny's lap, Firdevs Hanım (Uncle Vedat's wife),
Feride Hanım (my grandmother), an "ahretlik" girl, Şerif Hanım, my mother Nezihe and my aunt
Refika.

Leyla Hanım at the Beşiktaş mansion.

Imperial caiques at the Kanlıca Quey during a Flower Festival (from the Yusuf Razi collection).

Souvenir of Salonica. "Greetings from your brother Ismail". The card was mailed from Salonica. The White Tower still stands but the castle and the mosque are gone. On the reverse side the address is: To the virtuous Nezihe Hanım, daughter of the prosperous Governor of Ammare, Mehmet Ali Bey, Kızıltoprak, City of Felicity.

Souvenir de Salonique.

Rue du Vardar

By coincidence, among old postcards, I found one showing Vardar Street in Salonica. I decided to include it in this book of memoirs because it brings to mind the time my grandfather went to have his photo taken. The postcard is colored and the text is in French. There is no Ottoman script. Along with the horsedrawn tramcar and men wearing fezes, the minaret of a mesjid are visible. Salonica is important to us because it is the citiy where Atatürk was born. It was the second most important city in the European part of the Empire. Electricity was first installed in Salonica; also, th electrical tramway started working in Salonica before it did in Istanbul.

Below, the postcard sent to me by my grandfather from Europe expressing his pleasure to hear that I was enrolled at the St. Joseph school and recommending that I work hard.

Governor's mansion at Ammare, between Baghdad and Basra (above).
Yusuf Razi Bel in the study of his house in Nuruosmaniye, Istanbul, 1934-35 (right). Uncle Yusuf was very much interested in photography and he was very meticulous. I remember how this picture was taken. My uncle Sırrı and I had gone to visit Leyla Hanım. After taking her picture, my uncle wanted to take one of uncle Yusuf also. Uncle Yusuf thought his desk was very untidy, put his folders and typewriter in order and posed with an air of deep reflection which resembles Leyla Hanım's meditative poses. On the wall, exposed electric wires are visible which means that electricity was installed after the building had been constructed.

304

The invitation adressed to Yusuf Razi Bey reads, "You are cordially invited to lunch to be served at the Bağlarbaşı Residence in honor of the Poet Laurate Abdülhak Hamid Beyefendi to commemorate the publication of his new book titled Finten. Prince (signature)." The menu with the crown letterhead is attached to the invitation. "Lunch. October 28, 1332 (1914). Bean soup with cream - Pasha beurek with cheese - Sea bass with mayonnaise - Pilaf with pistachios and nuts - Cream of almonds - Ice cream - Fruits".

Rails for the tramway are being laid at Şişhane (left). This photograph, taken by Yusuf Razi Bey, shows many trees which were there in those days. The workers wear fezes or turbans, their supervisor wears a hat; he is probably a representative of the Tramway Company. Tools are limited to a wheelbarrow, pickaxes and shovels only. Below, the Halaskargazi Avenue at Osmanbey. "Hareket Ordusu" (the army which came to Istanbul from Thrace in 1909 to sudbue the anti-constituonial rebellion) as it arrived from Salonica. The Nazarian Mansion and the Greek Cemetery are visible in the background. The Mansion became Ecole Moderne later. This photo was also taken by Yusuf Razi Bey.

A. NİHAD VEDAD TEK

YÜKSEK MÜHENDİS MİMAR

DIPLOM INGENIEUR ARCHITEKT

ALMANYA SAKSONYA DRESDEN ŞEHRİNDEKİ
TECHNISCHE HOCHSCHULESİNDEN
(TEKNİK ÜNİVERSİTE)
EN ÜSTÜN DERECE İLE DİPLOMALI

AYRI TEKNİK ÜNİVERSİTEDEN
ÇELİK ve BETON-ARME KONSTRÜKSYON
ve HESAPSARI BİRİNCİ SINIF MÜTEHASSIS
EHLİYETİNE HAİZ.
MİLLİ EĞİTİM BAKANLIĞI YÜKSEK MÜH. MİMARLIK
VESİKASINA HAİZ No 2-920 Gün: 22-7-1944
BAYINDIRLIK BAKANLIĞI İCRAİ SAN'AT
RUHSATNAMESİ No. 415
İST. BELEDİYESİ İMAR SİCİL 91
T.N.M.O.B. MİMARLAR ODASI SİCİL 1937

BİL'UMUM MİMARİ ve DEKORASYON
PROJE ve TATBİKATLARI

BİL'UMUM SANAİ BİNALARINA AİT
PROJE ve TAAHÜD İŞLERİ

ÇELİK ve BETON-ARME İNŞAAT
PROJE ve STATİK HESAPLARI

MES'ULİYET ve FENNİ NEZARET
TEKNİK İSTİŞARE

ISTANBUL, *18 - IV - 1980*
Beyoğlu, İstiklâl Caddesi 390 numaralı Normanlı Yurdu
Kapı 8 daire 3 · Telefon : 44 19 57

Nihad Vedat Tek's letter of April
18, 1980 addressed to me
(above).
The Architect Vedat Tek when
he was a student in Paris.

The mother of Doctor Ismail Pasha, Kiveli Rodokanaki (left) in the local costume of Khios. Her maiden name was Metaxas. Below, Vedat Tek, Chief Architect of his Majesty the Sultan. His works include the main post office building at Sirkeci, the Bostancı Mosque, Ankara Palace (built as a hotel, now the official state guest house), Haydarpasha and Moda boat landings which still stand today.

مُظَفّرحَلِيم ١٥٧

تجهيزات عسكريه متعهدى

استانبول ـ بك اوغلى تقسيم نومرو ١١

تلغراف آدره ـ سى: استانبول ـ حليم

Muzaffer Halim's stationery with letterhead: Contractor for Military Supplies. Istanbul, Beyoğlu, Taksim No. 11. Cable: Istanbul Halim", 1923 or 1924 (left).

Members of the Union and Progress Party at Kızıltoprak (below). Standing: Muzaffer Halim on the left and Fuat Bey (his nickname was Fuat the Chin). Sitting (left to right): Rauf bey (my father's cousin). Zahit Bey (son of Zühtü Pasha, the patron of the Kızıltoprak mosque) and Saffet Bey.

Muzaffer Halim of Kızıltoprak, my father, who was one of the very first residents of Istanbul to be mobilized during the Dardanelles campaign (right).
Below, the Boat Landing Square at Kadıköy, 1935.

Kızıltoprak 1329 (1908) Front row, left to right: Uncle Sırrı, Sedat Arar, Hikmet Arar.
Middle row: Nezihe (my mother), Feride Ayni (my grandmother), Leyla Saz (Mimi), Aunt Refika, Kamer Hanım (Aunt Refika's mother-in-law).
Standing: Fuat Arar, Mehmet Ali Ayni (my grandfather), Ekrem Arar, Asım Arar (Aunt Refika's husband).

Leylâ Saz, 1928

312

Souvenir of a picnic to Pavli Island, 1933. Şerif Hanım (she had joined the family at Kastamonu as an "evlatlık"), Ali (the gardener), Emine (an "evlatlık"), Sıdıka (Şerif Hanım's daughter), İhsan (Sıdıka's son), Şükriye (a maid), "çengi hanım" (a dancer; I cannot remember her name, İhsan Efendi had brought her).

Refugees from Roumeli at Sultanahmet Square during the Balkan War (above). The photo was taken by Uncle Yusuf. Ahmet Halim and Nezih Halim wearing the St. Joseph College uniforms, 1933 (left).

COLLÈGE FRANÇAIS S⸱ JOSEPH de Kadi-Keui (Stamboul)

DIRIGÉ PAR LES FRÈRES DES ÉCOLES CHRÉTIENNES

2ᵉ Division (1°, 2°, 3°, 4°, et 5° Cl.)

3ᵉ **Classe**
ᵉ **DIVISION**

BULLETIN DE Mᵣ *Nzil Halim*

Notes obtenues au 2 ᵉ *Examen de l'année 19 33 — 19 34*

SPÉCIALITÉS	Notes	Max.	SPÉCIALITÉS	Notes	Max.
Langue turque	14	20	Calcul	29	40
Histoire	10	10	Arithmétique		
Géographie	9	10			
Instruction civique	10	10	Exercices de langage	8	10
Instruction morale	15	20	Leçons de choses	7	10
Grammaire-Conjugaison	16	20	Notions de sciences		
Analyse	6	10	Tenue des cahiers	8	10
Orthographe	10	20	Dessin à main levée	4	10
Lecture - Poésie	25	30	Calligraphie	8	10
Composition française	13	20	Solfège et Chant	9	10
Leçons illustrées de Français	8	10	Gymnastique	6	10

COURS FACULTATIFS :

Musique Inst⸱ᵉ : — Piano : — Violon : — Mandoline :

Moyenne gén⸱ᵉ : ~~14,16~~ sur 20 — **Place :** ~~1~~ sur *35* **Elèves**

Appréciation gén⸱ᵉ : **Conduite** *très bien* **Travail** *Bien* **Tenue** *très bien*

Observations : *Bon élève*

Kadi-Keuï, le *24 / 12* 19 *33*

Le Directeur :

F. Pierre

IMP. C. J. THÉOCHARI

My report card, College Français St Joseph, dated December 24, 1933.

315

My mother Nefise Nezihe and my grandfather, M. Ali Ayni at Kızıltoprak
(above) in 1935. Kalamış boat landing and Fenerbahche (below).

My mother's visiting cards (above). There is no address or telephone number on any of the five Nezihe Muzaffer cards, each printed in a different style of calligraphy.
Below, the "sea-bath" at Kalamış, 1934. "The left side for ladies, the right side for gentlemen. College St. Joseph and Mühürdar are visible in the background.

The Ahırkapı Lighthouse (above). A paddlewheel boat in the foreground. Behind, the Blue Mosque and St. Sophia. The building between the two exists no more. Now, a motorway passes in front of the lighthouse.

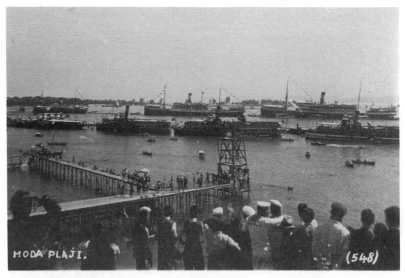

"Cabotage Day" at Kalamış Quey, July 1, 1934. On the left, the sea-bath of Moda. Three passenger ships, three ferry boats, one paddlewheel car ferry and tugboats are at for anchor celebrations.

318

Mehmet Ali Ayni with his family at Kızıltoprak, 1936. Standing: Ahmet Neyzi, Muzaffer Neyzi, Nezihe Neyzi, Nezih Neyzi, Asım Arar, Refika Arar, Sırrı Ayni. Sitting: Feride Ayni, Mehmet Ali Ayni, Nezihe Daniş. Sitting on the ground: Ali Neyzi.

319

Kızıltoprak, 1933. Leyla Hanım with her children and grandchildren. At the top of the stairs Nezih, next to him Hediye (my nanny), Ahmet (my brother), Selime, İsmail, Aunt Refika, Ali (seen partly). Firdevs Hanım, Uncle Vedat, Leyla Saz (Mimi), Yusuf Razi (my uncle), Nezihe (my mother), Feride Ayni (my grandmother), Nermin Taneri (Uncle Vedat's granddaughter).

Ankara Fotress, 1927 (above). Below, my father Muzaffer Halim Neyzi with Prime Minister İsmet İnönü at the Etimesgut "Air Field" on a spring day in 1936 at the presentation ceremony of two-propeller de Havilland passenger planes. One can see that there is no asphalt runway; the planes landed and took off from a field of weeds and grass. On İnönü's left are his sons Erdal and Ömer; the lady behind, wearing a coat and hat is Mevhibe İnönü. Further back, on the left is the Minister of Communications, Ali Çetinkaya ("Ali the Bald").

The rear gate of "Hacı Kamil Street No. 4, M. Ali Ayni House" (right). Sitting on the bumper of the car are Emin Sözeri (left) and my cousin Ismail Arar. My brother Ali used the name of this cobblestone street as the title of his book of memoirs. Today it is covered with asphalt and cluttered with apartment buildings.
Below, the Galata Bridge and the old Kadıköy boat landing (another photo by Yusuf Razi). In the foreground the Nilüfer and other passenger boats of Şirketi Hayriye (a private ferryboat company) alongside the bridge. Tramcars are visible on the bridge.

My daughters Furuğ and Füsun and myself by the bust of the Cretan Ahmet Fuat Pasha in Kütahya.
The governor's mansion covered with tiles and the Green Mosque was built on his orders. He was
influential in the progress and development of ceramics in the region.

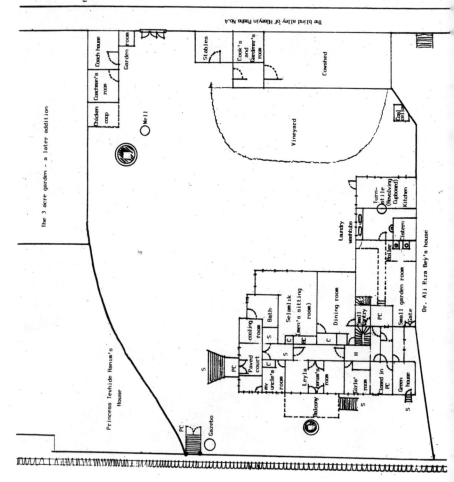

Legend:
- PC. Paved Court
- B. Basement staircase
- C. Built in closet
- S. Staircase
- H. Hall
- BC. Bookcase
- P. Pond

The blind alley of Hüseyin Pasha No.4

The 3 acre garden – a later addition

Well

Chicken coop | Coachman's room | Coach house
Garden room
Stables
Cook's and Gardner's room
Cowshed
Vineyard
Dog cell
Turn-stile (Revolving Cupboard)
Kitchen
Laundry workrub
Boiler
Cistern
Dr. Ali Riza Bey's house
cooling room
Bath
Selamlik (men's sitting room)
Dining room
Small pantry
PC
Small garden room
Gate
S
PC
Paved court
C
S
C
H
PC
Green house
Uncle's room
Leyla
Hanım's room
Girls' room
Closed in
S
Balcony
S
Princess Tevhide Hanım's House
PC
Gazebo

Kızıltoprak House Plan

324

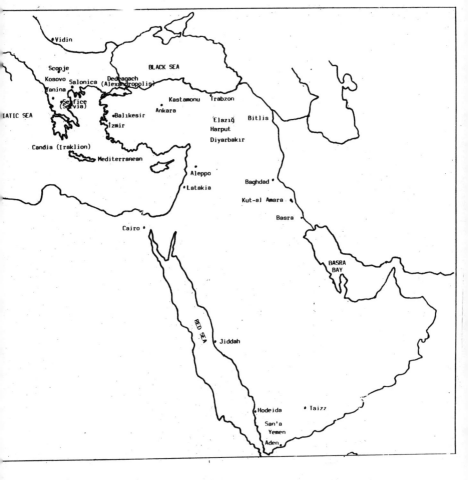

Locations where Family Members Held Office during the Ottoman Empire

325